DRUG
ABUSE

DRUG ABUSE

Its Natural History and Clinical Treatment

Marvin R. Burt

With Sharon Pines and Thomas J. Glynn

Transaction Publishers
New Brunswick (U.S.A.) and London (U.K.)

First paperback printing 2011
Copyright © 1979 by Schenkman Publishing Company, Inc.

This book is printed on acid-free paper that meets the American National Standard for Permanence of Paper for Printed Library Materials.

Library of Congress Catalog Number: 2010052851
ISBN: 978-1-4128-1826-1
Printed in the United States of America

Library of Congress Cataloging-in-Publication Data

Burt, Marvin R.
 Drug abuse : its natural history and clinical treatment / Marvin R. Burt; with Sharon Pines and Thomas J. Glynn.
  p. cm.
 Originally published as: Drug abuse, its natural history and the effectiveness of current treatments / by Marvin R. Burt, with Sharon Pines and Thomas J. Glynn. Cambridge, Mass. : Schenkman Pub. Co., c1979.
 Includes bibliographical references and index.
 ISBN 978-1-4128-1826-1
  1. Drug abuse--United States. 2. Drug abuse--Treatment--United States. I. Pines, Sharon. II. Glynn, Thomas J. III. Title.

HV5825.B87 2011
616.86'3206--dc22

                                                    2010052851

CONTENTS

PREFACE

Traditionally, drug treatment programs have been evaluated by assessing how well clients progress in treatment and their status upon leaving treatment. There has been increasing concern that this does not provide an adequate assessment of treatment outcome. A stronger evaluation should consider clients' status some time after leaving treatment. This book is concerned with the latter type of evaluation.

Follow-up studies have been conducted by other investigators,[1] but those were conducted a number of years ago. For a variety of philosophical and technical reasons, these investigators were unable to conduct follow-up studies making use of control or comparison groups. The use of such groups is difficult and often viewed as an undesirable or unmanageable task. Nevertheless, few question the desirability of obtaining such information. Interpreting the significance of change in addict behavior after leaving treatment is difficult in the absence of comparable information on clients who received no treatment.

This book is composed of recent follow-up studies on samples of former clients treated by two of the largest drug treatment agencies in the United States. The studies focus on comparing pre- and post-treatment behavior among clients receiving various types of treatment with persons who received little or no treatment.

---

[1] G. Hunt and M. Odoroff, "Follow-up of Narcotic Drug Addicts After Hospitalization," *Public Health Reports* 77 (1) : 41-54, 1962; O'Donnel, J., "A Follow-up of Narcotic Addicts," *American Orthopsychiatry* (34 (5) : 948-954, 1964; Ball, J.C. and Pabon, D., "Locating and Interviewing Narcotic Addicts in Puerto Rico," *Social Res.* 49: 401-411; Vaillant, G., "Twelve-year Follow-up of New York Narcotic Addicts: The Relation of Treatment to Outcome," *American Journal of Psychiatry* 122 (7) : 727-737, 1966.

ACKNOWLEDGMENTS

This study would not have been possible without the cooperation and participation of many individuals. Dr. Robert DuPont, M.D., Director of the National Institute on Drug Abuse (NIDA), recognized the significance of this study at an early stage and directed its extension into consideration of many issues critical to knowledge about drug treatment and the natural history of drug abuse. Without his constant support on behalf of this project, this study could not have been completed.

Barry Brown, Ph.D., formerly Director of Research, Statistics and Evaluation at the D. C. Department of Human Resources, helped conceive and design the project and provided direction, support, and assistance throughout it. He became NIDA project director upon becoming Chief of the Services Research Branch, Division of Resource Development. Dr. Brown made numerous helpful suggestions throughout the course of this project, critically reviewed earlier drafts of this report, and was particularly helpful in preparing Chapter XI.

David Nurco, D.S.W., was instrumental in suggesting further analysis after the study's initial phase. Ronald Gold was the NIDA Project Officer during the study's early phase. Mary Toborg helped to design and initiate the study.

Personnel in numerous agencies also cooperated in the study by giving the BAI staff access to records while, at the same time, being conscientious in protecting the confidentiality of all the NTA clients contacted for the study. Chapter IV describes confidentiality procedures.

Earl Stancil, Director of Central Medical Intake, NTA, and Robert Bailey, Chief, Legal Assistance Division, NTA, were most cooperative; they gave us access to CMI records throughout the study.

Special thanks are due to the two team leaders, Napoleon Turner and Calvin Tindal and to the following trackers/interviewers for their invaluable efforts and success in tracking and interviewing the clients in our sample:

- Gregory Anderson
- Alfred Belt
- Howard Brown
- Mary L. Clark
- Willie Ingram
- George Jackson
- Grace Jones
- Bruce King
- Edgar LaBat
- Gregory Lucas
- Clarence Minor
- Eli Morrison
- Edwin Preston

In addition to performing their supervisory role as team leaders, Napoleon Turner and Calvin Tindal provided numerous suggestions and helped modify some of the procedures for tracking. Napoleon Turner also trained the interviewers, helped construct the questionnaire, and provided insight into interpreting the results of the study.

Ronald Nolfi, formerly with NTA, assisted us in gaining access to computer printouts and facilitated picking the sample. He and Nicholas Kozel assisted by serving as liaison to numerous District of Columbia agencies.

Inspector Thomas Wolfry, Captain R. O. Winters, and Captain William I. Harlowe of the Metropolitan Police Department provided access to police records.

Norman Carlson, Director of the Federal Bureau of Prisons, provided assistance by giving us access to necessary information, clearance to interview residents of Federal prisons, and the support of two of his staff members: Jim Watts, who helped in finding the information we needed, and John Wash, who served as liaison with the Federal prisons where some respondents resided. John Wash also set up many of the interviews in the Federal prisons.

Wade Moore, Branch Chief of Medicaid Care, provided information on the location of some of our respondents.

Delbert Jackson, Director of the Department of Corrections, provided clearance to perform interviews in the penal institutions under his jurisdiction. Two of his staff members also helped: Bill Cooks, who served as liaison to the penal institutions, and Dewey Meadows, who assisted us in using the institution's computer to extract information on the location of some of our respondents.

Judge Greene, Chief Judge of the Superior Court of Washington, D.C., and Nancy Wynstra were most helpful in giving us clearance to obtain information on some of our respondents from the probation department. James Porter, Deputy Director of Adult Probation, and his staff provided information they had on our respondents.

Robert Leitman and Gilbert Peach of the Addiction Services Agency provided useful information on the ASA programs. George DeLeon, Ph.D., provided useful information on Phoenix House and other therapeutic communities. Nicholas Kozel of NIDA provided assistance in attempting to locate information on the changes in supply and price of heroin during the time periods in question.

Dick Eiswirth of COMNET performed an outstanding job in conducting the data processing.

Kenneth Webb, of the BAI staff, was instrumental in preparing the analysis plan and participated in data analysis.

Donna Van Arsdell was responsible for the graphic layout of the data tables.

Mary Cohen, Karen French, Gail Purruso, Cheryl Wysong, Susan Radcliff, and Barbara Kraft collected data from NTA Central Client Intake files on respondents and prepared tracking sheets. Mary Cohen and Barbara Kraft also located respondents, coded questionnaires, wrote computer instructions, and tabulated data.

The research leading to this book was supported under contracts SAODAP73-2, DA5PC023, and 271-76-4405 from the Special Action Office for Drug Abuse Prevention and the National Institute on Drug Abuse. This support is gratefully acknowledged. Interviewing of respondents in New York City was performed by Macro Systems, Incorporated.

This report benefited from comments on an earlier draft by Barry Brown, Ph.D., Robert L. DuPont, M.D., Frank Tims, and John O'Donnell, Ph.D.

The author is responsible for any errors.

MARVIN R. BURT, D.P.A.

PART I

FOLLOW-UP STUDY OF FORMER CLIENTS OF THE DISTRICT OF COLUMBIA'S NARCOTICS TREATMENT ADMINISTRATION

by
Marvin R. Burt
with
Sharon Pines

Chapter I

SUMMARY

This follow-up study assesses the experiences of clients who had contact with/or received treatment from the Narcotics Treatment Administration in Washington, D.C. The basic questions addressed are:

- What happened to former clients who left treatment?
- What influence did treatment seem to have on post-treatment outcomes of former clients?

The first question is answered by determining the status of former clients at the time of interview. The second question is considerably more difficult to answer. It requires that the effects of treatment be isolated from all other effects which might have influenced the post-treatment outcomes of the former clients.

Technically, answering the second question should require an experimental design in which prospective clients, who apply and are qualified for admission to NTA programs, are randomly assigned to treatment and control groups.

Of course, such a random assignment to experimental groups (i.e., modalities of treatment) and control groups (i.e., no treatment) is not feasible. Random assignment to treatment groups is not feasible because the determination of which treatment a client is assigned is a function of his own desires as well as professional judgement as to which treatment would be most effective for him. Assignment to a control group would be unconscionable. A responsible public program cannot refuse to treat a heroin addict simply because it desires to conduct an evaluation study. This would violate professional ethics as well as HEW regulations on protecting human subjects.

Due to the impossibility of employing a truly experimental design, a "next best" alternative was sought. It was decided to draw samples retrospectively (i.e., after the fact) of clients who actually entered methadone maintenance and abstinence programs. Due to the impossibility of randomly assigning prospective clients to control groups, it was decided to use as control groups individuals who applied for treatment, were accepted, but left within five days. The majority of the control group actually left within one or two days (prior to obtaining their first medication or counseling session).

Due to the belief that the period of time a client is out of treatment influences his post-treatment outcome, the sample was further segmented into the year in which the client left treatment. Three years were chosen: 1971, 1972, and 1973.

Sample Selection

The universe of clients was partitioned into six treatment groups and three nontreatment (control) groups. Because all clients who entered treatment subsequent to January 1970 were required to register at the Central Medical Intake (CMI), the initial universe consisted of all clients registered at the Central Medical Intake during the period of January 1971 through December 1973. Three time periods were specified during which the client must have left treatment: January to December 1971, January to December 1972, and January to December 1973. The universe was partitioned into type of treatment (or no treatment) received as well as the period during which clients left treatment. The following matrix shows that the sample was partitioned into those clients who left methadone maintenance,[1] left abstinence,[2] and those who registered at CMI and left within five days during each of the three years.

	1971	1972	1973	TOTAL
Methadone Maintenance	40	40	40	120
Abstinence	40	40	40	120
CMI Only (Control)	40	40	40	120
TOTAL	120	120	120	360

Three types of behavioral outcomes were investigated:
- Drug use
- Criminal activity
- Socioeconomic productivity

Comparisons were made during three time periods:
- The two-month period immediately prior to entering treatment
- The two-month period immediately after leaving treatment
- The two-month period immediately prior to being interviewed

---

[1]But who remained more than five days after registering at CMI.
[2]But who remained more than five days after registering at CMI.

Measurements were made to determine changes realized by each group comparing the three time periods. The measurements were then compared between the experimental and control groups to determine whether the changes appear to be attributable to the program in question or outside factors. Then comparisons were made among the three years to detect significant differences.

Because few NTA clients were enrolled in drug-free programs, "abstinence" was defined to include methadone detoxification from heroin as well as drug free programs. The overwhelming majority of the abstinence clients was enrolled in methadone detoxification.

The sample for each cell was randomly generated from the universe of all clients who left treatment (including dropouts as well as graduates) with the following exceptions:

- No client who was under eighteen years of age when first leaving NTA was included
- No client who was first admitted before January 1, 1970, was included

Forty names were randomly selected for each cell using the NTA computer listings and the data contained in the CMI files. Once the 40 names in each cell were finally determined, there were *no* substitutions for any reason.

The sample respondents were tracked, interviewed, and urine specimens were obtained to validate their responses to questions concerning their use of drugs.

The methodology is discussed in Chapter IV.

Natural History of Drug Abuse

The results of this study provide some insights into the natural history of drug abuse as well as direct answers to the questions concerned with differential outcomes of different client groups.

Chapter VI presents detailed data on the characteristics and backgrounds of the clients interviewed. In summary, the typical client was a black male, twenty-one to twenty-five years old, who had completed the 11th grade. He had used heroin daily for at least two years, had first participated in some type of crime by age eighteen, and was unemployed. Chapter VII analyzes clients' changes in behavior in terms of the various groups of interest.

The behavior of all the respondents (including the control and treatment groups) is shown in Tables I-1 and I-2. Substantial reductions in drug taking occurred between the two-month periods before

TABLE I-1

DRUG USE
(percentage)

Frequency of Use	2 Months Before NTA	2 Months After NTA	Last 2 Months
Heroin			
Not at all	3	52	64
Occasionally	28	34	29
Daily	69	14	7
Total	100	100	100
n =	289	289	289
Illegal Methadone			
Not at all	64	80	91
Occasionally	32	18	8
Daily	4	2	1
Total	100	100	100
n =	289	289	289
Cocaine			
Not at all	42	70	79
Occasionally	51	30	20
Daily	7	0	1
Total	100	100	100
n =	289	289	289
Amphetamines			
Not at all	72	79	85
Occasionally	21	17	14
Daily	7	4	1
Total	100	100	100
n =	289	289	289

TABLE I-2

EMPLOYMENT AND CRIMINAL ACTIVITY
(percentage)

Status	2 Months Before NTA	2 Months After NTA	Last 2 Months
Employment			
Paid job	34	37	45
Keeping house, student, job training	5	4	6
Illegal activities	44	38	24
All other activities	17	21	25
Total	100	100	100
n =	289	289	289
Arrests			
Not arrested	76	90	92
Arrested	24	10	8
Total	100	100	100
n =	288	288	288

entering treatment, after leaving treatment, and before being interviewed (Table I-1). Only 7 percent of the respondents used heroin
daily compared to 69 percent prior to entering NTA.[1]

Employment increased (Table I-2) but this was less dramatic than
the decrease in drug taking. Engagement in illegal activities decreased from 44 percent of the respondents before entering NTA to
24 percent during the period two months prior to the interview.
This reduction in reported illegal activities is confirmed by the substantial reduction in the percentage of clients arrested.[2]

These data show drug abusers progressing from frequent use of
heroin and other illicit drugs and engagement in other illegal activities to considerably less involvement in illicit drug use and illegal
activities. By the time they were interviewed, 22 percent of the respondents were fully recovered and 58 percent were "partially" or
"marginally" recovered (as defined in Chapter VII).

What Has Happened to Former Clients Who Left Treatment?

This discussion focuses on the three major groups of clients —
methadone maintenance, abstinence, and control — ignoring the year
in which they left treatment. Subgroups (as well as these major
groups) are addressed in Chapter VII.

Three types of behavioral outcomes were investigated:
- Drug use
- Criminal activity
- Socioeconomic productivity

Comparisons were made during three time periods:
- The two-month period immediately prior to entering treatment
- The two-month period immediately after leaving treatment
- The two-month period immediately prior to being interviewed

Drug use

Table I-3 summarizes the results. Heroin use declined dramatically
for clients leaving the program. This occurred immediately upon
leaving treatment and further improvement had occurred by the time

---

[1]Drug use information was confirmed by urine tests. However, it should be
noted that 27 percent of the urines were positive for preludin.

[2]Arrest information was confirmed by police arrest records.

the interviews were conducted. This pattern of immediate improvement followed by further improvement by the time the interviews were conducted occurred for all categories of drugs. While essentially all the respondents were using heroin at least some of the time prior to entering treatment, 63 to 66 percent stated that they were not using it at all during the two months prior to being interviewed. Only 4 to 6 percent of the respondents in any of the treatment groups admitted to using heroin daily during the two-month period prior to being interviewed. Sixty-two percent of these clients stated that they had been using heroin daily during the two months prior to treatment. Dramatic, statistically significant improvements occurred for both treatment groups; there is no statistically significant difference among the groups. The responses by the former clients were essentially confirmed by the urinalysis tests of specimens taken during the interviews.

A substantial statistically significant decline occurred in illegal methadone usage by all treatment groups for all years. Ninety-two percent of the treatment respondents indicated no illegal methadone usage at all during the two-month period prior to being interviewed, while from 61 to 69 percent used it during the two months prior to treatment. There is no statistically significant difference among the groups. In view of the concern over illegal methadone use by persons who don't use other opiates, it is reassuring that *none* of the respondents reported using only illicit methadone during the most recent two-month period.

Next to heroin, cocaine was the most popular drug used by these clients during the two-month period prior to entering NTA. Cocaine is not addictive and is rarely a primary drug of abuse. Only 41 to 43 percent of the clients did not use cocaine at all during this preprogram period, but few used it daily (4 to 8 percent). During the two months immediately prior to being interviewed, 77 to 78 percent of the respondents who had been through treatment programs did not use cocaine at all. Hardly any of these individuals used cocaine daily (0 to 3 percent), but a substantial percentage used cocaine occasionally (20 to 22 percent). The decline in use is statistically significant for both treatment groups; there is no statistically significant difference between the groups.

. Amphetamines were a relatively less popular drug as compared with heroin or cocaine. All treatment groups reported a reduction in amphetamines used between the two-month period prior to treatment and the two-month period prior to being interviewed.

Barbiturates were a comparatively unpopular drug of abuse among the clients sampled. Few of the clients used barbiturates during the two months prior to entering the program. Nevertheless, there was some improvement among these clients as reflected by the high percentage not using barbiturates at all during the two months immediately after treatment (89 to 93 percent). The improvement realized by the methadone maintenance group is statistically significant, but that of the abstinence group is not. However, there are no statistically significant differences between the two groups.

Hallucinogens, dilaudid, minor tranquilizers and other drugs were used very infrequently. The general pattern of reduction in use of drugs previously discussed is also reflected in these. However, none of the improvements in hallucinogen use is statistically significant. For dilaudid, improvements for methadone maintenance and abstinence groups are statistically significant between the period before treatment and the last two months.

The reduction in use of minor tranquilizers is not statistically significant.

Reductions in use of other drugs are statistically significant for both groups. There are no statistically significant differences among the groups.

The respondents were not specifically asked whether they used preludin, but whether they used other drugs. In any case, preludin was the drug that most frequently appeared in the urine results; 27 percent of the tests were positive for preludin, indicating widespread abuse of that drug.

Some reduction occurred in marijuana usage between pre- and postprogram periods. However, considerable use is indicated. This is hardly surprising in view of the widespread use of marijuana in our society, particularly by persons in the age groups represented in this sample. The reduction in marijuana use is statistically significant for the maintenance group, but not for the abstinence group. The difference between the two groups is not statistically significant.

A major concern among methadone programs is the belief that clients may tend to substitute alcohol for heroin. The data do not support this belief. There are only slight changes in drinking behavior. There is no significant difference between pretreatment and posttreatment drinking behavior or between the two groups.

Another form of substance substitution is increased use of cigarettes after withdrawing from heroin. The responses indicate that this has not occurred. The frequency of cigarette use changed little

TABLE I-3

DRUG USE
(percentage)

Frequency of Use	Methadone Maintenance			Abstinence			Control		
	2 Mo. Before NTA	2 Mo. After NTA	Last 2 Mo.	2 Mo. Before NTA	2 Mo. After NTA	Last 2 Mo.	2 Mo. Before NTA	2 Mo. After NTA	Last 2 Mo.
Heroin									
Not at all	0	52	66	4	57	63	5	46	63
Occasionally	28	38	30	24	29	31	32	34	27
Daily	72	10	4	72	14	6	63	20	10
Total	100	100	100	100	100	100	100	100	100
Illegal Methadone									
Not at all	69	84	92	61	81	92	62	76	89
Occasionally	26	14	8	38	17	6	33	21	9
Daily	5	2	0	1	2	2	5	1	2
Total	100	100	100	100	100	100	100	100	100
Cocaine									
Not at all	43	74	78	41	71	77	43	64	82
Occasionally	53	26	22	51	28	20	50	36	18
Daily	4	0	0	8	1	3	7	0	0
Total	100	100	100	100	100	100	100	100	100
Amphetamines									
Not at all	78	84	88	72	77	84	66	75	81
Occasionally	18	14	11	19	18	15	27	20	17
Daily	4	2	1	9	5	1	7	5	2
Total	100	100	100	100	100	100	100	100	100

n =	93	93	93	96	96	96	100	100	100

TABLE I-4

EMPLOYMENT AND CRIMINAL ACTIVITY
(percentage)

STATUS	Methadone Maintenance			Abstinence			Control		
	2 Mo. Before NTA	2 Mo. After NTA	Last 2 Mo.	2 Mo. Before NTA	2 Mo. After NTA	Last 2 Mo.	2 Mo. Before NTA	2 Mo. After NTA	Last 2 Mo.
Employment									
Paid job	38	33	38	28	40	57	37	38	40
Keeping house, student, job training	2	3	7	8	5	5	5	4	4
Illegal activities	42	35	29	50	41	20	38	36	25
All other activities	18	29	26	14	14	18	20	22	31
Total	100	100	100	100	100	100	100	100	100
n =	93	93	93	96	96	96	100	100	100
Arrests									
Not arrested	75	90	90	75	88	92	78	92	94
Arrested	25	10	10	25	12	8	22	8	6
Total	100	100	100	100	100	100	100	100	100
n =	93	93	93	95	95	95	100	100	100
Incarcerations									
Not incarcerated	89	88	86	87	94	89	85	90	93
Incarcerated	11	12	14	13	6	11	15	10	7
Total	100	100	100	100	100	100	100	100	100
n =	93	93	93	95	95	95	99	99	99

between the pre-treatment and post-treatment periods. Indeed, there is a slight reduction in heavy smoking (i.e., more than one pack each day). The differences are not statistically significant.

Employment

One of the desired results of a drug treatment program is employment or other prosocial activity (e.g., keeping house, going to school, job training). Table I-4 shows a general, but by no means consistent, pattern of improvement in comparing the two-month period prior to treatment with the most recent two-month period.

The abstinence group shows dramatic statistically significant improvement; the percentage of clients having a paid job doubled from 28 to 57 with the methadone maintenance group essentially unchanged. The percentage of abstinence clients who had a paid job or "keeping house, student, or job training" during the last two months was significantly greater than the methadone maintenance group. The abstinence group also experienced a dramatic reduction in illegal activities that was greater than the methadone maintenance group, although that group also showed improvement. Of course, during the period in question, the unemployment rate was increasing substantially. This should affect the results, especially during the most recent period.

A substantial influence on the data could have been exerted by a variety of programs underway in the District of Columbia during these periods, including some focusing on employment of ex-addicts by the U.S. Employment Service, Vocational Rehabilitation, various work-training programs, the Emergency Employment Act and NTA's policy of employing ex-addicts on its staff.

Criminal Behavior

Two measures of criminal behavior are used in this evaluation:
- Frequency of arrests
- Whether or not time was spent in jail

The percentage of clients who were arrested during the two-month period prior to being interviewed was substantially less than during the two months before treatment, indicating a reduction in criminal behavior as expressed by actual arrests (Table I-4). The reductions are statistically significant for both treatment groups. There is no statistically significant difference between the two groups.

Another indicator of criminal behavior is whether or not a client has spent time in jail during the periods in question. There is improvement, but it is not statistically significant.

What Influence Did Treatment Seem to Have on Post-Treatment Outcomes?

Drug Use

Comparisons were made, in terms of each drug, among the treatment and control groups. No statistically significant differences were found to exist.

During the period 1971-1974, substantial change occurred external to the treatment programs that could help to explain both the substantial decrease in heroin use and the lack of significant differences between the treatment and control groups. Of greatest significance is the substantial decrease in the supply and quality and the rise in the price of heroin. These factors made heroin usage by *all* groups more difficult whether they had received treatment or not.

The substantial reduction in use of illegal methadone by both treatment and control groups during the last two-month period is undoubtedly influenced by the tightening of Federal regulations governing the dispensing of methadone inaugurated late in 1972. Consequently, the supply of illegal methadone in Washington, D.C., was sharply curtailed. This is reflected in data on methadone overdose deaths.

Amphetamine use was severely restricted as the Federal Government initiated a significant policy reducing availability before the most recent time period.

Employment

The abstinence group showed a significantly greater improvement than the control group. Of course, employment is substantially influenced by economic conditions and government programs which may have little relationship to treatment.

Criminal Behavior

There are no statistically significant differences between treatment and control groups in frequency of arrests and whether time was spent in jail.

Multiple Behavioral Outcome Measures

Each respondent was classified (based on his drug use, criminal behavior, and employment) as:

- Fully recovered
- Partially recovered
- Marginally recovered, or
- A failure

As a whole, 22 percent of the respondents were fully recovered, 20 percent were failures and the remaining 58 percent were partially or marginally recovered. Fifty-seven percent achieved either full or partial recovery.

The differences in recovery status among treatment groups are not statistically significant, nor are the differences among the treatment and control groups. (Chapter VII).

Redefinition of Treatment and Control Groups (Chapter VIII)

The control group was "purified" to include only clients who had entered NTA for one day and did not subsequently re-enter treatment. All other clients were grouped according to the total length of time they remained in treatment, including all entries.

A remarkably consistent pattern of heroin use was shown among all groups. The differences between treatment groups and the control group are not statistically significant.

As in heroin use, the arrest patterns of the groups during the most recent two-month period are remarkably similar.

In terms of employment-type activities during the most recent two-month period, the patterns are again generally consistent among the groups; the differences are not statistically significant.

Explanatory Factors (Chapter IX)

A search was made for possible explanations as to why there are essentially no significant differences in the behavior of former clients sampled among treatment and control groups, and analyses were conducted of factors that might explain outcomes. A considerable number of clients' background and characteristic variables were examined; none of these was significantly different among the groups.

A number of client backgrounds, characteristics, and outcome variables (72) were analyzed through factor analysis and multiple regression analyses in attempting to establish relationships among the variables and to determine what variables might explain variance in the dependent (outcome) variables.

The most significant overall finding is that client outcomes are unrelated to any background or characteristic variables included in the study.

Client Attitudes and Perceptions (Chapter X)

Client attitudes and perceptions about treatment were not a principal focus of this study; therefore, only rather rudimentary questions were included in the interview instrument and the results should be regarded with caution.

This analysis shows that there are no significant differences among the treatment and control groups in terms of their personal reasons for participations in treatment. Clients in treatment for more than five days had generally favorable attitudes toward NTA. Approximately 70 percent of the treatment group clients stated that NTA was helpful to them and that the amount of time spent in treatment during their last month in NTA was adequate; 82 percent of them would recommend NTA to a friend with a drug problem.

A substantial percentage of the original control group believed that NTA helped (22 percent) and 20 percent of the clients in the control group subsequently re-entered treatment. Further, 58 percent of control group clients stated that they would recommend NTA to a friend who had a drug problem. Our data tend to show that many of the clients left NTA because they felt they could make changes or improvements in their lives without the help of NTA. However, client attitudes toward treatment were unrelated to outcomes.

The examination of client attitudes and perceptions regarding their treatment experiences suggests there are implications as to how NTA can enhance its ability to attract and affect changes in clients. It appeared that many clients quit not because they changed their commitment to seek change but rather because they questioned the means to achieve that change as offered by the treatment program. Thirty-nine percent of the treatment group and 31 percent of the control group clients responding felt that one of the most important changes needed was more and better counseling. Thus, perhaps clients would be more likely to make an appropriate investment in the treatment process at NTA if the supportive services such as individual counseling, group counseling, rehabilitative counseling, etc., received greater emphasis by the program. Their responses show that few supportive services were received.

A reason that 15 percent of the clients (13 percent of the methadone maintenance group, 8 percent of the abstinence group, and 23 percent of the control group) gave for quitting the program revolved around their suspicious and negative attitudes about methadone's role in the treatment process. This suggests that NTA could improve its ability to retain clients if it could attend more closely to community and client observations about methadone. This would require working with the community as well as the clients entering the treatment programs.

Discussion (Chapter XI)

This study has raised many issues and tested numerous hypotheses. The results raise questions with respect to some of the common assumptions pertaining to drug treatment programs.

One is struck first by the very large behavioral changes experienced by these clients. However, the data suggest that the effect of treatment cannot be separated from other factors. Moreover, clients' behavioral changes were not only unrelated to presence and type of treatment, but were also unrelated to demographic and background characteristics as well. This absence of differences is little short of baffling.

Chapter XI discusses several possible interpretations of this phenomenon. The "maturing-out" hypothesis seems inadequate to explain these findings; in fact, the data tend to ' dispute that theory. Forces entirely outside the traditional treatment process may be at work to help bring about change in addict behavior. The community may have changed. Or, as heroin use may have been tolerated in the community in the period preceding addicts' contact with NTA, it may have become increasingly unacceptable as the real dangers of the drug became known. Thus, if the addict was to remain acceptable to his community, he was forced to explore other avenues of behavior. Whether or not this describes the intellectual and behavioral changes in the decade 1965 to 1975 in Washington, D.C., is unknown, but there is evidence to support this theory.

A different explanation for the lack of differences between treatment and control groups may lie in the data. In this regard, we can hypothesize that persons having made a commitment to seek change, i.e., who enter treatment and then drop out of treatment immediately thereafter, represent a very select group of persons who are improperly cast into a control group. In this formulation, that group would consist, at least partly, of persons who had not given up their decision to seek behavioral change, but merely quit on the means to accomplish that change as posed by the treatment program. There is some support for this theory in our data.

Another explanation supported by our data lies in the criminal justice system's efforts to reduce the supply of illicit drugs and make the abuser's lifestyle more difficult to maintain. A substantial decrease in the purity of heroin occurred during this period and the price of heroin increased substantially, making it more difficult for an addict to obtain the drug. This probably helped to draw addicts into treatment programs.

The result of this study causes us to re-examine some commonly held assumptions about the treatment process. First is the common assumption that it is desirable to keep clients in treatment for extended periods of time. Our data show that clients did equally well whether they stayed in treatment one day or five years (or shorter periods of time). Perhaps, the clients felt they were the best judge of how long a period of treatment is sufficient.

The study raises questions with respect to the comparative virtues of methadone maintenance vs. detoxification. Neither modality was found to be clearly superior to the other. Again, perhaps treatment programs should be more flexible, as was NTA, with respect to the modality in which the clients should be placed.

There has been a great deal of interest in demographic and background correlates of success in drug treatment. Some studies have produced limited evidence showing that clients with certain characteristics do better in treatment than others. In this study, demographic and background factors failed to explain success in treatment or lack thereof. It is possible that these characteristics may be important in treatments other than methadone maintenance and detoxification. Nearly all the clients shared one characteristic — rather heavy involvement in heroin use. Possibly, if persons who were not heroin addicts were included, some characteristics could be significant; our data neither prove nor disprove this hypothesis.

Chapter II

INTRODUCTION

Background of Study

This study was initiated by the Narcotics Treatment Administration in Washington, D.C., and the Special Action Office for Drug Abuse Prevention. It was to determine the effectiveness of the Narcotics Treatment Administration's programs for treating heroin addicts and how post-treatment behavior was affected by the type of treatment modality and length of time out of treatment. Sponsorship of the study was shifted from the Special Action Office for Drug Abuse Prevention to the National Institute on Drug Abuse when the Federal Government's drug functions were reorganized. The initial study effort began on June 23, 1974, and concluded on February 28, 1975. A second phase of the study was conducted between July 1, 1975, and January 31, 1976; this resulted in a more refined analysis of the data.

The Special Action Office for Drug Abuse Prevention (SAODAP) specified the parameters of the study to assess the experiences of clients who had contact with and/or received treatment from the Narcotics Treatment Administration (NTA). It called for selecting a stratified random sample of 360 individuals, interviewing them, and obtaining urine samples. The basic issues addressed were:

- What happened to former clients who left treatment?
- What influence did treatment seem to have on post-treatment outcomes of former clients?

This report presents the final results of this study. Unfortunately, SAODAP specified an extremely short time span for tracking and interviewing former clients — only six months. In this brief time, some of the respondents could not be found. However, approximately 95 percent of the sample was located and 81 percent of the sample was successfully interviewed. To the best of our knowledge, this is

19

the highest response rate achieved for this type of study and this type of respondent. The backgrounds and characteristics of clients interviewed were compared to clients who were not interviewed. No significant differences were found.

The initial SAODAP contract allocated only one month to analyze the data and prepare the report. Of course, all the interesting questions could not be explored fully in this brief period. Nevertheless, the results were significant[1] and of considerable interest.

The National Institute on Drug Abuse awarded a contract to BAI to conduct further analyses of the data (including additional data contained in the NTA Central Client Intake files). This new research included regrouping clients and analyzing differential outcomes for the new groups and conducting more extensive multivariate analyses. Later, the focus was expanded to include a specific concern for the natural history of drug abuse.[2] This report is composed of the report published in February 1975, which concluded the initial contract, and the substantial additional analyses conducted pursuant to the subsequent NIDA contract.

Chapter III of this report describes the NTA program. Chapter IV develops the methodology employed. Chapter V defines objectives and evaluation criteria. Chapter VI presents a profile of clients upon entering NTA. Chapter VII analyzes the effectiveness of the treatment modalities in terms of post-treatment outcomes and compares the treatment groups to control groups. Chapter VIII analyzes different groupings of clients. Chapter IX explores hypotheses that could help to explain the results in Chapters VII and VIII. Chapter X analyzes clients' attitudes and perceptions about treatment. Some implications and interpretations are discussed in Chapter XI and conclusions are presented in Chapter XII.

_____

[1] Marvin R. Burt and Sharon Pines, *Evaluation of the District of Columbia's Narcotics Treatment Administration Programs*, 1970-1973 (Bethesda, Maryland: Burt Associates, Incorporated, 1975).

[2] For a recent example of a "natural history" approach, see: Lee H. Robins, *The Vietnam Drug Abuser Returns* (Washington, D.C.: Government Printing Office, 1973).

Chapter III

DESCRIPTION OF THE NARCOTICS TREATMENT ADMINISTRATION DURING THE TIME PERIODS UNDER STUDY

Background

Scope of the Problem

Estimates of the magnitude of drug addiction in Washington, D.C. have varied markedly and have not been subjected to reliable epidemiologic verification. At the time of the Tydings Committee Hearings (November 1969), the number of addicts in Washington was estimated at 10,400 (using the Baden Formula).[1] A more thorough study of mortality data prompted a more recent estimate (1971) of 17,000 (Baden Formula) or roughly 2.2 percent of the total D.C. population of 756,510. It was estimated that 20 percent of all males aged twenty to twenty-four in the city were heroin addicts. In the D.C. Model Cities area, it was estimated that 30 percent of all males aged twenty to twenty-four were heroin addicts.[2]

In 1970, at least 63 people died of opiate overdoses in Washington, D.C.[3] In a survey of 77 addict deaths recorded in 1969-1970 (only D.C. residents were included), the following profile was developed:

* 91 percent of deaths occurred among blacks

---

[1] Baden Formula assumes that one of every 200 heroin addicts dies of an overdose reaction each year (number of O.D. death x 200).

[2] Robert L. DuPont, "Profile of a Heroin-Addiction Epidemic," *New England Journal of Medicine*, 285 (August 5, 1971), 320-24. See also, Mark H. Greene, "An Epidemiologic Assessment of Heroin Use" in "The Epidemiology of Drug Abuse," eds. Mark H. Greene and Robert L. DuPont (Washington, D.C.: American Public Health Association, 1974), pp. 1-10.

[3] Drug screens were performed in 51 percent of all autopsied death. DuPont, op. cit.

- 74 percent of deaths occurred among males

- 60 percent of deaths occurred among individuals aged 21-30 years

- 48 percent of deaths occurred among individuals residing in D.C. service areas 6 and 7[1]

In 1971, 82 people died of opiate overdoses; 71 died in 1972; and 19 died in 1973.[2]

In 1972, addicts reported[3] spending $25-30 per day for drugs.[4] It was estimated that the annual value of property and services transferred because of addiction through robbery, theft, prostitution, drug sales, etc., was $328 million.[5] The indirect costs (e.g., fear) of drug addiction, while sizable, were impossible to measure.

Forty-five percent of the male offenders entering the D.C. Jail[6] were classified as narcotic users (based on urinalysis in 1969).[7] Thirty-seven percent of the addicts were charged with crimes against property as compared with 15 percent of nonaddicts. Also, three of four criminal homicides were committed by drug addicts.[8]

Treatment Programs

Washington, D.C., is served by a number of private and public treatment programs employing a range of treatment strategies. The

---

[1] DuPont, op. cit.

[2] District of Columbia Coroner's Office, Medical Examiner.

[3] Survey conducted at induction (prior to entering NTA); 100 randomly-selected patients were asked about their drug expenditures for the two-day period preceding induction.

[4] Interview conducted by Mr. Neal McKelvey with Dr. Barry Brown, April 13, 1972.

[5] John Holahan, "The Economics of Drug Addiction and Control in Washington, D.C.: A Model for Estimation of Costs and Benefits of Rehabilitation," Office of Planning and Research, D.C. Department of Corrections, Washington, D.C., 1970.

[6] Excludes those released at the precinct or released following arraignment in the D.C. Superior Court.

[7] Professional Advisory Committee on Heroin Addiction in D.C., "Report," May 1971.

[8] C. S. Campbell, et al., "The NTA: A Medical Approach with a Public Policy Guide," The George Washington University, Department of Public Administration, December 1, 1971.

overwhelming majority of addicts, however, are treated in programs operated by the Narcotics Treatment Administration, a division of the D.C. Department of Human Resources. The NTA programs rely heavily on methadone maintenance and detoxification. Most incoming clients choose to enter one of these two treatment modalities. Clients are not coerced into either treatment by the program staff.

Congressional authority for the initiation of a drug addiction treatment program in D.C. was granted in 1953. In 1956, the D.C. Department of Public Health began an inpatient abstinence program in a 35-bed unit of D.C. General Hospital. The Drug Addiction Treatment and Rehabilitation Center (DATRC), an outpatient abstinence program operated by the Department of Public Health and funded by OEO, was opened at D.C. General Hospital in 1968. In 1968, the Bureau of Rehabilitation opened a half-way house under contract to DATRC.

The Narcotics Addiction Rehabilitation Center (NARC) was established by the Department of Corrections in 1969 to provide methadone treatment for addicts leaving the D.C. prisons.

As a result of the Tydings Hearings and following a reorganization of the D.C. Government, the Narcotics Treatment Administration (NTA) was established in February 1970 to serve as an umbrella agency for publicly funded narcotic treatment programs (including the DATRC and NARC programs).[1]

Prior to the start of NTA in February 1970, there were a number of limited efforts launched by various D.C. Government agencies to cope with the mounting drug problem. NTA was established by the Department of Human Resources to lead and coordinate a comprehensive drug treatment effort.[2] All existing city-operated programs were incorporated into NTA.

Organizational Mechanisms

NTA is one of five divisions of the D.C. Department of Human Resources. In 1971, NTA was operating 11 facilities (eight outpatient and three inpatient). In addition, private contractors were operating two facilities. During 1972, there were 16 NTA-run facilities (13 outpatient and three inpatient). Three additional facilities

---

1 Campbell, op. cit.
2 Advisory Committee, op. cit.

were operated by contractors. In 1973, NTA operated 15 facilities (12 outpatient and three inpatient). An additional three units were operated by private contractors.

Philosophical Base

NTA operated a multi-modal program employing three treatment strategies:
- Abstinence
- Methadone detoxification
- Methadone maintenance

In addition, a three-week urine surveillance program was available for patients in the criminal justice system (referred from the court for drug use evaluation).

Each program combined a treatment effort with counseling services (drug counseling, vocational counseling). Provisions were also included to deal with clients who required hospitalization or with clients who were ill or pregnant. The client population is shown below

	May 1971		May 1972		May 1973
Total Number in Treatment	3,341	(100%)	4,176	(100%)	
Abstinence[1]	625	(19%)	665	(16%)	Not
Methadone Detox.	851	(25%)	1,018	(24%)	Available
Methadone Maint.	1,786	(54%)	2,493	(60%)	
Methadone Hold	79	(2%)	discontinued		

The philosophy of the program included:
- Extensive reliance on methadone[2]
- Extensive use of ex-addict counselors in all treatment strategies
- Primary emphasis on outpatient services, although inpatient beds are available

---

[1] Majority of clients enrolled in abstinence programs was under 18 years of age.

[2] The client distribution within treatment modalities was changing. The influx of younger, less "hard core" addicts resulted in an input mix of 60 percent detoxification, 20 percent maintenance and 20 percent abstinence. Given the high discharge rate for detox programs, the picture at any point in time would probably not be too much different from the one in the table above.

- Clear and limited program goals
  - Cessation of illegal drug use
  - Cessation of participation in illegal activities
  - Participation in jobs, education, job training
- Retention in treatment

Treatment Model

Admission Criteria

- Methadone maintenance
  - Must volunteer for maintenance
  - Must have used heroin continuously for at least two years
  - Must be at least eighteen years old
  - Cannot meet previous two requirements, but failed in an adequate detox attempt
- Methadone detoxification (detox from heroin or methadone)
  - Any client who has a history of *less* than two years addiction to heroin without prior attempts at detoxification; or
  - Any client who is under eighteen years old; or
  - Any client who requests detoxification
- Abstinence
  - Any client who requests this type of treatment (or clients who, in the estimation of the counselor, do not have serious addiction problems)

Figure III-1 shows the flow of patients through the NTA program.

Central Medical Intake (CMI)

All new clients and readmissions (clients who had not had contact with an NTA treatment program for 28 days) reported to CMI. CMI was open from 9:00 a.m. to 7:00 p.m., five days a week. It provided uniform, standardized initial client orientation, multi-phasic health screening and referral to appropriate treatment modalities. The central intake facility began operation in October of 1971. The entire facility, including equipment and the 24-hour personnel, was funded by the Department of Human Resources.

The following activities were performed at CMI:
- Identification screen — checked to see if client was already under treatment in NTA, contacted program or cooperating program

PATIENT FLOW

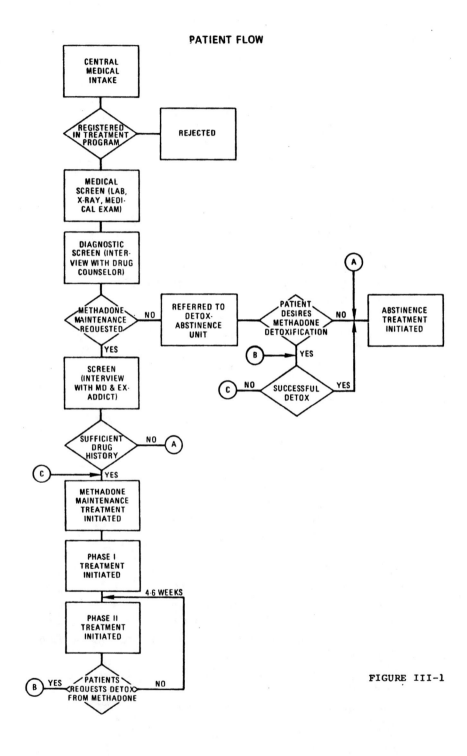

FIGURE III-1

- Medical screen — medical history, urinalysis including tests for drugs; hematocrit; sickle cell and hepatitis test; serology; lower function studies; X-ray; EKG and complete medical examination
- Diagnostic screening — counselors took social and drug history, explained various treatment modalities, and assisted clients in selection of treatment modality
- Provided identification card with unique number assigned to each patient
- Data collection point — a copy of each client's drug history and social and medical summary was sent to Computer Services Division of NTA
- Assignment to treatment modality and treatment center
- Annual review of NTA clients to update initial medical and social history and to evaluate treatment experience

Treatment Programs

All clients referred to a methadone detoxification or maintenance treatment program were interviewed upon arrival by a physician and counselor. This session was conducted primarily to verify addiction. Thus, the screening for addiction was as follows:

- Medical examination at CMI — urinalysis and physical
- Interview at CMI with drug counselor — collect drug history
- Interview at treatment center with physician
- Interview at treatment center with ex-addict counselor

These steps were taken to preclude methadone administration to non-addicts. A client failing to establish a record of addiction was referred (if he so desired) to an abstinence unit.

Methadone Maintenance

The initial daily dosage level was 15-50 mg. This dose was increased gradually on one of three maintenance dosage schedules over a two- to six-week period until the client was stabilized on 50-80 mg. per day.[1] The dosage level depended on age, size, duration of habit,

---

[1] There was evidence that low dose (less than 50 mg.) methadone maintenance was sometimes employed. Rather than a treatment option, this appeared to be a physician-related decision. The physician sometimes was not convinced the client was an addict. Other times, the physician was concerned about the short- or long-term side effects of methadone.

and side effects. Dosage levels above 80-100 mg. were discouraged and dosage levels above 100-130 mg. were forbidden. Clients in Phase I maintenance were required to come to the treatment center five times per week. After the client was stabilized on methadone, he was transferred to a Phase II maintenance clinic. Based on his performance (discontinued use of illegal drugs, employment or school, home life, etc.), the number of visits could be reduced to two per week until Federal regulations were revised late in 1972. While NTA initially believed that methadone maintenance would continue for an indefinite period, they began to detoxify methadone clients whose life situation had been stable for six to twelve months. Clients who requested detoxification were transferred to a detoxification unit and slowly withdrew from methadone.[1] Clients were then strongly urged to enroll in an abstinence program (urine testing and counseling) for at least three months.

Methadone Detoxification

The initial dose was 15-25 mg. of methadone.[2] Depending on the client's response, this dose may have been increased up to 50-60 mg. until the client was stabilized (comfortable and had ceased heroin use). Then the client was placed on one of nine detoxification schedules, and the stabilization dose was gradually reduced. Abstinence could be achieved somewhere between two weeks (administrative detox) and 25 weeks following the start of treatment.[3] Detoxification clients were not permitted to take medication home. Clients who failed at detoxification were aggressively counseled toward accepting maintenance treatment, provided they met the admission requirements. Clients completing the detoxification program were encouraged to enter the abstinence program for at least six months and participate in regular surveillance, individual, and group counseling.

Abstinence

Clients in abstinence programs received no methadone but re-

---

[1] Patients reported it more difficult to kick methadone than heroin. This apparently resulted from the impure nature of street heroin and from the longer duration of the action of methadone.

[2] Maintenance patients who attempted to detox had to begin at their current level (50-100 mg.).

[3] All but two schedules called for completion of detox within 90 days.

ceived regular urine surveillance, individual and group counseling, and vocational counseling. The majority of clients entering abstinence directly (as opposed to entering from detoxification) were under eighteen years old.

Youth

The majority of clients seventeen years of age and under were referred to abstinence programs (outpatient and inpatient clinics and a modified therapeutic community for males). Limited attempts were made with detoxification (low doses over three to twenty-four weeks) and maintenance (low dose, 60-70 mg., over a three to twelve month period). In addition to medical treatment, if indicated, youths received individual and group counseling. A weekly family therapy session was also scheduled.

Criminal Justice System

A firm relationship was established between NTA and the criminal justice system. NTA handled all clients who were formally referred by the courts or D.C. Department of Corrections as a condition of their release to the community. Liaison and surveillance of CJS patients was maintained by the Criminal Justice Surveillance Unit.

Staff Ratios

Methadone maintenance clinics were operated on a 21/300 (approximately 1/14) staff to patient ratio. The following staffing pattern was employed:

- Administration
  1 administrator
  1 clinic manager specialist
  1 information specialist
  1 secretary
  1 clerk-typist
- Treatment
  .5 physician
  1.5 nurse
  3 medical assistants

- Counseling
  1 chief counselor
  7 drug counselors
  2 vocational counselors
  1 community coordinator

Chapter IV

METHODOLOGY

Evaluation Design

The Special Action Office for Drug Abuse Prevention specified the parameters of the follow-up study to assess the experiences of clients who had contact with and/or received treatment from the Narcotics Treatment Administration in Washington, D.C. It called for selecting a sample of 360 individuals, interviewing them, and obtaining urinalysis specimens. The basic issues to be addressed as previously noted were:[1]

- What happened to former clients who left treatment?
- What influence did treatment seem to have on post-treatment outcomes of former clients?

The first question can be answered by determining the status of former clients at the time they were interviewed. The second question was more difficult to answer in that the effects of treatment must be isolated from all other effects which might have influenced the post-treatment outcome of the former clients.

Technically, answering the second question required an experimental design in which prospective clients, who applied and were qualified for admission to NTA programs, were randomly assigned to treatment and control groups. This type of design may be expressed in the following matrix form where R represents random assignment, O represents periodic observations and X represents introduction of treatment.

---

[1] Although not clearly specified at the outset of the project, a third issue was addressed in this analysis: How were post-treatment outcomes influenced by type of treatment modality and by time elapsed since leaving treatment?

$$RO_1 \ X \ O_2$$
$$RO_3 \ X \ O_4$$
$$RO_5 \ X \ O_6$$
etc.

Of course, such a random assignment to experimental groups (i.e., modalities of treatment) and control groups (i.e., no treatment) was not feasible. Random assignment to treatment groups was not feasible because the determination as to which treatment a client was assigned was a function of his own desires as well as professional judgment as to which treatment would be most effective. Assignment to a control group would be unconscionable. A responsible public program cannot refuse to treat a heroin addict simply because it desires to conduct an evaluation study. This would violate professional ethics as well as HEW regulations on protecting human subjects.

Due to the impossibility of employing a truly experimental design, a "next best" alternative was sought. It was decided to draw samples retrospectively (i.e., after the fact) of clients who actually entered methadone maintenance and abstinence programs. Due to the impossibility of randomly assigning prospective clients to control groups, it was decided to use as control groups individuals who applied for treatment, were accepted, but who left within five days. The overwhelming majority of this group actually left within one or two days prior to obtaining their first medication or counseling session.

Because the period of time a client has been out of treatment may influence his post-treatment outcome, the sample was further segmented into the year in which the client left treatment. Three years were chosen: 1971, 1972, and 1973. As interviews were conducted from August 1974 through January 1975, the respondents had been out of treatment for roughly one to three years. Although it would have been desirable to stratify the sample by time spent in treatment, this could not be done with reasonable precision. NTA records did not necessarily record the date when a client left treatment, although it was usually possible to determine the *year* of departure.

Sample Selection

The universe of clients was partitioned into six treatment groups and three nontreatment (control) groups. Because all clients who entered treatment subsequent to January 1970 were required to register at the Central Medical Intake unit (later called Central Client Intake), the initial universe consisted of all clients registered at the Central Medical Intake unit during the period January 1971 through December 1973 — 10,807 clients. Three time periods were specified during which the client must have left treatment: January to December 1971, January to December 1972, and January to December 1973. The universe was partitioned into type of treatment (or no treatment received) and time period during which clients left treatment. The following matrix shows that the sample was partitioned into those clients who left methadone maintenance,[1] those who left abstinence,[2] and who registered at Central Medical Intake and left within five days[3] during each of the three years. A methadone maintenance client is defined as one who spent a minimum of 51 percent of his time in a methadone maintenance regimen. An abstinence client is defined as one who spent a minimum of 51 percent of his time in a detoxification-abstinence regimen.

	1971	1972	1973	Total
Methadone Maintenance	40	40	40	120
Abstinence	40	40	40	120
CMI Only (Control)	40	40	40	120
Total	120	120	120	360

Because clients were not assigned randomly to experimental and control groups, the design employed is a type of quasi-experimental design termed a "nonequivalent control group design."[4] Referring to the matrix below, two experimental (E) and one control group (C) are selected for each of the three years. Periodic observations are made during three time periods: (1) two months prior to entering treatment, (2) two months after leaving treatment, and (3) two months prior to being interviewed. Measurements are made to determine changes realized by each group comparing the three time periods. The measurements between the experimental and and control groups are then compared to determine whether the

---

[1] But who remained more than five days after registering at CMI.

[2] But who remained more than five days after registering at CMI.

· [3] The sample was formed by successively drawing all clients who left within one day, two days, three days, four days, and five days for each of the three years until a sufficient number of clients was obtained.

[4] Donald T. Campbell and Julian C. Stanley, *Experimental and Quasi-Experimental Designs for Research* (Chicago: Rand McNally, 1963).

NONEQUIVALENT CONTROL GROUP DESIGN

Group	1971	1972	1973	
E^1_1	O. . .XO			O
E^1_2	O. . .XO			O
C^1_1	O O			O
E^2_1		O. . .XO		O
E^2_2		O. . .XO		O
C^1_2		O O		O
E^3_1			O. . .XO	O
E^3_2			O. . .XO	O
C^3_1			O O	O

changes appear to be attributable to the program in question or outside factors. Then comparisons are made among the three years to detect significant differences.

Because few NTA clients were enrolled in drug-free programs, "abstinence" was defined to include methadone detoxification as well as drug-free programs. The overwhelming majority of these clients were enrolled in methadone detoxification programs.

The sample for each cell was randomly generated from the universe of all clients who left treatment (including dropouts as well as graduates) with the following exceptions:

- No client who was under 18 years of age when first leaving NTA was included

- No client who was first admitted before January 1, 1970, was included

Forty names were randomly selected for each cell using the NTA computer listings and the data contained in the CMI files. Once the 40 names in each cell were finally determined, there were *no* substitutions for any reason.

During the tracking of the respondents, it was discovered that two of the respondents were actually the same person, using different names. Therefore, the sample size was reduced from 360 to 359.

Questionnaire Design

SAODAP specified that the questionnaire design follow a questionnaire developed by the Johns Hopkins University in conducting a previous study.[1] We revised this questionnaire substantially: (1) the number of questions was reduced, (2) nearly all questions were made close-ended, (3) the format was changed considerably to facilitate interviewing and coding, (4) the language was changed to "street language" in order to facilitate understanding between the respondents and interviewers, and (5) it was completely recoded.

The instrument was pretested with nine respondents who were former clients of NTA and were readily accessible.

---

[1] The Johns Hopkins University School of Hygiene and Public Health, "Interdrug, Final Report: An Evaluation of Treatment Programs for Drug Abusers," a study conducted under OEO Contract B2C-5409, July 31, 1973.

Interviewing

The interviewers were predominantly ex-addicts who had become NTA staff counselors. The initial group of interviewers received 12 hours of formal training including practice with actual interviewing using videotape playback. Later, as more interviewers were added to the project, the formal sessions were limited to three hours and more emphasis was placed upon field experience under supervision. As a final test to qualify as a member of the interviewing staff, the interviewer was given a tracking sheet containing information on the whereabouts of a client and $15 for the purpose of paying the client for the interview. Successful completion of the interview resulted in being accepted as a member of the staff. The clients were paid $10 each for completing the interview and an additional $5 for providing a urine specimen.

The typical interviewer was a rehabilitated ex-addict, with counseling experience, who was "street wise."

Sources of Locational Data

At the inception of the project, numerous sources of information on the whereabouts of the clients in the sample were investigated. Principal sources were:

- Central Client (Medical) Intake
- D.C. Vocational Rehabilitation Administration
- Medicaid
- D.C. Department of Vital Statistics
- D.C. Department of Corrections
- Superior Court of the District of Columbia
- Washington, D.C., Metropolitan Police Department
- Federal Bureau of Prisons
- The telephone directory and criss-cross telephone directory

In addition to the above official sources, numerous unofficial sources were used by the interviewer including:

- Personal contacts
- Relatives, friends, employers, etc., who were identified either by the official sources or by personal contacts
- The "wire" on the streets
- Former NTA counselors of the client

Field Tracking Procedures

Following the data extraction and sample selection procedures, the interviewers were given sheets with the target client's name, address, telephone number (if available), work location (if available), as well as the names, addresses, telephone numbers of relatives or friends listed to be contacted in an emergency. The interviewers first made telephone calls to the numbers listed for the client. If the client answered the telephone call, the interviewer explained the purpose of the interview and made an appointment to see the client. No interviewing was conducted by telephone because of the need to validate the respondent's identity and obtain a urine specimen to validate answers to questions concerning drug use.

Where telephone contacts were not usable, the interviewer traveled to the listed address and tried to contact the client. If contact was not made but the target client appeared to live there, the interviewer returned as often as possible. In a few cases, as many as 15 return visits were made. If a friend or relative could be located at the target client's address, the client's current status was ascertained and an appointment was made through the friend or relative. The interviewer also visited the alternate addresses listed on the tracking sheet. In addition, the interviewers were trained to follow up on any leads that might have emerged during the tracking process. The interviewer or team leader also made contacts with treatment units in order to find additional useful information. Any inability of the interviewer to find a client was checked by the team leader, who reviewed the tracking experience and helped to obtain further leads. The team leaders validated the responses in selected cases.

Intensive tracking procedures were conducted during the last six weeks of the period. The tracking sheet for each client not successfully interviewed was reviewed in a group session led by the Project Director. The interviewer explained his tracking progress. Suggestions were made by the Project Director, team leaders, and other interviewers as to what further steps might be taken to locate and interview the target client. Some clients were reassigned to another interviewer. Tracking was ordered ceased only where all leads as to the client's location had been exhausted, the client had repeatedly intentionally eluded the interviewer, denied his identity, or flatly refused to be interviewed.

Approximately 95 percent of the sample clients were located and 81 percent were successfully interviewed. In the majority of cases

where the client was not located, the records indicated nonexistent or otherwise fictitious addresses and telephone numbers, false next of kin, and/or the client had assumed a fictitious identity. However, the target client was tracked under all of his known aliases. The results of tracking and interviewing are shown in Table IV-1.

TABLE IV-1

RESULTS OF TRACKING AND INTERVIEWING

	Number	Percent
Initial sample	360	
Client using two sampled names	1	
Revised sample	359	100
Client deceased	2	1
Client located	342	95
Client refused to be interviewed or interview incomplete	50	14
Successful interviews	291 [a]	81

	1971	1972	1973	Total
In institutions	23 [b]			
Elsewhere	268			
Methadone Maintenance	27	29	37	93
Abstinence	34	33	29	96
Control	34	36	30	100
Total	95	98	96	289

[a] Two interviews were received too late to include in the analysis; therefore only 289 were used.

[b] Twenty respondents were interviewed in jails or prisons; three in hospitals.

We anticipated that the clients who left treatment early and members of the control groups would be more difficult to locate and interview. This is because the information useful for tracking "older" clients was more out of date, and information on control group members was often less complete than that on clients in treatment for longer periods of time. However, the data below, showing the number of completed interviews by cell, indicate little difference be-

tween the groups. This is probably due to the priorities used in assigning respondents to interviewers. Clients who left treatment earlier or who were members of control groups were generally assigned earlier; thus, more time was allowed for tracking and interviewing them.

Characteristics of clients interviewed were compared to those of clients not interviewed. There were no significant differences.

Confidentiality of Data

All data extracted from program records, collected in interviews, or gathered from corroboratory sources were treated as confidential in order to protect all cooperating individuals and agencies. Identification numbers only were key punched on the data processing cards; a list of names and identification numbers was separately maintained and protected.

More important than the confidentiality of responses was the protection of the clients' addiction history during the field tracking efforts. The interviewers were trained to ensure that none of the clients' friends, relatives, etc., knew that the client had a history of addiction or was treated in a drug abuse program — even if they were listed as persons to be contacted in an emergency. The interviewers were trained to probe gently to see if the person indicated such knowledge; if such recognition was not forthcoming, the interviewers were instructed to terminate the discussion by asking the person to have the client contact the interviewer about "some health program she/he was in." The interviewers were continually reminded that they must avoid revealing the client's identity, even if this meant not completing an interview. This confidentiality of identity was a vital component of the field tracking process.

Quality Control

Completed interviews were checked to determine: (1) whether the correct person had been interviewed, (2) whether the information obtained was internally consistent and (3) whether the information obtained was complete.

A concern was the problem of floating identities among addicts (i.e., where identities, including various identification cards, are passed about). This problem was exacerbated by the monetary in-

centive the interviewers were using. In several instances, imposters attempted to pose as the respondent, presumably in order to obtain the $15. Some of these ruses were successful despite the procedures established to thwart them. Interviewers were supplied with certain information including the client's age, Social Security number, next of kin, address, date of birth, etc. They were instructed to ask the respondent to provide this information and to show specific identification cards as a device for verifying his identity.

Verification that the proper respondent was interviewed was accomplished by comparing his signature (obtained on the receipt he signed for the $15) with the signature in the file at Central Medical Intake. Secondly, the interview responses were compared to certain known data obtained from other sources: personal and family characteristics and drug usage history obtained from the CMI files; and arrest history obtained from the police files. If none of these checked out, the respondent was judged to be the wrong person and the interview was rejected as invalid.

Interviews that were incomplete or internally inconsistent were rejected as invalid. In these instances, the tracking sheet and questionnaires were returned to the interviewer and he was required to reinterview the client. This was a time-consuming process, particularly uring the first few months of the tracking and interviewing period. However, as a result of these strict quality control procedures, the data were unusually complete as demonstrated by the consistent "n's" in the tables throughout the report.

The experience in this follow-up study points to the need for strict procedures for validating the responses. Without such procedures, the data would be of questionable validity.

Data Reduction and Analysis

All questionnaires were checked for completeness and internal consistency and coded for data processing immediately upon receipt.

Analysis was conducted on each variable to determine its distribution, properties, and whether it was statistically significant among the three groups within each year. Chi-square tests were used initially, testing for significance at the .05 level. The data were then grouped by: (1) input variables — client background and demographic characteristics and (2) outcome variables — drug use, criminal activity and socioeconomic productivity.

The outcome variables then were compared by time periods:

- The two-month period before treatment
- The two-month period after treatment
- The two-month period before being interviewed

The means and distributions were tested for significance at the .05 level using "F," "t," and Chi-square tests.[1]

Because the F and Chi-square tests showed htat the nine groups of respondents were homogeneous, the groups were collpased into one for purposes of multivariate analysis. Factor analyses were conducted using 72 variables. The multivariate analyses are discussed in Chapter IX. Numerous stepwise multiple regressions were run using various combinations of independent variables. and alternative dependent variables for the entire sample and selected subgroups.

---

[1] Technically, the analysis of variance (F test) assumptions are that the distributions of the variables are normal and the variances of distributions from the mean are equal. Because variances are almost never quite equal or distributions quite normal, some error is introduced, the magnitude of which is not known. The F and t tests were used to determine whether differences between the three successive two-month periods and differences among treatment and control groups were statistically significant. The F test was used for each variable to check for differences in means among treatments, years, and their interaction in one analysis of variance. F tests were not used where distributions were binominal because of the skewed distributions and small sample sizes. Chi-square tests, which make no assumptions as to distribution and variances from the mean, were employed for all variables in comparing treatment and control groups within each of the three years.

Chapter V

OBJECTIVES AND EVALUATION CRITERIA

Objectives

The objectives of the Narcotics Treatment Administration are simple and straightforward:
- Reduce heroin usage
- Reduce other drug usage
- Reduce criminal activity
- Increase employment and income

These simple and straightforward objectives make possible straightforward evaluation criteria:

- Frequency of heroin usage prior to the program compared to that after the program
- Frequency of other drug usage before the program compared to that after the program
- Employment before the program compared to that after the program

Thus, the criteria of effectiveness focus on the changes in behavior in the above four categories as measured before and after the program. This study focuses on the following periods:

- Preprogram — The two-month period immediately prior to entering NTA treatment
- Postprogram — The two-month period immediately after leaving treatment
- Postprogram — The period two months immediately prior to being interviewed.

As arrests were infrequent, arrest data were also gathered for six-month periods prior to entering treatment, six months after leaving treatment, and six months prior to being interviewed.

Chapter VI

PROFILE OF CLIENTS UPON ENTERING NTA

What type of person entered NTA? We drew random samples of clients entering NTA who met the criteria specified in Chapter IV during each of the three years, 1971, 1972, and 1973. This chapter presents a composite of the characteristics upon entering treatment of the sample clients who were interviewed. These data are subjected to detailed statistical analysis in later chapters.

Client Characteristics

Table VI-1 shows that the clients were typically male (82 percent), black (86 percent), and relatively young (21 to 25). Clearly, clients interviewed had characteristics similar to those in the total sample.[1]

Backgrounds

Table VI-2 depicts the backgrounds of these clients. More than half of the clients for whom data are available were born in Washington, D.C., and 89 percent of the clients lived until at least age 15 with one or both parents. Eighty-two percent of the clients had caretakers who worked regularly, and 49 percent of the clients had parents who had at least graduated from high school. Only 11 percent

---

[1] No further data are available for clients not interviewed.

TABLE VI-1

CLIENT CHARACTERISTICS
(percentage)

	Total Sample (n=359)	Clients Interviewed (n=289)
Sex		
Male	81	82
Female	19	18
Race		
Black	82	86
White	18	14
Age		
Less than 18	0	0
18 — 20	24	26
21 — 25	44	42
26 — 30	20	20
31 — 36	5	5
Over 36	7	7

TABLE VI-2

CLIENT BACKGROUNDS
(percentage)

Birthplace (n=151) *	
Washington, D.C.	59
Other	41
Client Caretakers Until Age 15 (n=289)	
Parents	89
Other	11
Caretakers Work History (n=288)	
Never worked	3
Worked occasionally	15
Worked regularly	82
Educational Level Attained by Clients' Parents (n=289)	
Grades 1-8	18
Grade 9	11
Grade 10	11
Grade 11	11
Grade 12	28
Above grade 12	21
Illegal Drug Use by Clients' Family (n=288)	
No	89
Yes	11
Highest Grade Completed (n=288)	
Grades 1-8	6
Grade 9	7
Grade 10	25
Grade 11	22
Grade 12	33
Above 12	7
Veteran Status (n=233) *	
Not a veteran	89
Veteran	11
Mental Health Treatment Prior to First Entry (n=227) *	
Never treated	95
Treated	5

* Source: CCI Files.

of the clients had family members who used illegal drugs. Forty percent of the clients had graduated from high school; the average client had completed the eleventh grade. Only 11 percent of the clients were veterans and only 5 percent had been treated in a mental health program prior to first entering NTA.

Client Status Upon Entering NTA

Table VI-3 depicts the clients' statuses upon entering NTA as recorded by the Central Client Intake Files. As shown by the "n's," data were not available for all clients.

Approximately one half of the clients had one or more dependents, 76 percent of the clients indicated that their health status was "excellent" or "good." At the time they entered NTA, about two thirds of the clients stated that they had used heroin daily for more than two years; and 45 percent claimed that they were spending more than $40 per day for heroin. Sixty percent of the clients had never been incarcerated; 22 percent had been incarcerated for at least one year. Seventy-four percent of the clients entered voluntarily. Table VI-4 shows the age of the clients when they first participated in each type of crime. Nearly all had participated in a drug-related crime, more than half of them before age eighteen. Fifty-two percent had participated in a property crime, 24 percent of these before age eighteen. Participation in violent and victimless crimes was relatively rare; 73 percent stated they had never been involved in violent crimes; and 69 percent, never involved in victimless crimes.

TABLE VI-3

CLIENT STATUS UPON ENTERING NTA
(percentage)

Living Arrangement (n=208) *
  Alone   13
  Spouse   14
  Parents   35
  Other relatives   11
  Friends   19
  Institution (hospital, halfway house, etc.)   7
  No stable arrangement and other   1

Number of Dependents (n=162) *
  None   49
  One   22
  Two   20
  Three or more   9

General Health Status (n=183) *
  Excellent   23
  Good   53
  Fair   20
  Poor   4

Duration of Daily Heroin Use (n=162) *
  No days   1
  16-180 days   3
  181-365 days   7
  1-2 years   22
  Over 2 years   67

Daily Heroin Use (in dollars) (n=106) *
  Less than $6   13
  $6-40   42
  $41-100   31
  $101-150   10
  More than $150   4

Time Incarcerated (n=198) *
    Never   60
    1-5 days   3
    6 days-1 year   15
    1-2 years   7
    2-4 years   4
    4-10 years   9
    More than 10 years   2

Type of Participation (n=286)
    Voluntary   74
    Forced by legal authorities   26

* Source: CCI Files.

TABLE VI-4
AGE OF CLIENT WHEN FIRST PARTICIPATED IN CRIME
(percentage)

Age When First Involved

Type of Crime	Never Involved	Less Than 13	14-15	16-17	18-19	20-25	Over 25	Total*
Drug Related	2	4	20	30	23	19	2	100
Property	48	6	8	10	13	11	4	100
Violent	73	1	1	5	7	11	2	100
Victimless	69	1	3	5	6	13	3	100
Other	96	0	0	1	1	2	0	100

*n=288 for all rows.

Client Behavior During the Two Months Immediately
Prior to Entering NTA

Table VI-5 shows that during the two-month period immediately prior entering NTA, nearly all the clients used heroin at least occasionally and 69 percent used it daily. Most of the clients also used cocaine occasionally and marijuana. Alcohol and cigarettes were used by most of the clients at least occasionally. Illegal methadone was used at least occasionally by 36 percnet of the clients, but use of the remaining drugs in Table VI-5 was relatively infrequent.

According to Table VI-6, 24 percent of the clients were arrested and 13 percent incarcerated during this two-month period. Table VI-7 shows that only 34 percent of the clients had a paid job. Forty-three percent admitted to being engaged in illegal activities.

TABLE VI-5
FREQUENCY OF DRUG USE — TWO-MONTH PERIOD
PRIOR TO ENTERING NTA
(percentage)

Drugs	Not at All	Frequency of Use Occasionally	Daily	Total*
Heroin	3	28	69	100
Illegal Methadone	64	32	4	100
Cocaine	42	51	7	100
Amphetamines	72	21	7	100
Barbiturates	82	16	2	100
Hallucinogens	87	12	1	100
Dilaudid	86	11	3	100
Minor Tranquilizers	90	9	1	100
Other Drugs	91	8	1	100
Marijuana	26	43	31	100
Alcohol	36	54	10	100
Cigarettes	12	53	35	100

* n=289 for all rows.

TABLE VI-6

ARRESTS AND INCARCERATIONS — TWO-MONTH PERIOD PRIOR TO ENTERING NTA
(percentage)

Arrests	
Not arrested	76
Arrested	24
Total	100
n =	288
Incarcerations	
Not incarcerated	87
Incarcerated	13
Total	100
n =	287

TABLE VI-7

EMPLOYMENT — TWO-MONTH PERIOD PRIOR TO ENTERING NTA
(percentage)

Status	Percent
Paid job	34
Keeping house	5
Student, job training	0
Illegal activities	43
All other activities	18
Total	100
n =	289

Chapter VII

EFFECTIVENESS — CHANGE IN BEHAVIOR

This chapter addresses each of the evaluation criteria that were discussed in the previous chapter. For each evaluation criterion, the research questions initially posed are answered:

- What happened to former clients who left treatment?
- What influence did treatment seem to have on post-treatment outcomes of former clients?

For each effectiveness measure, we will first show what happened to clients in terms of the behavioral elements defined and then compare their behavior with that of individuals in the control group.

Chi-square, t, and F tests (as appropriate) were performed on the tables contained in this chapter. *These were not significant at the .05 level, except in the instances specifically noted in the text.* Complete results of these tests are contained in Appendix A.

Two types of analyses are presented in this chapter. First, all clients in the sample entering methadone maintenance modalities are grouped irrespective of the year in which they entered treatment (all entreed in 1971, 1972, or1973). Similarly, all clients entering abstinence modalities are placed in a second group; and all clients in the contro group are grouped irrespective of the year in which they entered NTA.[1]

---

[1] T tests were performed on: (1) the differences between behavior two months before entering NTA and two months after leaving for each group; (2) the differences between behavior two months before entering NTA and two months before being interviewed; (3) comparing the differences in behavioral changes in (1) and (2) for each of the three groups (correcting probabilities for degrees of freedom). F tests were performed among groups. Statistically significant results (p = <.05) are reported in the text and attendant data presented with each table. Complete results of all ests are in Appendix A. Chi-square tests were performed on skewed binominal distributions.

TABLE VII-1

HEROIN USE
(percentage)

Frequency of Use	Methadone Maintenance			Abstinence			Control		
	2 Mo. Before NTA	2 Mo. After NTA	Last 2 Mo.	2 Mo. Before NTA	2 Mo. After NTA	Last 2 Mo.	2 Mo. Before NTA	2 Mo. After NTA	Last 2 Mo.
Not at all	0	52	66	4	57	63	5	46	63
Occasionally	28	38	30	24	29	31	32	34	27
Daily	72	10	4	72	14	6	63	20	10
TOTAL	100	100	100	100	100	100	100	100	100
n =	93	93	93	96	96	96	100	100	100

SIGNIFICANT TESTS

Variable Description	Group	T-Test	DF	Significance
2 Before vs 2 After	Maintenance	13.2	92	<.001
	Abstinence	14.0	95	<.001
	Control	11.2	99	<.001
2 Before vs Last 2	Maintenance	16.1	92	<.001
	Abstinence	18.1	95	<.001
	Control	15.0	99	<.001

After completion of the above analysis, the three groups are further divided by year in which the client initially entered NTA. The methadone maintenance group consists of three subgroups — 1971, 1972, and 1973. Similarly, the abstinence and control groups each consist of three groups -- 1971, 1972, and 1973. Thus, there are nine groups.

Comparison of Methadone Maintenance,
Abstinence, and Control Groups

Heroin Use

Table VII-1 shows that heroin use declined dramatically for clients leaving the program. This occurred immediately upon leaving treatment and further improvement occurred by the time the interviews were conducted. While essentially all the clients were using heroin at least some of the time prior to entering treatment, 63 to 66 percent stated that they were not using it at all during the two-month period prior to being interviewed. Only 4 to 6 percent of the clients in either of the treatment groups admitted to using heroin daily during the two months prior to treatment. Dramaitc statistically significant improvement occurred for both groups, but there are no dramatic statistically significant differences between the two groups.

Dramatic statistically significant improvements were also achieved by the clients who had not received treatment (i.e., left within five days of acceptance at CMI). There are no statistically significant differences in improvement experienced by the treatment groups and the control groups. The responses by the former clients, as indicated in Table VII-1, were essentially confirmed by urinalysis tests of specimens taken during the interviews.[1]

During the period 1971-1974, a major change occurred external to the treatment programs that could help explain both the decrease in heroin use and the lack of significant differences between the treatment and control groups. This change was the decrease in the supply and quality and the rise in price of heroin. The change would decrease heroin usage by *all* groups whether in treatment or not.

Evidence of a general reduction in heroin use comes from several sources. First, the number of heroin overdose deaths dropped substantially as indicated in Chapter III. Secondly, the percent of urine

---

[1] These tests showed that 88 percent of the respondents gave answers that were consistent with the urinalysis tests.

56   DRUG ABUSE

specimens tested among arrestees in the D.C. Central Lock-up that
were positive for heroin decreased from 25 percent during the first
half of 1972 to about 10 percent during the second half of 1973.
During the period when the interviews were conducted (roughly the
second half of 1974)), about 15 percent were positive. District of
Columbia police reported that in June 1973, the average price of
heroin purchased on the street was $8.38 per milligram, compared
to $2.08 during the first half of 1972. The purity of heroin purchased
on the street by D.C. narcotics agents declined from 6 percent in
the second half of 1969 to 2 percent during the first quarter of 1973.
The purity increased gradually thereafter; during the period when
our interviews were conducted, roughly the second half of 1974,
purity was about 4 percent.[1] The shapes of the supply and demand
curves and the effect of price on them are not precisely clear, but
such changes in price and quality could be expected to affect demand for the drug. A general downturn in the heroin epidemic in
Washington, D.C., has been reported elsewhere.[2]

It would be interesting and instructive to compare, on a monthly
basis, rates of reported heroin use, overdose rates, and purity and
price of heroin. This would provide some notion of the relationship
between the availability, purity and price, and actual use in the
community. This is not feasible due to the lack of trend data on
actual use and the small number of overdose cases reported.

Another factor that could act to reduce heroin usage is a change
in police activity, other than that aimed at reducing the supply of
heroin. This could influence heroin use by: (1) incarcerating pushers and users or (2) increasing the perceived risk of arrest and incarceration. Police strength was essentially constant during the period
as indicated below:

[1] Ladrence Feinberg, "City's Heroin Addicts Decrease, Center Says," *Washington
Post*, July 22, 1973; Metropolitan Police Department, "Average Purity of Street
Level Heroin Purchased by D.C. Narcotics Agents."

[2] Robert L. DuPont and Mark H. Green, "Patterns of Heroin Addiction in the
District of Columbia," National Association for the Prevention of Addiction to
Narcotics; *Proceedings of the 5th National Conference on Methadone Treatment*
(Washington, D.C., 1973). The sharp decline in heroin use from 1969 through
1973 in Washington, D.C. is also documented in Mark H. Greene and Robert
L. Dupont "Heroin Addiction Trends," *American Journal of Psychiatry*, Vol. 131,
1974, pp. 545-550.

For a discussion of the impact of a drug treatment program on incidence and
prevalence of heroin addiction, see: Patrick H. Hughes, Edward C. Senay, and
Richard Parker, "The Medical Management of a Heroin Epidemic," *Archives of
General Psychiatry*, Vol. 27, November 1972, pp. 585-591.

Police Strength[1]
(Number of Officers)

	FY 1971	FY 1972	FY 1973	FY 1974
Total Strength	4,920	5,070	4,895	not
Patrol Strength	3,535	3,650	3,862	available

Therefore, it is unlikely that police strength could have been a significant factor unless there were changes in allocation of effort such as more emphasis on arresting pushers. No changes occurred. The number of arrests did not change substantially during this period as indicated below:

Arrests[2]
(000)

	FY 1971	FY 1972	FY 1973	FY 1974
Part I Offenses	12.3	12.5	12.6	
Part II Offenses[3]	18.6	17.9	18.3	not
Drug Offenses	(3.1)	(3.0)	(3.5)	available
Total	30.9	30.4	30.9	

Illegal Methadone Usage

Table VII-2 shows statistically significant declines in illegal methadone usage by both treatment groups. Ninety-two percent of each group indicated no illegal methadone usage during the two-month period immediately prior to being interviewed, while 61 to 69 percent used it during the two months immediately prior to treatment.

The control group also shows statistically significant improvement (i.e., reductions in illegal methadone use), and there are no statistically significant differences in improvement between the treatment groups and the control group.

This reduction in use of illegal methadone by both treatment and control groups during the last two-month period was undoubtedly influenced by the tightening of Federal regulations inaugurated late in 1972 governing the dispensing of methadone. Consequently, the supply of illegal methadone in Washington, D.C., was sharply cur-

---

1 Metropolitan Police Department, Washington, D.C., *Annual Reports*: Fiscal Year 1971, 1972, 1973.

2 Metropolitan Police Department, op. cit.

3 Excludes drunk and disorderly arrests which were distorted by civil disturbances in Fiscal Year 1971.

tailed. This is reflected in the following data on methadone overdose deaths.

Opiate Overdose Deaths[1]

Cause	1971	1972	1973
Heroin	60	20	5
Methadone	17	33	14
Combination of Methadone & Heroin	5	18	0

[1] Source: District of Columbia Medical Examiner.

TABLE VII-2

ILLEGAL METHADONE USE
(percentage)

Frequency of Use	Methadone Maintenance			Abstinence			Control		
	2 Mo. Before NTA	2 Mo. After NTA	Last 2 Mo.	2 Mo. Before NTA	2 Mo. After NTA	Last 2 Mo.	2 Mo. Before NTA	2 Mo. After NTA	Last 2 Mo.
Not at all	69	84	92	61	81	92	62	76	89
Occasionally	26	14	8	38	17	6	33	21	9
Daily	5	2	0	1	2	2	5	1	2
TOTAL	100	100	100	100	100	100	100	100	100
n =	93	93	93	96	96	96	100	100	100

SIGNIFICANT TESTS

Variable Description	Group	T-Test	DF	Significance
2 Before vs 2 After	Maintenance	3.5	92	<.001
	Abstinence	3.3	95	.002
	Control	3.5	99	<.001
2 Before vs Last 2	Maintenance	4.9	92	<.001
	Abstinence	5.4	95	<.001
	Control	5.3	99	<.001

TABLE VII-3

AT LEAST ONE ILLICIT OPIATE USED--
MOST RECENT TWO MONTHS
(percentage)

Opiate(s) Used	Methadone Maintenance	Abstinence	Control
Yes	37	41	41
No	63	59	59
TOTAL	100	100	100
n =	93	96	100

TABLE VII-4

LEGAL METAHDONE USE
(percentage)

Frequency of Use	Methadone Maintenance			Abstinence			Control		
	2 Mo. Before NTA	2 Mo. After NTA	Last 2 Mo.	2 Mo. Before NTA	2 Mo. After NTA	Last 2 Mo.	2 Mo. Before NTA	2 Mo. After NTA	Last 2 Mo.
Not at all	86	94	90	84	96	94	89	93	93
Occasionally	5	2	3	3	1	0	5	3	1
Daily	9	4	7	13	3	6	6	4	6
TOTAL	100	100	100	100	100	100	100	100	100
n =	93	93	93	96	96	96	100	100	100

SIGNIFICANT TESTS

Variable Description	Group	T-Test	DF	Significance
2 Before vs 2 After	Abstinence	3.1	95	.003

TABLE VII-5

COCAINE USE
(percentage)

Frequency of Use	Methadone Maintenance			Abstinence			Control		
	2 Mo. Before NTA	2 Mo. After NTA	Last 2 Mo.	2 Mo. Before NTA	2 Mo. After NTA	Last 2 Mo.	2 Mo. Before NTA	2 Mo. After NTA	Last 2 Mo.
Not at all	43	74	78	41	71	77	43	64	82
Occasionally	53	26	22	51	28	20	50	36	18
Daily	4	0	0	8	1	3	7	0	0
TOTAL	100	100	100	100	100	100	100	100	100
n =	93	93	93	96	96	96	100	100	100

SIGNIFICANT TESTS

Variable Description	Group	T Test	DF	Significance
2 Before vs 2 After	Maintenance	5.9	92	<.001
	Abstinence	5.1	95	<.001
	Control	5.8	99	<.001
2 Before vs Last 2	Maintenance	6.7	92	<.001
	Abstinence	5.6	95	<.001
	Control	7.7	99	<.001

Illicit Opiates

Table VII-3 indicates the percentage of clients using at least one illicit opiate (heroin, illegal methadone, or dilaudid) during the most recent two-month period. From 37 to 41 percent of treatment group respondents used at least one of these drugs occasionally. The slight differences among treatment groups are not statistically significant.

There is some fear that individuals might use illicit methadone who do not use other opiates, but *none* of the respondents in this study reported using only illicit methadone during the most recent two-month period.

Legal Methadone

By definition, legal methadone could be obtained only by enrollment in a program dispensing the drug. Few respondents were enrolled in such a program during the two-month period prior to entering the NTA program and the two months after leaving.[1] Table VII-4 shows that for those few respondents who had been enrolled in such a program, there is a statistically significant change ony for abstinence clients between the periods immediately prior to entering NTA and after leaving. There are no statistically significant differences among the groups.

Cocaine

Next to heroin, cocaine was the most popular drug used by respondents during the two-month period immediately prior to entering the NTA program. Cocaine is not addictive and is rarely a primary drug of abuse. Table VII-5 shows that 41 to 43 percent of the clients did not use cocaine during this preprogram period; only a few used it daily (4 to 7 percent). During the two months immediately prior to being interviewed, 77 to 78 percent of the respondents who had been through treatment programs did not use cocaine. Hardly any of these individuals used cocaine daily (0 to 3 percent) but a substantial percentage used cocaine occasionally (20 to 22 percent).

----

[1] See Tables VIII-8 and VIII-9 for the percentage of clients who were enrolled in drug treatment programs prior to and subsequent to NTA respectively.

TABLE VII-6

AMPHETAMINE USE
(percentage)

Frequency of Use	Methadone Maintenance			Abstinence			Control		
	2 Mo. Before NTA	2 Mo. After NTA	Last 2 Mo.	2 Mo. Before NTA	2 Mo. After NTA	Last 2 Mo.	2 Mo. Before NTA	2 Mo. After NTA	Last 2 Mo.
Not at all	78	84	88	72	77	84	66	75	81
Occasionally	18	14	11	19	18	15	27	20	17
Daily	4	2	1	9	5	1	7	5	2
TOTAL	100	100	100	100	100	100	100	100	100
n =	93	93	93	96	96	96	100	100	100

SIGNIFICANT TESTS

Variable Description	Group	T-Test	DF	Significance
2 Before vs 2 After	Control	2.9	99	.006
2 Before vs Last 2	Maintenance	2.7	92	.008
	Abstinence	4.2	95	<.001
	Control	4.3	99	<.001

TABLE VII-7

BARBITURATE USE
(percentage)

Frequency of Use	Methadone Maintenance			Abstinence			Control		
	2 Mo. Before NTA	2 Mo. After NTA	Last 2 Mo.	2 Mo. Before NTA	2 Mo. After NTA	Last 2 Mo.	2 Mo. Before NTA	2 Mo. After NTA	Last 2 Mo.
Not at all	80	88	93	89	90	93	79	83	89
Occasionally	18	12	6	8	9	5	21	17	11
Daily	2	0	1	3	1	2	0	0	0
TOTAL	100	100	100	100	100	100	100	100	100
n =	93	93	93	96	96	96	100	100	100

SIGNIFICANT TESTS

Variable Description	Group	T-Test	DF	Significance
2 Before vs 2 After	Maintenance	3.2	92	.002
	Control	2.5	99	.01
2 Before vs Last 2	Maintenance	3.5	92	<.001
	Control	2.9	99	.004

As with heroin, all the groups show substantial statistically significant reductions in usage. There are no statistically significant differences in reductions in usage.

Amphetamines

Table VII-6 shows that amphetamines were less popular drugs than heroin or cocaine. All treatment groups reported a reduction in amphetamine usage between the two-month period prior to treatment and the two months prior to being interviewed.

There is no statistically significant difference between the treatment and control groups. It should be noted that a significant policy was initiated by the Federal Government prior to the most recent two-month period which considerably restricted the availability of amphetamines and reduced their potential for abuse. Preludin, a non-amphetamine stimulant, was the drug that was most frequently present in the urines taken during the interviews — appearing in 27 percent of the urines. Late in 1972, the District of Columbia Medical Society obtained a voluntary reduction of amphetamine shipments in Washington by the drug manufacturers and established rigorous guidelines for physicians designed to severely limit the use of amphetamines.[1] This could have further restricted the availability of amphetamines and also caused substitution of preludin, which was not considered in the Medical Society's action. However, it cannot be determined to what extent substitution took place due to the lack of data on preludin use during prior periods.

Barbiturates

Barbiturates were a comparatively unpopular drug of abuse among the clients sampled. According to Table VII-7, few clients used barbiturates during the two months immediately prior to entering the program (from 79 to 89 percent did not use them at all). Nevertheless, there are statistically significant improvements for the methadone maintenance and control groups (but not for the abstinence group).

There are no statistically significant differences in improvement among the treatment and control groups.

Hallucinogens, Dilaudid, Minor Tranquilizers, and Other Drugs

Tables VII-8, VII-9, VII-10, and VII-11 indicate infrequent use of these drugs. The general pattern of improvement shown on previous

TABLE VII-8

HALLUCINOGEN USE
(percentage)

Frequency of Use	Methadone Maintenance			Abstinence			Control		
	2 Mo. Before NTA	2 Mo. After NTA	Last 2 Mo.	2 Mo. Before NTA	2 Mo. After NTA	Last 2 Mo.	2 Mo. Before NTA	2 Mo. After NTA	Last 2 Mo.
Not at all	89	94	95	88	93	91	86	91	91
Occasionally	10	6	5	12	7	9	13	8	8
Daily	1	0	0	0	0	0	1	1	1
TOTAL	100	100	100	100	100	100	100	100	100
n =	93	93	93	96	96	96	100	100	100

TABLE VII-9

DILAUDID USE
(percentage)

Frequency of Use	Methadone Maintenance			Abstinence			Control		
	2 Mo. Before NTA	2 Mo. After NTA	Last 2 Mo.	2 Mo. Before NTA	2 Mo. After NTA	Last 2 Mo.	2 Mo. Before NTA	2 Mo. After NTA	Last 2 Mo.
Not at all	89	96	96	82	88	89	87	92	93
Occasionally	9	4	3	14	11	11	11	6	6
Daily	2	0	1	4	1	0	2	2	1
TOTAL	100	100	100	100	100	100	100	100	100
n =	93	93	93	96	96	96	100	100	100

SIGNIFICANT TESTS

Variable Description	Group	T-Test	DF	Significance
2 Before vs Last 2	Maintenance	2.2	92	.03
	Abstinence	2.8	95	.006

TABLE VII-10

MINOR TRANQUILIZER USE
(percentage)

Frequency of Use	Methadone Maintenance			Abstinence			Control		
	2 Mo. Before NTA	2 Mo. After NTA	Last 2 Mo.	2 Mo. Before NTA	2 Mo. After NTA	Last 2 Mo.	2 Mo. Before NTA	2 Mo. After NTA	Last 2 Mo.
Not at all	95	96	98	93	93	92	82	87	93
Occasionally	4	4	2	5	7	7	17	12	7
Daily	1	0	0	2	0	1	1	1	0
TOTAL	100	100	100	100	100	100	100	100	100
n =	93	93	93	96	96	96	100	100	100

SIGNIFICANT TESTS

Variable Description	Group	T-Test	DF	Significance
2 Before vs 2 After	Control	2.2	99	.03

tables is also reflected in these. However, none of the improvements in hallucinogen use is statically significant. For dilaudid, improvements for methadone maintenance and abstinence groups are statistically significant between the period before treatment and the last two months. The improvement for the control group is not statistically significant.

The reduction in use of minor tranquilizers is statistically significant between the period two months before treatment and the last months only for the control group.

Reductions in use of other drugs are statistically significant for all three groups between the period before treatment and the last two months.

As for other drugs, none of the changes in drug usage are statistically significant between the treatment and control groups.

Marijuana

Table VII-12 shows some reductions in marijuana usage among the periods in question, although considerable use is indicated. This is hardly surprising in view of the widespread use of marijuana in our society, particularly by persons in the age groups represented in the sample. However, reductions in marijuana use are statistically significant for the methadone maintenance and control groups but not for the abstinence group.

There are no statistically significant differences in the changes in marijuana usage between the two types of treatment or between the treatment and control groups.

Alcohol

A major concern among methadone programs is the belief that clients may tend to substitute alcohol for heroin. Table VII-13 does not support this belief. There are slight changes in drinking behavior after treatment compared to before treatment, but these are not statistically significant.

There are no statistically significant differences in drinking behavior among the two types of treatment or between the treatment and control groups.

Cigarette Use

Another form of substance substitution is increased use of cigarettes after withdrawing from heroin. Table VII-14 does not support this

TABLE VII-11

OTHER DRUG USE
(percentage)

Frequency of Use	Methadone Maintenance			Abstinence			Control		
	2 Mo. Before NTA	2 Mo. After NTA	Last 2 Mo.	2 Mo. Before NTA	2 Mo. After NTA	Last 2 Mo.	2 Mo. Before NTA	2 Mo. After NTA	Last 2 Mo.
Not at all	92	98	98	95	97	98	85	93	95
Occasionally	7	2	2	5	3	2	13	5	3
Daily	1	0	0	0	0	0	2	2	2
TOTAL	100	100	100	100	100	100	100	100	100
n =	93	93	93	96	96	96	100	100	100

SIGNIFICANT TESTS

Variable Description	Group	T-Test	DF	Significance
2 Before vs 2 After	Maintenance	2.3	92	.03
	Control	2.6	99	.01
2 Before vs Last 2	Maintenance	2.1	92	.04
	Abstinence	2.0	95	.05
	Control	2.9	99	.005

TABLE VII-12

MARIJUANA USE
(percentage)

Frequency of Use	Methadone Maintenance			Abstinence			Control		
	2 Mo. Before NTA	2 Mo. After NTA	Last 2 Mo.	2 Mo. Before NTA	2 Mo. After NTA	Last 2 Mo.	2 Mo. Before NTA	2 Mo. After NTA	Last 2 Mo.
Not at all	33	41	42	21	30	30	24	36	35
Occasionally	37	35	33	49	46	41	42	39	35
Daily	30	24	25	30	24	29	34	25	30
TOTAL	100	100	100	100	100	100	100	100	100
n =	93	93	93	96	96	96	100	100	100

SIGNIFICANT TESTS

Variable Description	Group	T-Test	DF	Significance
2 Before vs 2 After	Maintenance	2.0	92	.05
	Control	3.4	99	.002
2 Before vs Last 2	Maintenance	2.3	92	.02
	Control	2.0	99	.05

TABLE VII-13

ALCOHOL USE
(percentage)

Frequency of Use	Methadone Maintenance			Abstinence			Control		
	2 Mo. Before NTA	2 Mo. After NTA	Last 2 Mo.	2 Mo. Before NTA	2 Mo. After NTA	Last 2 Mo.	2 Mo. Before NTA	2 Mc. After NTA	Last 2 Mo.
Never	33	37	38	40	43	40	36	33	30
Occasionally	57	56	54	51	47	52	55	55	55
At least once each day	10	7	8	9	10	8	9	12	15
TOTAL	100	100	100	100	100	100	100	100	100
n =	93	93	93	96	96	96	100	100	100

TABLE VII-14

CIGARETTE USE
(percentage)

Frequency of Use	Methadone Maintenance			Abstinence			Control		
	2 Mo. Before NTA	2 Mo. After NTA	Last 2 Mo.	2 Mo. Before NTA	2 Mo. After NTA	Last 2 Mo.	2 Mo. Before NTA	2 Mo. After NTA	Last 2 Mo.
Not at all	10	11	11	14	12	12	11	11	10
One pack or less per day	57	63	64	50	57	63	53	53	55
More than one pack per day	33	26	25	36	31	25	36	36	35
TOTAL	100	100	100	100	100	100	100	100	100
n =	93	93	93	96	96	96	100	100	100

TABLE VII-15

EMPLOYMENT
(percentage)

Status	Methadone Maintenance			Abstinence			Control		
	2 Mo. Before NTA	2 Mo. After NTA	Last 2 Mo.	2 Mo. Before NTA	2 Mo. After NTA	Last 2 Mo.	2 Mo. Before NTA	2 Mo. After NTA	Last 2 Mo.
Paid job	38	33	38	28	40	57	37	38	40
Keeping house, student, job training	2	3	7	8	5	5	5	4	4
Illegal activities	42	35	29	50	41	20	38	36	25
All other activities	18	29	26	14	14	18	20	22	31
TOTAL	100	100	100	100	100	100	100	100	100
n =	93	93	93	96	96	96	100	100	100

SIGNIFICANT TESTS

Variable Description	Group	T Test	F Test	x^2 Test	DF	Significance
2 Before vs 2 After	Abstinence	-2.2	--		95	.028
2 Before vs Last 2	Abstinence	-4.7	--		95	<.001
	Maint. vs Abstinence	3.5	--		185	.003*
	Abstinence vs Control	-2.9	--		194	.014*
	Among Groups	--	7.0		2	.002
Last 2	Maint. vs Abstinence			4.8	1	.05
	Abstinence vs Control			4.2	1	.05

*Probabilities corrected for degrees of freedom.

belief. The frequency of cigarette use changed little between the pre-treatment and post-treatment periods. Indeed, for all the years in question, there is some reduction in heavy smoking (i.e., more than one pack each day) in the treatment groups. These reductions are not statistically significant.

Again, there are no statistically significant differences between the treatment modalities or between the treatment and control groups.

Employment

One of the desired results of a drug treatment program is employ-ment or other prosocial activity such as keeping house, going to school, or job training. Table VII-15 shows that there is a general, but not consistent, pattern of improvement in compraing the two-month period prior to treatment with the most recent two-month period. The abstinence group showed dramatic improvement; the percentage of clients having a paid job doubled from 28 to 57, while methadone maintenance and control groups were essentially un-changed. The improvement for the abstinence group is statistically significant but not for the other groups. The improvement for the abstinence group is significantly greater than the methadone main-tenance and control groups. The percentage of abstinence clients having a paid job or "keeping house, student, or job training" during the last two months was significantly greater than both the methadone maintenance[1] and the control groups.[2] The abstinence group also experienced a dramatic reduction in illegal activities that was greater than the methadone maintenance and control groups, although these groups also showed improvement.

---

[1] The difference in distributions between abstinence and methadone mainte-nance groups for the last two months is significant only when the data are col-lapsed into two status categories: (1) paid job and keeping house, student, and job training; (2) illegal activities and all other activities ($X^2 = 4.8$, df $= 1$ p $= .05$). When three categories are used — (1) employment and keeping house, student, and job training; (2) illegal activities; (3) all other activities — the difference is not significant ($X^2 = 4.5$, df $= 2$, p$>$ .05).

[2] The difference between abstinence and control groups is significant when the data are collapsed into two groups as specified in the previous footnote ($X^2 = 4.2$, df $= 1$, p $= .05$). The difference is also significant when the three categories are used ($X^2 = 6.2$, df $= 2$, p$<$ .05).

During the period in question, the unemployment rate was increasing substantially, and the problem was most severe among young black males such as the respondents. This should have affected the results, especially during the most recent two-month period. The data could have been influenced also by a variety of programs underway in the District of Columbia during these periods. The U.S. Employment Service, Vocational Rehabilitation, various work-training programs, the Emergency Employment Act, and NTA's policy of employing ex-addicts all increased employment opportunities for ex-addicts.

Criminal Behavior

Two measures of criminal behavior are used in this study:
• Frequency of arrests
• Whether or not time has been spent in jail

Table VII-16 shows that the percentage of clients who were arrested during the two-month period prior to bieng intreviewed was substantially less than during the two months before treatment. The percentage of clients who were arrested varied between 6 and 10 percent during the most recent period in contrast to 22 to 25 percent during the period before treatment. This indicates a very substantial reduction in criminal behavior as expressed by actual arrests. These reductions are statistically significant.

Thre are no statistically significant differences between types of treatment or treatment and control groups.[1] Table VII-17 shows a very similar pattern in comparing three six-month periods. Again, these reductions are statistically significant; but there are no statistically significant differences among the treatment and control groups.

---

[1] The number of arrests reported by respondents was compared to the Metropolitan Police Department records. Eighteen percent of the respondents reported fewer arrests than were recorded in police records. Many respondents were arrested frequently and within short time periods making it difficult for them to remember the exact number.

In several instances, the number of arrests reported by the respondents was greater than the number appearing in police records. One reason for this may be that the police records did not always contain the exact number of arrests and in some cases did not record any at all. Furthermore, the records examined did not include arrests for jurisdictions outside of Washington, D.C., while the respondents included these arrests in their answers.

TABLE VII-16

ARRESTS--TWO-MONTH PERIODS
(percentage)

Status	Methadone Maintenance			Abstinence			Control		
	2 Mo. Before NTA	2 Mo. After NTA	Last 2 Mo.	2 Mo. Before NTA	2 Mo. After NTA	Last 2 Mo.	2 Mo. Before NTA	2 Mo. After NTA	Last 2 Mo.
Not arrested	75	90	90	75	88	92	78	92	94
Arrested	25	10	10	25	12	8	22	8	6
TOTAL	100	100	100	100	100	100	100	100	100
n =	93	93	93	95	95	95	100	100	100

SIGNIFICANT TESTS

Variable Description	Group	X^2-Test	DF	Significance
2 Before vs Last 2	Maintenance	10.5	1	<.005
	Abstinence	14.5	1	<.005
	Control	14.0	1	<.005

TABLE VII-17

ARRESTS--SIX-MONTH PERIODS
(percentage)

Status	Methadone Maintenance			Abstinence			Control		
	6 Mo. Before NTA	6 Mo. After NTA	Last 6 Mo.	6 Mo. Before NTA	6 Mo. After NTA	Last 6 Mo.	6 Mo. Before NTA	6 Mo. After NTA	Last 6 Mo.
Not arrested	63	89	84	68	79	78	70	90	87
Arrested	37	11	16	32	21	22	30	10	13
TOTAL	100	100	100	100	100	100	100	100	100
n =	93	93	93	95	95	95	100	100	100

SIGNIFICANT TESTS

Variable Description	Group	X^2 Test	DF	Significance
6 Before vs Last 6	Maintenance	18.1	1	<.005
	Abstinence	4.2	1	.05
	Control	12.9	1	<.005

TABLE VII-18

INCARCERATIONS--TWO-MONTH PERIODS
(percentage)

Time Spent in Jail	Methadone Maintenance			Abstinence			Control		
	2 Mo. Before NTA	2 Mo. After NTA	Last 2 Mo.	2 Mo. Before NTA	2 Mo. After NTA	Last 2 Mo.	2 Mo. Before NTA	2 Mo. After NTA	Last 2 Mo.
No	89	88	86	87	94	89	85	90	93
Yes	11	12	14	13	6	11	15	10	7
TOTAL	100	100	100	100	100	100	100	100	100
n =	93	93	93	95	95	95	99	99	99

SIGNIFICANT TESTS

Variable Description	Group	x^2 Test	DF	Significance
2 Before vs Last 2	Control	4.5	1	.05

TABLE VII-19

INCARCERATIONS--SIX-MONTH PERIODS
(percentage)

Time Spent in Jail	Methadone Maintenance			Abstinence			Control		
	6 Mo. Before NTA	6 Mo. After NTA	Last 6 Mo.	6 Mo. Before NTA	6 Mo. After NTA	Last 6 Mo.	6 Mo. Before NTA	6 Mo. After NTA	Last 6 Mo.
No	82	85	88	82	84	86	80	86	90
Yes	18	15	12	18	16	14	20	14	10
TOTAL	100	100	100	100	100	100	100	100	100
n =	93	93	93	95	95	95	99	99	99

SIGNIFICANCE TESTS

Variable Description	Group	x^2 Test	DF	Significance
6 Before vs Last 6	Control	5.6	1	.05

TABLE VII-20

EXTENT OF RECOVERY
(percentage)

Extent of Recovery	Methadone Maintenance	Abstinence	Control	Total
Fully	15	26	26	22
Partially	38	35	32	35
I	(23)	(11)	(20)	(18)
II	(5)	(1)	(2)	(3)
III	(7)	(11)	(3)	(7)
IV	(3)	(12)	(7)	(7)
Marginally	28	18	23	23
I	(23)	(11)	(17)	(17)
II	(1)	(6)	(2)	(3)
III	(4)	(1)	(4)	(3)
Failure	19	21	19	20
TOTAL	100	100	100	100
n=	93	96	100	289

TABLE VII-21
HEROIN USE
(percentage)

Frequency of Use	Methadone Maintenance			Abstinence			Control		
	2 Mo. Before NTA	2 Mo. After NTA	Last 2 Mo.	2 Mo. Before NTA	2 Mo. After NTA	Last 2 Mo.	2 Mo. Before NTA	2 Mo. After NTA	Last 2 Mo.
1971									
Not at all	0	48	67	0	53	62	6	53	65
Occasionally	26	37	29	21	32	38	32	30	20
Daily	74	15	4	79	15	0	62	17	15
Total	100	100	100	100	100	100	100	100	100
n=	27	27	27	34	34	34	34	34	34
1972									
Not at all	0	38	59	3	58	64	3	33	50
Occasionally	31	48	38	24	33	24	36	45	39
Daily	69	14	3	73	9	12	61	22	11
Total	100	100	100	100	100	100	100	100	100
n=	29	29	29	33	33	33	36	36	36
1973									
Not at all	0	67	70	10	62	62	7	53	77
Occasionally	27	30	25	28	21	31	26	27	20
Daily	73	3	5	62	17	7	67	20	3
Total	100	100	100	100	100	100	100	100	100
n=	37	37	37	29	29	29	30	30	30

TABLE VII-22
ILLEGAL METHADONE USE
(percentage)

Frequency of Use	Methadone Maintenance			Abstinence			Control		
	2 Mo. Before NTA	2 Mo. After NTA	Last 2 Mo.	2 Mo. Before NTA	2 Mo. After NTA	Last 2 Mo.	2 Mo. Before NTA	2 Mo. After NTA	Last 2 Mo.
1971									
Not at all	82	93	100	68	73	94	50	71	88
Occasionally	18	7	0	32	24	6	44	26	9
Daily	0	0	0	0	3	0	6	3	3
Total	100	100	100	100	100	100	100	100	100
n =	27	27	27	34	34	34	34	34	34
1972									
Not at all	52	79	90	55	85	88	70	72	83
Occasionally	38	17	10	42	12	9	22	22	14
Daily	10	4	0	3	3	3	8	6	3
Total	100	100	100	100	100	100	100	100	100
n =	29	29	29	33	33	33	36	36	36
1973									
Not at all	73	81	89	62	86	93	67	87	97
Occasionally	22	16	11	38	14	4	33	13	3
Daily	5	3	0	0	0	3	0	0	0
Total	100	100	100	100	100	100	100	100	100
n =	37	37	37	29	29	29	30	30	30

Another indicator of criminal behavior is whether or not a client has spent time in jail during the periods in question. Table VII-18 shows no consistent pattern of improvement or degradation, but rather is mixed. Table VII-19, using six-month periods, presents a less distorted picture; all groups show improvement. However, only the control group's reduction is statistically significant.

There are no statistically significant differences between the types of treatment or between treatment and control groups.

Consistency should not necessarily be expected among arrests and incarcerations during a two- or six-month period. An individual could have been arrested prior to a period in question but not incarcerated until convicted during that period, or arrested and incarcerated prior to the period in question and still incarcerated durin that period.

Multiple Behavioral Outcomes

Thus far, this analysis has focused on one behavior at a time. Now, it will address multiple behavioral outcomes expressed in terms of each respondent's:

- Drug use
- Arrests and incarcerations
- Employment

We define as a fully recovered person a respondent who, during the most recent two-month period, was:

- Using no illicit drugs (except marijuana)
- Not arrested or incarcerated
- Either employed, keeping a house, in school, or in vocational training

A respondent is defined as a program failure if, during the most recent two-month period, he:

- Used an illicit drug daily, or
- Was incarcerated

Between these two extremes of success and failure are several types of partial and marginal success. The following matrix defines nine mutually exclusive and collectively exhaustive categories ranging from success to failure.[1]

---

[1] This is a modification of categories suggested by Barry S. Brown, "The Role of Research in a Narcotics Treatment Program," *Drug Forum*, Volume 3 (2), Winter, 1974, and G. E. Vaillant, "A Twelve-Year Follow-up of New York City Addicts: Volume I, The Relation of Treatment to Outcome," *American Journal of Psychiatry*, 122:727-736, 1966.

Categories of Success (Recovery)

Extent of Recovery	Engages in Illicit Drug Use[1]	Arrested	Prosocial Employment
Full	No	No	Yes
Partial-I	No	No	No
Partial-II	No	Yes	Yes
Partial-III	No	Yes	No
Partial-IV	Yes, but not daily	No	Yes
Marginal-I	Yes, but not daily	Yes	Yes
Marginal-II	Yes, but not daily	Yes	No
Marginal-III	Yes, but not daily	No	No
Failure	Yes, daily or incarcerated		

Table VII-20 indicates the behavioral outcomes, expressed in terms of extent of recovery, achieved by each of the nine groups. The category "Partial" includes all four Partial categories and "Marginal" includes all three Marginal categories. The methadone maintenance group experienced a lower rate of full recovery than the abstinence group, but a slightly lower rate of failure. The differences between the treatment groups are not statistically significant.

The control groups experienced about the same extent of recovery as the treatment groups; the differences are not statistically significant.

As a whole, 22 percent of the respondents were fully recovered, 20 percent were failures, and the remaining 58 percent were partially or marginally recovered. Fifty-seven percent achieved either full or partial recovery.

*Comparison of Methadone, Abstinence
and Control Groups for 1971, 1972, and 1973*

Each of the three groups is partitioned by the year in which the client initially entered NTA. Thus, the methadone maintenance group consists of three subgroups — 1971, 1972, and 1973. Similarly, the abstinence and control group each consisted of three subgroups

---

[1] Except for marijuana.

— 1971, 1972, and 1973. The analysis will proceed as in the previous section.[1]

Heroin Use

Table VII-21 shows that heroin use declined dramatically for clients leaving the program in all three years. This occurred immediately upon leaving treatment and further improvement occurred by the time the interviews were conducted. This pattern of immediate improvement followed by further improvement by the time the interviews were conducted occurred for all categories of drugs. While essentially all the clients were using heroin at least some of the time prior to entering treatment, 50 to 70 percent stated that they were not using it at all during the two-month period prior to being interviewed. No more than 12 percent (range: 0-12 percent) of the clients in any of the treatment groups admitted to using heroin daily during the two-month period prior to being interviewed. Sixty-two to 79 percent of these clients stated that they had been using heroin daily during the two months prior to treatment. Dramatic improvement occurred for all the treatment groups in all years, but there is no statistically significant difference *among* the groups.

Dramatic improvements also were achieved by the clients who had not received treatment (i.e., left within five days of acceptance at CMI). There is no statistically significant difference in heroin usage achieved by the treatment groups and the control group. There are no statistically significant differences if the period two months before treatment is compared to the period two months after treatment. The response by the former clients, as indicated in Table VII-21, were essentially confirmed by urinalysis tests of specimens taken during the interviews.[2]

Illegal Methadone

Table VII-22 shows a decline in illegal methadone usage by all treatment groups for all years. From 88 to 100 percent of the respondents indicated no illegal methadone usage at all during the two-month period immediately prior to being interviewed compared to

---

[1] F tests were performed for total distribution, among groups, and among years. Chi-square tests were performed comparing methadone maintenance, abstinence, and control groups for each year.

[2] These tests showed that 88 percent of the respondents gave answers that were consistent with the results of the urinalysis tests.

TABLE VII-23

AT LEAST ONE ILLICIT OPIATE USED--MOST RECENT TWO MONTHS

(percentage)

Opiate(s) Used	1971			1972			1973		
	Meth. Maint.	Absti- nence	Control	Meth. Maint.	Absti- nence	Control	Meth. Maint.	Absti- nence	Control
Yes	37	38	41	38	39	53	35	45	27
No	63	62	59	62	61	47	65	55	73
TOTAL	100	100	100	100	100	100	100	100	100
n =	27	34	34	29	33	36	37	29	30

TABLE VII-24
LEGAL METHADONE USE
(percentage)

Frequency of Use	Methadone Maintenance			Abstinence			Control		
	2 Mo. Before NTA	2 Mo. After NTA	Last 2 Mo.	2 Mo. Before NTA	2 Mo. After NTA	Last 2 Mo.	2 Mo. Before NTA	2 Mo. After NTA	Last 2 Mo.
1971									
Not at all	89	92	85	82	94	91	82	91	91
Occasionally	7	4	8	0	0	0	6	6	3
Daily	4	4	7	18	6	9	12	3	·6
Total	100	100	100	100	100	100	100	100	100
n =	27	27	27	34	34	34	34	34	34
1972									
Not at all	86	100	90	82	97	97	92	94	92
Occasionally	4	0	0	6	3	0	5	3	0
Daily	10	0	10	12	0	3	3	3	8
Total	100	100	100	100	100	100	100	100	100
n =	29	29	29	33	33	33	36	36	36
1973									
Not at all	84	89	94	90	97	93	93	93	97
Occasionally	5	3	3	3	0	0	4	0	0
Daily	11	8	3	7	3	7	3	7	3
Total	100	100	100	100	100	100	100	100	100
n =	37	37	37	29	29	29	30	30	30

82 percent during the two months immediately prior to treatment.

The control groups also showed improvement (i.e., reductions in illegal methadone use), and there is no statistically significant difference between the treatment groups and the control group for any of the years. Further, there are no statistically significant differences among the three years.[1]

Illicit Opiates

Table VII-23 indicates the percentage of clients using at least one illicit opiate (heroin, illegal methadone, or dilaudid) during the most recent two-month period. From 35 to 45 percent of treatment group respondents used at least one of these drugs occasionally. Differences among treatment groups within years are not statistically significant.

The 1971 and 1972 groups experienced somewhat higher illicit opiate use, but the 1973 control group indicated lower use. These differences between treatment and control groups within each year are not statistically significant.

Legal Methadone

By definition, legal methadone could be obtained only by enrollment in a program dispensing the drug. Few respondents were enrolled in such a program during the two-month period prior to entering the NTA program and the two months after leaving. Table VII-24 shows that of those few respondents who had been enrolled in such a program, there are no statistically significant differences among the groups or among the years.

Cocaine

Table VII-25 shows that 28 to 50 percent of the treatment clients did not use cocaine during this preprogram period. Only a few used it daily (0 to 12 percent). During the two months immediately prior to being interviewed, 66 to 92 percent of the respondents who had been through treatment programs did not use cocaine. Hardly any of these individuals used cocaine daily (0 to 6 percent), but a sub-

---

1 There is a statistically significant result in the F test of the interaction among the groups in different years for the period two months before entering NTA, but this does not modify the statement in the text.

stantial percentage used cocaine occasionally (8 to 34 percent).

There are no statistically significant differences in usage among the treatment and control groups. As with heroin, all the groups showed substantial reductions in usage.

Amphetamines

Table VII-26 shows that all treatment groups reported a reduction in amphetamine usage between the two-month period prior to treatment and the two months prior to being interviewed.

There is no statistically significant difference between the treatment and control groups or among the three years. The significant policy initiated by the Federal Government prior to the most recent two-month period which considerably restricted the availability of amphetamines was previously noted.

Barbiturates

According to Table VII-27, few clients used barbiturates during the two months immediately prior to entering the program (from 73 to 93 percent did not use them at all). Nevertheless, there was some improvement among these clients as reflected by the high percentage not using barbiturates during the two months immediately after treatment (83 to 100 percent).

There is no statistically significant difference in barbiturate usage among the treatment and control groups within each year.[1]

Hallucinogens, Dilaudid, Minor Tranquilizers,
and Other Drugs

Tables VII-28, VI-29, VII-30, and VII-31 indicate infrequent use of these drugs. The general pattern of improvement shown on previous tables is also reflected in these.

As for other drugs, none of the differences in drug usage are statistically significant between the treatment and control groups and within years.[1]

---

[1] There are statistically significant differences in F tests results comparing different groups among the years for the periods two months after NTA and the most recent two months, but not significant differences among groups within years.

Marijuana

In contrast to the generally reduced frequency of usage shown for other drugs, Table VII-32 shows little change in marijuana usage among the periods in question. The percentage of those respondents who abstained from the use of marijuana during the most recent two-month period varies from 27 to 56 percent.

There is no statistically significant difference in marijuana usage among the years, between the two types of treatment, or the treatment and control groups.

Alcohol Use

A major concern among methadone programs is the belief that clients may tend to substitute alcohol for heroin. Table VII-33 does not support this belief. There is a slight decrease for some groups in the percentage of clients who stated that they never drank during the two-month period immediately after treatment as compared to the period immediately prior to treatment, but increases for other groups. There is little difference between pre-treatment and post-treatment drinking behavior.

There is no significant difference in drinking behavior among the two types of treatment, among the years, or between the treatment and control groups.

Cigarette Use

Another belief is that cigarette use increases after withdrawing from heroin. Table VI-34 does not support this belief. The frequency of cigarette use changed little between the pre-treatment and post-treatment periods. Indeed, for all the years in question, there is a slight reduction in heavy smoking (i.e., more than one pack each day) in the treatment groups.

Again, there is no significant difference between the treatment modalities, among the years, or between the treatment and control groups.

---

1 The F test of interaction between treatments in digerent years was significant at the .05 level for the last two-month period for minor tranquilizers, but not significant among treatment groups and among like groups in different years. This does not affect the conclusion.

TABLE VII-25
COCAINE USE
(percentage)

Frequency of Use	Methadone Maintenance			Abstinence			Control		
	2 Mo. Before NTA	2 Mo. After NTA	Last 2 Mo.	2 Mo. Before NTA	2 Mo. After NTA	Last 2 Mo.	2 Mo. Before NTA	2 Mo. After NTA	Last 2 Mo.
1971									
Not at all	40	67	74	50	70	79	32	62	85
Occasionally	60	33	26	41	27	15	59	38	15
Daily	0	0	0	9	3	6	9	0	0
Total	100	100	100	100	100	100	100	100	100
n =	27	27	27	34	34	34	34	34	34
1972									
Not at all	38	72	66	42	73	76	50	67	75
Occasionally	59	28	34	46	27	24	47	33	25
Daily	3	0	0	12	0	0	3	0	0
Total	100	100	100	100	100	100	100	100	100
n =	29	29	29	33	33	33	36	36	36
1973									
Not at all	49	81	92	28	69	76	47	63	87
Occasionally	43	19	8	69	31	21	43	37	13
Daily	8	0	0	3	0	3	10	0	0
Total	100	100	100	100	100	100	100	100	100
n =	37	37	37	29	29	29	30	30	30

TABLE VII-26
AMPHETAMINE USE
(percentage)

Frequency of Use	Methadone Maintenance			Abstinence			Control		
	2 Mo. Before NTA	2 Mo. After NTA	Last 2 Mo.	2 Mo. Before NTA	2 Mo. After NTA	Last 2 Mo.	2 Mo. Before NTA	2 Mo. After NTA	Last 2 Mo.
1971									
Not at all	81	89	100	79	79	85	59	74	79
Occasionally	8	7	0	12	12	12	29	17	15
Daily	11	4	0	9	9	3	12	9	·6
Total	100	100	100	100	100	100	100	100	100
n =	27	27	27	34	34	34	34	34	34
1972									
Not at all	76	79	79	76	82	85	69	75	81
Occasionally	24	21	21	24	18	15	25	19	19
Daily	0	0	0	0	0	0	6	6	0
Total	100	100	100	100	100	100	100	100	100
n =	29	29	29	33	33	33	36	36	36
1973									
Not at all	78	84	87	59	69	83	70	77	83
Occasionally	19	13	10	20	24	17	27	23	17
Daily	3	3	3	21	7	0	3	0	0
Total	100	100	100	100	100	100	100	100	100
n =	37	37	37	29	29	29	30	30	30

TABLE VII-27
BARBITURATE USE
(percentage)

Frequency of Use	Methadone Maintenance			Abstinence			Control		
	2 Mo. Before NTA	2 Mo. After NTA	Last 2 Mo.	2 Mo. Before NTA	2 Mo. After NTA	Last 2 Mo.	2 Mo. Before NTA	2 Mo. After NTA	Last 2 Mo.
1971									
Not at all	93	96	100	91	94	100	71	77	85
Occasionally	7	4	0	6	6	0	29	23	15
Daily	0	0	0	3	0	0	0	0	0
Total	100	100	100	100	100	100	100	100	100
n =	27	27	27	34	34	34	34	34	34
1972									
Not at all	73	76	86	82	79	82	78	81	83
Occasionally	24	24	14	12	18	12	22	19	17
Daily	3	0	0	6	3	6	0	0	0
Total	100	100	100	100	100	100	100	100	100
n =	29	29	29	33	33	33	36	36	36
1973									
Not at all	76	92	92	93	97	97	90	93	100
Occasionally	21	8	5	7	3	3	10	7	0
Daily	3	0	3	0	0	0	0	0	0
Total	100	100	100	100	100	100	100	100	100
n =	37	37	37	29	29	29	30	30	30

TABLE VII-28
HALLUCINOGEN USE
(percentage)

Frequency of Use	Methadone Maintenance			Abstinence			Control		
	2 Mo. Before NTA	2 Mo. After NTA	Last 2 Mo.	2 Mo. Before NTA	2 Mo. After NTA	Last 2 Mo.	2 Mo. Before NTA	2 Mo. After NTA	Last 2 Mo.
1971									
Not at all	100	96	100	88	94	94	85	85	88
Occasionally	0	4	0	12	6	6	15	15	12
Daily	0	0	0	0	0	0	0	0	0
Total	100	100	100	100	100	100	100	100	100
n =	27	27	27	34	34	34	34	34	34
1972									
Not at all	86	93	93	85	88	91	86	94	92
Occasionally	14	7	7	15	12	9	14	6	8
Daily	0	0	0	0	0	0	0	0	0
Total	100	100	100	100	100	100	100	100	100
n =	29	29	29	33	33	33	36	36	36
1973									
Not at all	84	92	92	90	97	86	87	93	93
Occasionally	13	8	8	10	3	14	10	4	4
Daily	3	0	0	0	0	0	3	3	3
Total	100	100	100	100	100	100	100	100	100
n =	37	37	37	29	29	29	30	30	30

Employment

One of the desired results of a drug treatment program is employment or other prosocial activity such as keeping house, going to school, or job training. Table VII-35 shows there is a general, but by no means consistent, pattern of improvement in comparing the two-month period prior to treatment with the most recent two-month period. The most marked improvement is in the 1971 group. There were improvements in all years in all groups with the exception of methadone maintenance in 1972 and 1973, in which there are only slight changes, indicating a persistent problem needing attention.

Particularly striking is the sharp reduction in illegal activity. All groups show improvement, most of them very substantial improvement. Some factors that could have influenced this performance were previously discussed.[1]

There is no statistically significant difference between the treatment modalities, among the years, or between the treatment and control groups.

Criminal Behavior

Table VII-36 shows that the percentage of clients who were arrested during the two-month period prior to being interviewed was substantially less than during the two months before treatment. The percentage of clients who were arrested varied between 4 and 12 percent during the most recent period in contrast to 13 to 41 percent during the period before treatment. This indicates a very substantial reduction in criminal behavior as expressed by actual arrests. Table VII-37, using six-month periods, shows the same pattern of improvement.

There are no statistically significant differences between types of treatment, treatment and control groups, and among years.

---

[1] Only one activity was recorded for each respondent and some could have been engaged in more than one activity. Approximately 5 percent of clients reported that they had income from both a paid job and also illegal activities during the most recent two months.

TABLE VII-29
DILAUDID USE
(percentage)

Frequency of Use	Methadone Maintenance			Abstinence			Control		
	2 Mo. Before NTA	2 Mo. After NTA	Last 2 Mo.	2 Mo. Before NTA	2 Mo. After NTA	Last 2 Mo.	2 Mo. Before NTA	2 Mo. After NTA	Last 2 Mo.
1971									
Not at all	89	97	100	82	88	91	94	94	91
Occasionally	7	3	0	12	9	9	6	6	9
Daily	4	0	0	6	3	0	0	0	0
Total	100	100	100	100	100	100	100	100	100
n =	27	27	27	34	34	34	34	34	34
1972									
Not at all	97	93	97	88	88	94	89	92	94
Occasionally	3	7	3	12	12	6	11	8	6
Daily	0	0	0	0	0	0	0	0	0
Total	100	100	100	100	100	100	100	100	100
n =	29	29	29	33	33	33	36	36	36
1973									
Not at all	84	97	92	76	86	80	77	90	94
Occasionally	13	3	5	17	14	20	16	3	3
Daily	3	0	3	7	0	0	7	7	3
Total	100	100	100	100	100	100	100	100	100
n =	37	37	37	29	29	29	30	30	30

TABLE VII-30
MINOR TRANQUILIZER USE
(percentage)

Frequency of Use	Methadone Maintenance			Abstinence			Control		
	2 Mo. Before NTA	2 Mo. After NTA	Last 2 Mo.	2 Mo. Before NTA	2 Mo. After NTA	Last 2 Mo.	2 Mo. Before NTA	2 Mo. After NTA	Last 2 Mo.
1971									
Not at all	100	100	100	88	94	85	79	85	94
Occasionally	0	0	0	9	6	12	18	12	6
Daily	0	0	0	3	0	3	3	3	0
Total	100	100	100	100	100	100	100	100	100
n =	27	27	27	34	34	34	34	34	34
1972									
Not at all	97	97	100	94	91	94	83	92	92
Occasionally	3	3	0	6	9	6	17	8	8
Daily	0	0	0	0	0	0	0	0	0
Total	100	100	100	100	100	100	100	100	100
n =	29	29	29	33	33	33	36	36	36
1973									
Not at all	89	92	95	97	93	97	83	83	93
Occasionally	8	8	5	0	7	3	17	17	7
Daily	3	0	0	3	0	0	0	0	0
Total	100	100	100	100	100	100	100	100	100
n =	37	37	37	29	29	29	30	30	30

TABLE VII-31
OTHER DRUG USE
(percentage)

Frequency of Use	Methadone Maintenance			Abstinence			Control		
	2 Mo. Before NTA	2 Mo. After NTA	Last 2 Mo.	2 Mo. Before NTA	2 Mo. After NTA	Last 2 Mo.	2 Mo. Before NTA	2 Mo. After NTA	Last 2 Mo.
1971									
Not at all	93	100	100	100	100	100	85	88	91
Occasionally	7	0	0	0	0	0	12	9	6
Daily	0	0	0	0	0	0	3	3	3
Total	100	100	100	100	100	100	100	100	100
n =	27	27	27	34	34	34	34	34	34
1972									
Not at all	97	97	97	91	94	94	83	94	97
Occasionally	0	3	3	9	6	6	17	6	3
Daily	3	0	0	0	0	0	0	0	0
Total	100	100	100	100	100	100	100	100	100
n =	29	29	29	33	33	33	36	36	36
1973									
Not at all	89	97	97	93	97	100	87	97	97
Occasionally	11	3	3	7	3	0	10	0	0
Daily	0	0	0	0	0	0	3	3	3
Total	100	100	100	100	100	100	100	100	100
n =	37	37	37	29	29	29	30	30	30

TABLE VII-32
MARIJUANA USE
(percentage)

Frequency of Use	Methadone Maintenance			Abstinence			Control		
	2 Mo. Before NTA	2 Mo. After NTA	Last 2 Mo.	2 Mo. Before NTA	2 Mo. After NTA	Last 2 Mo.	2 Mo. Before NTA	2 Mo. After NTA	Last 2 Mo.
1971									
Not at all	44	48	56	27	29	27	24	41	41
Occasionally	37	37	33	49	50	44	38	32	30
Daily	19	15	11	24	21	29	38	27	29
Total	100	100	100	100	100	100	100	100	100
n =	27	27	27	34	34	34	34	34	34
1972									
Not at all	31	38	35	24	27	30	28	31	31
Occasionally	41	41	41	46	52	40	36	38	36
Daily	28	21	24	30	21	30	36	31	33
Total	100	100	100	100	100	100	100	100	100
n =	29	29	29	33	33	33	36	36	36
1973									
Not at all	27	38	38	10	31	35	20	37	33
Occasionally	33	30	27	52	38	37	53	46	40
Daily	40	32	35	38	31	28	27	17	27
Total	100	100	100	100	100	100	100	100	100
n =	37	37	37	29	29	29	30	30	30

Another indicator of criminal behavior is whether or not a client has spent time in jail during the periods in question. Table VII-38 shows no pattern of improvement or degradation, but rather is mixed. A less distorted picture is presented in Table VII-39 which uses six-month periods. This shows no degradation and generally slight improvement.

Again, there are no statistically significant differences between the types of treatment, among the years, or between treatment and control groups.

Summary

Table VII-40 summarizes this discussion of the nine groups by presenting for each behavioral outcome measure whether:

- Improvements were realized by treatment groups comparing the most recent two-month period to the two-month period immediately prior to treatment
- There are significant differences among treatment groups — methadone maintenance and abstinence (predominantly methadone detoxification)
- There are significant differences among treatment and control groups
- There are significant differences among years

Multiple Behavioral Outcomes

Table VII-41 indicates the behavioral outcomes, expressed in terms of extent of recovery,[1] achieved by each of the nine groups. Methadone maintenance groups experienced a somewhat lower rate of failure in two of the three years. The differences between treatment groups are not statistically significant.

The control groups experienced about the same extent of recovery as the treatment groups; the differences are not statistically significant.

---

[1] As defined earlier in this chapter.

TABLE VII-33
ALCOHOL USE
(percentage)

Frequency of Use	Methadone Maintenance			Abstinence			Control		
	2 Mo. Before NTA	2 Mo. After NTA	Last 2 Mo.	2 Mo. Before NTA	2 Mo. After NTA	Last 2 Mo.	2 Mo. Before NTA	2 Mo. After NTA	Last 2 Mo.
1971									
Never	26	33	48	44	47	47	38	23	23
Occasionally	67	60	48	50	44	47	63	65	59
At least once each day	7	7	4	6	9	6	9	12	18
Total	100	100	100	100	100	100	100	100	100
n =	27	27	27	34	34	34	34	34	34
1972									
Never	38	38	31	36	30	30	39	39	33
Occasionally	52	48	55	52	58	61	50	47	56
At least once each day	10	14	14	12	12	9	11	14	11
Total	100	100	100	100	100	100	100	100	100
n =	29	29	29	33	33	33	36	36	36
1973									
Never	35	38	35	38	52	42	33	37	33
Occasionally	54	59	57	52	38	48	57	53	50
At least once each day	11	3	8	10	10	10	10	10	17
Total	100	100	100	100	100	100	100	100	100
n =	37	37	37	29	29	29	30	30	30

TABLE VII-34
CIGARETTE USE
(percentage)

Frequency of Use	Methadone Maintenance			Abstinence			Control		
	2 Mo. Before NTA	2 Mo. After NTA	Last 2 Mo.	2 Mo. Before NTA	2 Mo. After NTA	Last 2 Mo.	2 Mo. Before NTA	2 Mo. After NTA	Last 2 Mo.
1971									
Not at all	11	11	15	18	18	18	9	6	6
1 pack or less per day	52	67	67	44	50	55	47	53	59
More than 1 pack per day	37	22	18	38	32	27	44	41	35
Total	100	100	100	100	100	100	100	100	100
n =	27	27	27	34	34	34	34	34	34
1972									
Not at all	7	7	7	9	3	6	8	8	8
1 pack or less per day	55	62	65	58	70	76	64	61	58
More than 1 pack per day	38	31	28	33	27	18	28	31	34
Total	100	100	100	100	100	100	100	100	100
n =	29	29	29	33	33	33	36	36	36
1973									
Not at all	11	14	11	14	14	14	17	20	17
1 pack or less per day	62	62	62	48	52	55	47	44	46
More than 1 pack per day	27	24	27	38	34	31	36	36	37
Total	100	100	100	100	100	100	100	100	100
n =	37	37	37	29	29	29	30	30	30

TABLE VII-35
EMPLOYMENT
(Percentage)

STATUS	Methadone Maintenance			Abstinece			Control		
	2 Mo. Before NTA	2 Mo. After NTA	Last 2 Mo.	2 Mo. Before NTA	2 Mo. After NTA	Last 2 Mo.	2 Mo. Before NTA	2 Mo. After NTA	Last 2 Mo.
1971									
Paid Job	33	41	52	15	27	59	29	32	41
Keeping House, Student, Job Training	0	4	4	15	12	12	0	0	0
Illegal Activities	48	33	26	62	50	21	50	47	24
All Other Activities	19	22	18	8	11	8	21	21	35
Total	100	100	100	100	100	100	100	100	100
n =	27	27	27	34	34	34	34	34	34
1972									
Paid Job	31	21	24	39	52	61	47	42	39
Keeping House, Student, Job Training	0	0	10	3	0	0	6	6	8
Illegal Activities	55	48	41	46	30	15	31	28	28
All Other Activities	14	31	25	12	18	24	16	24	25
Total	100	100	100	100	100	100	100	100	100
n =	29	29	29	33	33	33	36	36	36
1973									
Paid Job	46	38	38	31	38	52	33	40	40
Keeping House, Student, Job Training	5	5	8	7	3	3	10	7	3
Illegal Activities	27	27	22	41	45	24	33	33	23
All Other Activities	22	30	32	21	14	21	24	20	34
Total	100	100	100	100	100	100	100	100	100
n =	37	37	37	29	29	29	30	30	30

TABLE VII-36
ARRESTS--TWO-MONTH PERIODS
(percentages)

	Methadone Maintenance			Abstinence			Control		
	2 Mo. Before NTA	2 Mo. After NTA	Last 2 Mo.	2 Mo. Before NTA	2 Mo. After NTA	Last 2 Mo.	2 Mo. Before NTA	2 Mo. After NTA	Last 2 Mo.
1971									
Not Arrested	59	89	89	85	91	91	65	91	94
Arrested	41	11	11	15	9	9	35	9	6
Total	100	100	100	100	100	100	100	100	100
n =	27	27	27	34	34	34	34	34	34
1972									
Not Arrested	79	86	90	76	91	88	83	94	94
Arrested	21	14	10	24	9	12	17	6	6
Total	100	100	100	100	100	100	100	100	100
n =	29	29	29	33	33	33	36	36	36
1973									
Not Arrested	84	95	92	61	82	96	87	90	93
Arrested	16	5	8	39	18	4	13	10	7
Total	100	100	100	100	100	100	100	100	100
n =	37	37	37	28	28	28	30	30	30

TABLE VII-37
ARRESTS--SIX-MONTH PERIODS
(Percentage)

ARRESTED	Methadone Maintenance			Abstinence			Control		
	6 Mo. Before NTA	6 Mo. After NTA	Last 6 Mo.	6 Mo. Before NTA	6 Mo. After NTA	Last 6 Mo.	6 Mo. Before NTA	6 Mo. After NTA	Last 6 Mo.
1971									
NO	52	89	78	74	82	82	62	91	91
YES	48	11	22	26	18	18	38	9	9
TOTAL	100	100	100	100	100	100	100	100	100
n =	27	27	27	34	34	34	34	34	34
1972									
NO	55	79	83	76	85	82	72	94	89
YES	45	21	17	24	15	18	28	6	11
TOTAL	100	100	100	100	100	100	100	100	100
n =	29	29	29	33	33	33	36	36	36
1973									
NO	78	97	89	54	68	68	77	83	80
YES	22	3	11	47	32	32	23	17	20
TOTAL	100	100	100	100	100	100	100	100	100
n =	37	37	37	28	28	28	30	30	30

TABLE VII -38
INCARCERATIONS--TWO-MONTH PERIODS
(percentage)

Time Spent in Jail	Methadone Maintenance			Abstinence			Control		
	2 Mo. Before NTA	2 Mo. After NTA	Last 2 Mo.	2 Mo. Before NTA	2 Mo. After NTA	Last 2 Mo.	2 Mo. Before NTA	2 Mo. After NTA	Last 2 Mo.
1971									
NO	85	85	70	94	94	97	70	88	91
YES	15	15	30	6	6	3	30	12	9
TOTAL	100	100	100	100	100	100	100	100	100
n =	27	27	27	34	34	34	34	33	33
1972									
NO	93	83	90	88	94	91	91	91	97
YES	7	17	10	12	6	9	9	9	3
TOTAL	100	100	100	100	100	100	100	100	100
n =	29	29	29	33	33	33	35	35	35
1973									
NO	89	95	95	79	93	79	93	90	90
YES	11	5	5	21	7	21	7	10	10
TOTAL	100	100	100	100	100	100	100	100	100
n =	37	37	37	28	28	28	30	30	30

TABLE VII-39

INCARCERATIONS--SIX-MONTH PERIODS
(Percentage)

IN JAIL	Methadone Maintenance			Abstinence			Control		
	6 Mo. Before NTA	6 Mo. After NTA	Last 6 Mo.	6 Mo. Before NTA	6 Mo. After NTA	Last 6 Mo.	6 Mo. Before NTA	6 Mo. After NTA	Last 6 Mo.
1971									
NO	78	82	78	91	85	91	70	85	85
YES	22	18	22	9	15	9	30	15	15
TOTAL	100	100	100	100	100	100	100	100	100
n =	27	27	27	34	34	34	34	34	34
1972									
NO	83	79	93	79	85	91	86	91	97
YES	17	21	7	21	15	9	14	9	3
TOTAL	100	100	100	100	100	100	100	100	100
n =	29	29	29	33	33	33	35	35	35
1973									
NO	84	92	92	75	82	75	83	80	87
YES	16	8	8	25	18	25	17	20	13
TOTAL	100	100	100	100	100	100	100	100	100
n =	37	37	37	28	28	28	30	30	30

TABLE VII-40

SUMMARY OF BEHAVIORAL OUTCOMES

Behavioral Outcome Measure	Improvement in Treatment Groups Most Recent 2 Months Compared to 2 Months Before Treatment	Significant Differences Among Treatment Groups?	Significant Differences Among Treatment and Control Groups?	Significant Differences Among Years?
DRUG USE				
Heroin	Yes	No	No	No
Illegal Methadone	Yes	No	No	No
Cocaine	Yes	No	No	No
Amphetamines	Yes	No	No	No
Barbiturates	Yes	No	No	No
Hallucinogens, Dilaudid, Minor Tranquilizers and Other Drugs	Yes	No	No	No
Marijuana	No	No	No	No
Alcohol	No	No	No	No
Cigarettes	No	No	No	No
Employment[1]	Yes[2]	No	No	No
Criminal Activity				
Arrests	Yes	No	No	No
Incarcerations	Mixed	No	No	No

_____

[1]Includes holding a job, keeping a house, attending school or vocational training.

[2]Except methadone maintenance 1972 and 1973.

As a whole, 22 percent of the respondents were fully recovered, 20 percent were failures, and the remaining 58 percent were partially or marginally recovered. Fifty-seven percent achieved either full or partial recovery.

TABLE VII-41

EXTENT OF RECOVERY
(Percentage)

EXTENT OF RECOVERY	1971			1972			1973			TOTAL
	Meth. Maint.	Absti- nence	Control	Meth. Maint.	Absti- nence	Control	Meth. Maint.	Absti- nence	Control	
Fully	22	23	35	7	36	19	16	17	23	22
Partially	33	44	24	38	28	31	40	35	43	35
Margin- ally	19	15	21	38	15	31	28	24	17	23
Failure	26	18	20	17	21	19	16	24	17	20
TOTAL	100	100	100	100	100	100	100	100	100	100
n =	27	34	34	29	33	36	37	29	30	289

Chapter VIII

ANALYSIS OF DIFFERENT CLIENT GROUPINGS

As was discussed in Chapter IV, two of the specific hypotheses tested in this study were:

- Client outcomes will be effected by length of time elapsed since the client left treatment
- Client outcomes will be sensitive to the type of treatment that the client received

The analysis to this point has found few significant differences among the client groups. Now we will test the following hypotheses that different groupings of clients will result in significant differences among groups:

- There is no significant difference in outcomes among clients as a function of the total time they spent in treatment
- There is no significant difference in outcomes among clients as a function of their status upon leaving treatment

Redefinition of Treatment and Control Groups

The definition of treatment and control groups in this study was, necessarily, rather arbitrary. We assigned clients in the sample to methadone maintenance or abstinence groups on the basis of the modality in which they spent most time. Some maintenance clients probably were reassigned to abstinence and vice versa during the course of treatment. And some clients who were in methadone maintenance could have dropped out and re-entered treatment as abstinence clients and vice versa. We attempted to regroup clients in accordance with their switching modalities, but NTA records did not necessarily record changes in modality; therefore, this type of regrouping was impossible.

It was originally planned to assign to control groups only those clients who had entered NTA and left within one day. Because the

TABLE VIII-1

HEROIN USE PAST 2 MONTHS
(Percentage)

FREQUENCY OF USE	Total Time in Treatment							TOTAL
	1 Day	2-14 Days	15-120 Days	121-364 Days	1-5 Years	Over 5 Years		
Not at all	66	62	64	68	63	53		64
Occasionally	19	29	32	25	35	40		29
Daily	15	9	4	7	2	7		7
TOTAL	100	100	100	100	100	100		100
n =	55	34	73	41	41	30		274

TABLE VIII-2

ARRESTS PAST 2 MONTHS
(Percentage)

ARRESTED LAST 2 MONTHS	Total Time in Treatment							TOTAL
	1 Day	2-14 Days	15-120 Days	121-364 Days	1-5 Years	Over 5 Years		
No	96	94	92	93	83	97		92
Yes	4	6	8	7	17	3		8
TOTAL	100	100	100	100	100	100		100
n =	55	34	73	41	41	30		274

TABLE VIII-3

EMPLOYMENT LAST 2 MONTHS
(Percentage)

ACTIVITY LAST 2 MONTHS	Total Time in Treatment						TOTAL
	1 Day	2-14 Days	15-120 Days	121-364 Days	1-5 Years	Over 5 Years	
Paid Job	38	47	45	54	37	50	45
Keeping House, Student, or Job Training	7	--	8	2	7	--	5
Illicit Activities	26	24	25	20	22	40	25
All Other Activities	29	29	22	24	34	10	25
TOTAL	100	100	100	100	100	100	?.00
n =	55	34	73	41	41	30	274

number of clients who had left that soon did not provide sufficiently large control groups, the definition was changed to include clients who had left within five days. We required 40 clients for each of the three control groups for a total of 120. During the course of the analysis, it was found that some of these clients had subsequently reentered treatment. Thus, the control groups were not as "pure" as one would like.

In view of this switching among modalities and "contamination" of the control groups, a different type of grouping seemed to be of interest. Because the analysis showed few significant differences in characteristics or significant differences in outcomes among years, the three years were collapsed into one. And because of control group contamination, a pure control group was established consisting of clients who never received more than one day of treatment.[1]

The new comparison can be made more interesting by partitioning clients who received more than one day of treatment into groups depending upon *total* length of time spent in treatment. Thus, if a client entered treatment once for ten days and a second time for 50 days, his total time in treatment would be 60 days. Groupings were determined by first examining frequency distributions and forming groups having no less than 30 clients.

Formally stated, the following hypothesis is tested:

- There is no difference in outcomes between groups differentiated by length of time in treatment

Heroin Use

Table VIII-1 depicts frequency of heroin use during the most recent two-month period comparing clients grouped in terms of *total* time spent in drug treatment. A remarkably consistent pattern is shown among all the groups. The differences between treatment groups and the control group are not statistically significant.

Arrests

Table VIII-2 shows the percentage of clients arrested during the most recent two-month period for each of the groups. As in heroin use, the patterns are remarkably similar for each of the groups. The

---

[1] Practically speaking, this is equivalent to no treatment at all.

TABLE VIII-4

ALL CLIENTS INTERVIEWED COMPARED TO REDUCED SET*
EMPLOYMENT, ARRESTS, INCARCERATIONS, HEROIN USE
(percentage)

Variable	2 Months Before NTA		2 Months After NTA		Past 2 Months	
	All	Reduced Set*	All	Reduced Set*	All	Reduced Set*
Employed	34	35	37	39	45	49
Not Employed	66	65	63	61	55	51
Total n =	100	100	100	100	100	100
	289	249	289	249	289	249
Arrested	24	22	10	8	8	7
Not Arrested	76	78	90	92	92	93
Total n =	100	100	100	100	100	100
	288	248	288	248	288	248
Jailed	13	11	9	7	10	1
Not Jailed	87	89	91	93	90	99
Total n =	100	100	100	100	100	100
	287	247	287	247	287	247
Heroin Used Daily	69	69	14	13	7	8
Heroin Used Occasionally	28	28	34	34	29	30
Heroin Never Used	3	3	52	53	64	62
Total n =	100	100	100	100	100	100
	289	249	289	249	289	249

*Consists of all clients interviewed less those institutionalized or in treatment at any time during the two-month period immediately prior to the interview.

DISTRICT OF COLUMBIA 111

differences between treatment and control groups do not appear to be significant.

Employment

Table VIII-3 focuses upon the client's employment-type activities during the most recent two-month period. Again, the patterns are generally consistent among the groups, particularly when "paid job" and "keeping house, student, or job training" are combined as prosocial activities.[1] As in the previous two tables, clients in treatment more than five years showed a somewhat different pattern from other groups. The difference in distribution between the control group and that group is not statistically significant.[2]

Conclusion

This analysis shows that even when a "pure" (although nonequivalent)[3] control group is used, there are still no significant differences between treatment and control groups. Further, it raises questions with respect to the common assumptions regarding there being a strong association between length of time in treatment and prosocial activities.

Redefinition of Population at Risk

The population at risk in this study has consisted of all 289 clients interviewed, irrespective of their status during the two-month period immediately prior to the interview. It may be argued that some of these individuals should not be considered at risk because they are institutionalized (in jail, in prison, or hospitalized) or in a drug treatment program. There are 40 individuals in this category of

---

[1] As noted previously, only one activity category was coded for each respondent and some could have been engaged in more than one activity (e.g., paid job and illicit activities). About 5 percent of the clients reported incomes from both a paid job and illegal activities.

[2] Due to the low cell frequencies, a Chi-square test was conducted combining prosocial activities into one cell and illicit activities and all other activities into another for each of two groups (control compared to over five years of treatment). The result is not statistically significant. $X^2 = .1$, df $= 1$, p ► .05.

[3] As stated in Chapter IV, the control group is considered nonequivalent because clients were not randomly assigned at intake to treatment (experimental) and control groups.

whom 25 were in jail or prison, 3 hospitalized, and 12 in drug treatment.[1]

Table VIII-4 compares the pre- and post-treatment behavior for two groups of clients:

- All respondents
- A reduced set which excludes the 40 clients institutionalized or in treatment.

Differences between the two groups are slight and not statistically significant.

We conclude that excluding respondents who are institutionalized or in drug treatment programs from the population at risk has no effect on the results of this study.

Clients' Status Upon Leaving Compared to Later Drug Use

There has been considerable attention in the drug treatment field to client's status upon leaving treatment. Clients who leave against medical advice or "split" are commonly viewed as failures, although there has been some evidence that many "splittees" do rather well.

We sought to determine the status of clients in the sample in order to test the hypothesis that status upon leaving treatment is related to outcome. Unfortunately, it proved to be very difficult to determine clients' status upon leaving NTA. The clinical records did not necessarily record this. Clients were asked why they left NTA,[2] but we doubt that this is a valid indicator and the data showed few graduates.

A more sensitive indicator of status would be the methadone dosage level upon termination. A threshold level could be established of (say) 5-10 milligrams; clients achieving this level upon termination would be considered essentially graduated. This method proved impossible to administer because methadone dosage data were not available.

Another method was used which was less satisfactory. NTA regularly took urine samples and subjected them to tests for the following drugs: quinine, morphine, methadone, cocaine, codeine, amphet-

---

[1] Some of these individuals were not in that category during the entire two month period, but the data do not indicate who they are or how long they did not have that status.

[2] See Table X-6.

amines, and barbiturates. The results of these tests were available for 1973, 1974, and 1975 but not for previous years. We decided to analyze the urine results for those clients who were in treatment during those three years. The three urinalysis test results recorded immediately prior to leaving NTA were used as a basis for determining a client's drug-taking status upon leaving NTA. This is an inadequate substitute for graduation, but it at least provides some indication of the extent to which the program was successful in altering drug-taking behavior as of the time the client left treatment.

Urinalysis test results were found for 85 of the 289 clients. These results were compared to the clients' interview responses and the urinalysis test results on urine samples taken during the interview.[1]

Table VIII-5 shows the results of this analysis. Forty-seven percent of clients with positive urine results immediately prior to leaving NTA also were using drugs during the two-month period immediately prior to being interviewed. The precentage of clients with negative urine results who were using drugs later was exactly the same. Thus, the clients' use of drugs after treatment is unrelated to drug use shortly before leaving treatment.

A single urinalysis test is an inadequate indication of a client's status because it only indicates whether a drug was taken during a rather brief period of time (e.g., roughly 24 hours). It says nothing about frequency of use and quantity.[2] Ths, we used urinalysis results taken at the time of interview principally to corroborate answers to questions concerning current drug use. NIDA has expressed considerable interest in a more detailed presentation of urine results. Table VIII-6 compares results of the *last* urine test prior to leaving NTA with the urine results at the time of the interview. This procedure roughly equalizes the probability that a drug being used less than daily will be detected, although we cannot control for whatever differences might exist in the accuracy of urinalysis tests conducted during the different time periods.

Table VIII-6 shows a very mixed picture.[3] For example, only three

---

[1] In those few cases where the questionnaire results and urinalysis test results were inconsistent (e.g., the respondent stated he was not using drugs, but the urinalysis test was positive for heroin) it was asssumed that the respondent was using the drugs indicated.

[2] There are also, of course, important limitations on the accuracy of the tests.

[3] The total number of clients reflected in this table is slightly smaller than in Table VIII-5 because urine results were not available for all clients inter-

TABLE VIII-5

CLIENT DRUG USE IMMEDIATELY PRIOR TO LEAVING
NTA COMPARED TO PAST TWO MONTHS

Drug Use Past Two Months	Urine Results Before Leaving NTA					
	Positive		Negative		Total	
	#	%	#	%	#	%
Yes	18[a]	47	22	47	40	47
No	20	53	25	53	45	53
Total	38	100	47	100	85	100

[a]Sixteen of these clients were using the same drugs at the time of the interview for which they were positive before leaving NTA; 2 were not using the same drugs.

of the 21 clients who were positive for morphine or quinine in their last NTA urinalysis test were also positive for them at the time of the interview.

Results of tests conducted on urines taken at intake were not available. If they were, an interesting analysis would be to compare these to test results during treatment and at the interview.

------

viewed. And some clients appeared more than once because they were positive for more than one drug.

TABLE VIII-6

COMPARISON OF URINE TESTS

Last NTA Urine-- Client Positive For:	Urine Status at Interview--Client Positive For:											
	Morph./ Quinine	Meth.	Cocaine	Amph.	Barb.	Hall.	Dil.	Minor Tranq.	Pre.	Other Drugs	Clean	Total
Morphine/Quinine	3	1	1						4	1	11	21
Methadone											1	1
Cocaine											2	2
Amphetamines												0
Barbiturates												0
Hallucinogens												0
Dilaudid												0
Minor Tranquilizers												0
Preludin												0
Other Drugs											1	1
Clean	9	6		1					5	1	36	58
Total	12	7	1	1	0	0	0	0	9	2	51	83

Chapter IX
A SEARCH FOR EXPLANATORY FACTORS

This chapter discusses possible reasons why there are essentially no significant differences in the behavior of former clients sampled among treatment and control groups and searches for factors that might explain outcomes. First to be examined are the backgrounds and characteristics of the clients to determine whether there are significant differences among groups. Second, possible differences in the control group and the treatment groups are examined in terms of subsequent treatment and type of participation in NTA. Third, possible interpretations are analyzed through multivariate analyses. Finally, an analysis is made of the services actually received by the clients.

Client Backgrounds and Characteristics

The following client background and characteristic variables are examined in this section:
- Sex
- Race
- Age
- Highest grade completed in school
- Marital status
- Living with someone
- Age first used heroin
- Treatment prior to entering NTA
- Treatment after leaving NTA
- Type of participation in NTA

Reference to the tables in Chapter VII will demonstrate that there are no significant differences in these groups of clients prior to treatment in terms of their drug use, arrests or jail time, or socioeconomic productivity (expressed in terms of employment, school status, and whether they are keeping a home).

117

Sex

Table IX-1 shows that the percentage of respondents who are males varies between 76 and 97 percent among the groups. These differences are not significant.

Race

Table IX-2 shows that the percentage of clients who are black varied from 72 to 97. These differences are not significant. Note that there is more correspondence (i.e., the differences are less) between the control group and treatment groups within each year than among the years.

Age

The age distributions among the various groups are roughly similar, but Table IX-3 shows some differences in the distributions. These are significantly different among groups.[1] The multivariate analysis (discussed later in this chapter) shows no significant relationship between age and outcome.

Highest Grade Completed

Table IX-4 shows very similar distributions in highest grade completed among each of the groups. The percentage of respondents who completed at least the twelfth grade varies substantially but the differences in distributions are not statistically significant.

Marital Status

According to Table IX-5, the percentage of clients who are married is essentially the same for each of the groups, varying from 21 to 41 percent. The differences are not statistically significant.

Living with Someone

Living with someone is believed to be a measure of stability in

---

[1] The F test is significant at the .05 level among groups. Only the Chi-square test among groups in 1973 is significant at the .05 level (see Appendix A). When the 1971, 1972, and 1973 groups are collapsed into one, the differences in distributions are not significant.

TABLE IX-1

SEX
(percentage)

SEX	1971			1972			1973		
	Meth. Maint.	Absti-nence	Control	Meth. Maint.	Absti-nence	Control	Meth. Maint.	Absti-nence	Control
MALE	89	82	82	79	97	81	76	76	77
FEMALE	11	18	18	21	3	19	24	24	23
TOTAL	100	100	100	100	100	100	100	100	100
n =	27	34	34	29	33	36	37	29	30

TABLE IX-2

RACE
(percentage)

RACE	1971			1972			1973		
	Meth. Maint.	Absti-nence	Control	Meth. Maint.	Absti-nence	Control	Meth. Maint.	Absti-nence	Control
BLACK	96	97	88	90	91	72	73	93	80
WHITE	4	3	12	10	9	28	27	7	20
TOTAL	100	100	100	100	100	100	100	100	100
n =	27	34	34	29	33	36	37	29	30

TABLE IX-3

AGE
(percentage)

AGE	1971			1972			1973		
	Meth. Maint.	Absti- nence	Control	Meth. Maint.	Absti- nence	Control	Meth. Maint.	Absti- nence	Control
< 18	0	0	0	0	0	0	0	0	0
18 - 20	0	3	3	0	6	0	3	21	13
21 - 25	45	65	53	41	52	58	49	38	40
26 - 30	33	17	23	38	27	28	11	31	33
31 -36	11	0	15	17	6	6	16	10	7
> 36	11	15	6	4	9	8	21	0	7
TOTAL	100	100	100	100	100	100	100	100	100
n =	27	34	34	29	33	36	37	29	30

TABLE IX-4

HIGHEST GRADE COMPLETED
(percentage)

HIGHEST GRADE COMPLETED	1971			1972			1973		
	Meth. Maint.	Absti-nence	Control	Meth. Maint.	Absti-nence	Control	Meth. Maint.	Absti-nence	Control
1 - 8	0	3	6	10	3	8	11	3	7
9	7	12	15	3	12	6	0	0	10
10	30	29	29	35	24	28	17	21	17
11	33	24	26	28	15	17	19	17	17
12	26	29	18	17	40	33	45	52	33
13 or more	4	3	6	7	6	8	8	7	16
TOTAL	100	100	100	100	100	100	100	100	100
n =	27	34	34	29	33	36	36	29	30

TABLE IX-5

MARITAL STATUS
(percentage)

Marital Status	1971			1972			1973		
	Meth. Maint.	Absti-nence	Control	Meth. Maint.	Absti-nence	Control	Meth. Maint.	Absti-nence	Control
Single	59	76	79	72	79	72	62	72	67
Married	41	24	21	28	21	28	38	28	33
TOTAL	100	100	100	100	100	100	100	100	100
n =	27	34	34	29	33	36	37	29	30

TABLE IX-6

LIVING WITH SOMEONE
(percentage)

Living with Someone	1971			1972			1973		
	Meth. Maint.	Absti- nence	Control	Meth. Maint.	Absti- nence	Control	Meth. Maint.	Absti- nence	Control
No	30	15	15	28	15	17	19	31	20
Yes	70	85	85	72	85	83	81	69	80
TOTAL	100	100	100	100	100	100	100	100	100
n =	27	34	34	29	33	35	37	29	30

TABLE IX-7

AGE FIRST USED HEROIN
(percentage)

Age	1971			1972			1973		
	Meth. Maint.	Absti-nence	Control	Meth. Maint.	Absti-nence	Control	Meth. Maint.	Absti-nence	Control
<12	0	0	0	0	0	0	0	0	3
12-13	0	0	0	0	0	0	6	3	3
14-15	4	12	9	17	15	6	16	17	7
16-17	15	44	32	21	21	30	16	31	27
18-19	41	18	32	28	31	36	24	21	23
20-25	33	23	27	31	30	25	27	28	37
26-30	7	3	0	3	3	0	11	0	0
>31	0	0	0	0	0	3	0	0	0
TOTAL	100	100	100	100	100	100	100	100	100
n =	27	34	34	29	33	36	37	29	30

TABLE IX-8

DRUG TREATMENT BEFORE NTA
(percentage)

Treatment Prior to NTA	1971			1972			1973		
	Meth. Maint.	Absti- nence	Control	Meth. Maint.	Absti- nence	Control	Meth. Maint.	Absti- nence	Control
NO	89	94	79	76	73	86	70	64	87
YES	11	6	21	24	27	14	30	36	13
TOTAL	100	100	100	100	100	100	100	100	100
n =	27	34	34	29	33	36	37	28	30

the individual's life style. The percentage of clients in this category, shown in Table IX-6, varies only from 70 to 85 percent and the differences are not statistically significant.

Age First Used Heroin

The earlier the age that an individual first uses heroin, the more he is believed to have adopted heroin use as a long-term life style. Table IX-7 presents the distribution of ages at which the respondent first used heroin. There is no significant differences in the pattern among the groups and the differences are not statistically significant.

Treatment Prior to Entering NTA

Table IX-8 shows that there are some differences in terms of the percentage of respondents who had been in a drug treatment program prior to entering NTA. The percentage ranges from 6 to 36 and tends to be somewhat higher for clients who left treatment in 1972 or 1973. However, there is no significant difference among the groups in each year.

Treatment After NTA

Another hypothesis that could explain the lack of statistically significant differences in effectiveness among the groups would be that members of the control groups obtained treatment subsequent to their leaving the Central Medical Intake. Table IX-9 shows that the members of the control groups were generally no more likely to enter treatment subsequent to NTA than the treatment groups. Again, these differences are not significant.

Type of Participation

It is believed that a person whose participation in a drug treatment has been forced by legal authorities is less likely to be successful than one who participates voluntarily. Thus, one hypothesis that could help explain the lack of differences between the treatment and control groups is that there are differences in the type of participation. Table IX-10 shows that there are no substantial, consistent differences; these differences are not statistically significant.

TABLE IX-9

DRUG TREATMENT AFTER LEAVING NTA
(percentage)

Treatment After NTA	1971			1972			1973		
	Meth. Maint.	Absti-nence	Control	Meth. Maint.	Absti-nence	Control	Meth. Maint.	Absti-nence	Control
NO	67	82	74	90	94	86	95	90	80
YES	33	18	26	10	6	14	5	10	20
TOTAL	100	100	100	100	100	100	100	100	100
n =	27	34	34	29	33	36	37	29	30

TABLE IX-10

TYPE OF PARTICIPATION IN NTA
(percentage)

Participation in NTA	1971			1972			1973		
	Meth. Maint.	Absti-nence	Control	Meth. Maint.	Absti-nence	Control	Meth. Maint.	Absti-nence	Control
Voluntary	67	82	65	76	69	86	78	64	80
Forced by Legal Authorities	33	18	35	24	31	14	22	36	20
TOTAL	100	100	100	100	100	100	100	100	100
n =	27	34	34	29	32	36	36	28	30

Multivariate Analysis

Initial Analysis

Thus far, the behavior of the treatment and control groups has been analyzed in terms of a single variable at a time. None of the differences among the treatment and control groups proved to be statistically significant in terms of change of drug use, criminal activity, and social productivity.

Since all of the characteristics examined in Tables IX-1 to IX-10 suggest that the nine groups are homogeneous, the nine groups can be collapsed into one and examined to see whether combinations of characteristics can explain the differences in outcome.

The following independent variables are considered:
- Sex
- Age
- Race
- Highest grade completed
- Married
- Living with someone
- Drug treatment before NTA
- Drug treatment after NTA
- How many close associates used drugs two months prior to NTA
- Lived at one place in the last two months
- Used heroin in the last two months[1]
- Total arrests in the last two months[1]
- More than one drug used in the last two months[1]
- Employed in the last two months[1]

The following dependent variables are defined:
- Used heroin in the last two months
- Used more than one drug in the last two months
- Used alcohol in the last two months
- Total arrests in the last two months

---

[1] Indicates also used alternatively as a dependent variable.

TABLE IX-11

STEPWISE MULTIPLE REGRESSIONS

Independent Variables	Multiple Regressions				
	1	2	3	4	5
Sex	X	X	X	X	X
Age	X	X	X	X	X
Race	X	X	X	X	X
Highest grade completed	X	X	X	X	X
Married	X	X	X	X	X
Living with someone	X	X	X	X	X
Drug treatment after NTA	X	X	X	X	X
Drug treatment before NTA	X	X	X	X	X
Heroin used last 2 months	No	X	X	X	X
Total arrests last 2 months	X	X	X	X	No
> 1 drug used last 2 months	X	No	X	X	X
Employed last 2 months	X	X	X	X	X
Alcohol used last 2 months	X	X	X	No	X

Dependent Variables	1	2	3	4	5	$R_2 =$
Used Heroin last 2 months	X					.13
> 1 drug used last 2 months		X				.04
Cigarettes used last 2 months			X			.08
Alcohol used last 2 months				X		.07
Total arrests last 2 months					X	.05

Table IX-11 shows the independent and dependent variables included in each of the stepwise multiple regressions. An X indicates the variable was included. The *highest* multiple correlation coefficient squared (R^2) was .13,[1] indicating that none of the independent variables, when used in a linear relationship, showed a useful reduction of the dependent variable variance. The correlation coefficients (R) also were quite low, indicating no useful reduction in the dependent variable. Therefore, none of these independent variables explain these behavioral outcomes.

Factor Analysis

A factor analysis was conducted for the purpose of determining what variables are correlated with each other and, conversely, what variables are not. The procedure used drew out factors that are orthogonal or uncorrelated (using the Verimax rotation). Thus, any variable that is in *no* factors is uncorrelated with all 15 factors presented. Any variable that is on different factors represents different dimensions uncorrelated with each other.

The complete results of the factor analysis are contained in Appendix B. This section highlgihts the most important findings. The following variables were included in the factor analysis:
- Sex
- Race
- Age
- Highest grade completed
- Additional school years
- Marital status
- Living with someone
- Longest time at one address
- Residences last three years
- Days sick in bed
- Caretakers until age 15
- Caretakers' work history
- Caretakers' education
- Drug use by family
- Heroin use two months before NTA

---

[1] All F tests were significant at the .05 level.

- Heroin use past two months
- Drug program before NTA
- Adequacy of time at NTA
- Participation in NTA
- Type of service received at NTA
  - Individual counseling
  - Group counseling
  - Tranquilizers, muscle relaxers
  - Methadone maintenance
  - Methadone detoxification
  - Vocational rehabilitative counseling
- Most helpful activity
- Did NTA program help?
- Did anything other than NTA help in life change?
- Would recommend NTA to a friend
- Further contact with NTA
- Frequency of contact
- Treatment after NTA
- Number of times busted
- Busted six months before NTA
- Number of times incarcerated
- Incarcerated past two months
- Incarcerated past six months
- Incarcerated two months after NTA
- Incarcerated six months after NTA
- Incarcerated six months before NTA
- Longest time held a job
- Days worked two months before NTA
- Days worked two months after NTA
- Days worked past two months
- NTA helped get job two months after
- Source of income two months before
  - Illegal activities
  - Job
  - Social Security, VA benefits, unemployment
  - Welfare
  - Spouse
  - Relatives or friends
- Source of income two months after
  - Illegal activities

- Job
- Social Security, VA benefits, unemployment
- Welfare
- Spouse
- Relatives or friends
- Source of income last two months
  - Illegal activities
  - Job
  - Social Security, VA benefits, unemployment
  - Welfare
  - Spouse
  - Relatives or friends
- Number of associates entered NTA two months before
- Number of associates entered NTA two months after
- Number of associates entered NTA past two months
- Number of associates using drugs two months before
- Number of associates using drugs two months after
- Number of associates using drugs past two months

Source of Income

Clients whose source of income was Social Security, Veterans Administration (VA), unemployment, welfare, spouse, relatives, or friends during the period two months prior to entering NTA tended to have the same source during the period two months after leaving and during the most recent two months. Further, the source of income *was not related to any other behavior* (e.g., drug use, etc.).

Most Helpful Activity

Methadone maintenance clients tended to identify methadone maintenance itself as the most helpful activity. They did not identify other choices — individual counseling; group counseling; tranquilizers, muscle relaxers, etc.; job training, referral and placement counseling; vocational rehabilitation counseling; or other activities. This could indicate that they placed a relatively high value on methadone maintenance itself, compared to supportive services. This could be attributable to their having received supportive services and found them to be not helpful, or to their having not received supportive services. Later in this chapter, it will be shown that the only supportive srevices receved by a large percentage of clients was individual counseling. Thus, this factor should be regarded with caution.

Associates' Drug Use

The number of a client's associates using drugs during the period two months prior to entering NTA correlates slightly with the number during the period two months after leaving NTA and the two months prior to being interviewed. The factor loadings deteriorate over time, indicating fewer associates using drugs. Similarly, the number of a client's associates entering NTA during each of the three periods is slightly correlated. However, the loadings deteriorated for the most recent period indicating fewer associates entering NTA.

This factor suggests changes in many clients' associational patterns after treatment.

Incarcerations

As the data show, clients incarcerated during the period six months prior to treatment are likely to be incarcerated during the period six months prior to being interviewed. This factor is unrelated to drug use or arrests, possibly because opportunities for drug use should be relatively limited while incarcerated. Thirty-four of the respondents indicated that they were incarcerated during this period; 20 of them were interviewed in jail or prison.

Employment

Clients who were employed prior to entering NTA are likely to be employed after leaving NTA. And clients whose source of income before entering NTA was a job are likely to have the same source after leaving. There is no noticeable correlation between other activities prior to entering NTA and post-treatment employment. However, there is a slight correlation between NTA helping a client get a job and a client working, indicating that this activity was helpful to some clients. Employment is unrelated to drug use or arrests.

Illegal Activities

There is a correlation between being engaged in illegal activities during the period two months before entering NTA, the period two months after leaving NTA, and the most recent two-month period. However, the factor loadings are not extremely high (.64, .68, and .61 for each of the three successive periods), indicating that many clients engaged in illegal activities before treatment were not engaged in them after treatment. This is verified by Table VII-15 which shows substantial reductions in illegal activities. Heroin use during the past two months is slightly correlated with illegal activities during all three two-month periods (factor loading .41).

Adequacy of Time at NTA

Clients who stated that something other than methadone maintenance was the most helpful activity tended to state that the amount of time spent at the clinic during each visit was enough to help them become rehabilitated. Clients participating in methadone detoxification tended to state that the amount of time spent at the clinic during each visit was adequate and that something other than methadone maintenance was the most helpful activity.

Arrests and Involuntary Participation

Not surprisingly, being arrested during the period six months prior to entering NTA is correlated with entering NTA involuntarily. However, these variables are not associated with any others (e.g., heroin use or arrests after leaving NTA). To express the point more succinctly, clients who are forced by legal authorities to enter the program do as well as those who enter voluntarily.

Conclusions

Several variables had very low communalities and are not related to any of the factors (i.e., communality < .1):
- Highest grade completed
- Living with someone
- Caretakers until age 15
- Caretakers' work history
- Caretakers' education
- Drug use by family members
- Would you recommend NTA to a friend with a drug problem?

Further, the following variables that had communalities of > .1

had factor loading of < .35, indicating only slight correlation with other variables:

- **Sex**
- **Race**
- **Age**
- Schooling after leaving NTA
- Marital status
- Longest time spent at one address
- Number of residences during last three years
- Number of days sick in bed
- Heroin use, two months before entering NTA
- Drug treatment before entering NTA
- Adequacy of time spent at NTA
- Was participation in NTA voluntary or involuntary?
- Was vocational rehabilitation counseling received?
- Would client recommend NTA to a friend?
- Client incarcerated two months after NTA
- Longest time client held a job
- Number of days worked past two months

The variables indicating output or response to treatment — heroin use, employment, arrests, and incarcerations during the past two months — showed little correlation with each other or with other variables. The only instance where one of these output variables has a factor loading of > .35 is for heroin use during the past two months. It shows a factor loading of only .41 as indicated previously.

The factor analysis results raise questions with respect to a number of commonly accepted beliefs. For example, it is believed that such variable as age, sex, and voluntary/involuntary participation affect treatment outcomes. We found no such correlations. Further, these variables were generally uncorrelated with each other. For example, clients whose participation in NTA was forced by legal authorities did as well as clients participating voluntarily. These involuntary clients were not substantially different from voluntary clients in terms of any of the variables included in the factor analysis (e.g., age, sex, etc.).

No demographic or background variables had a factor loading of > .35. This suggests that such variables are unrelated to outcome and of little predictive value for these types of clients in these programs.

Multiple Regression Analyses

Stepwise multiple regression analyses were conducted upon completion of the factor analysis. In accordance with accepted procedures, the variable with the highest factor loading in each of the factors was selected for inclusion in the multiple regression, as well as other variables of interest that had low communalities in the factor analysis ($< .1$). The elimination of other variables in each factor helped to minimize problems of multicolinearity.

The following independent variables were used:
- Sex
- Race
- Age
- Highest grade completed
- Number of years gone to school since leaving NTA
- Marital status
- Living with someone
- The longest period of time client lived in one place during two months prior to being interviewed
- Number of places lived during last three years
- Days sick in bed during two months prior to being interviewed
- What adults the client lived with most of the time until age fifteen (parents, other)
- Work history of parents
- Years of school by client
- Drug use by persons in clients' household when growing up
- Heroin use two months before entering NTA
- Drug treatment before entering NTA
- Was the amount of time spent in the clinic at each visit enough?
- Participation in NTA voluntary or involuntary
- Was methadone maintenance or another activity most helpful?
- Number of arrests
- Was client incarcerated during the six months prior to first entering NTA?
- Longest time client held a job
- Number of days client worked during the two months before first going to NTA
- Source of funds two months before first going to NTA (illegal activities or other)

- Source of funds first two months at NTA (Social Security, VA benefits or unemployment; other)

The following dependent variables were used:

- Heroin use during the past two months
- Number of days employed during past two months
- Source of funds during the past two-months (illegal activities, other)

The results of these multiple regressions were quite similar to the ones previously described. The multiple correlation coefficient squared (R^2) for each dependent variable was:

Dependent Variable	R^2
Heroin past two months	.13
Number of days worked past two months	.08
Illegal activities past two months	.18

The highest R^2 was .18[1] indicating that none of the independent variables, when used in a linear relationship, showed a useful reduction of the dependent variables' variance. The correlation coefficients also were quite low, indicating no useful reduction in the independent variable. Therefore, none of these independent variables explain these behavioral outcomes.

Next, multiple regressions were conducted using only members of treatment groups — clients in the control groups were omitted. The same independent and dependent variables were used. The results were not substantially different from the previous ones. The multiple correlation coefficient squared (R^2) for each dependent variable was:

Dependent Variable	R^2
Heroin past two months	.18
Number of days worked past months	.16
Illegal activities past two months	.23

The highest R^2 was .23[2] indicating that none of the independent variables, when used in a linear relationship, showed a useful reduction of the dependent variables' variance. The correlation coef-

---

[1] All F tests were significant at the .001 level. Stepping was stopped when the coefficient of the last variable entered was not significant at the .01 level.

[2] All F tests were significant at the .001 level. Stepping was stopped when the coefficient of the last variable entered was not significant at the .05 level.

TABLE IX-12
CLIENT PARTICIPATION IN INDIVIDUAL COUNSELING
(Percentage)

PARTICIPATION	Methadone Maintenance	Abstinence	Control	Total
No	57	45	85	63
Yes	43	55	15	37
TOTAL	100	100	100	100
n=	92	94	100	286

TABLE IX-13
CLIENT PARTICIPATION IN GROUP COUNSELING
(Percentage)

PARTICIPATION	Methadone Maintenance	Abstinence	Control	Total
No	87	80	95	87
Yes	13	20	5	13
TOTAL	100	100	100	100
n=	93	93	100	286

TABLE IX-14
CLIENT PARTICIPATION IN CHEMICAL TREATMENT--
USE OF TRANQUILIZERS, MUSCLE RELAXERS, ETC.
(Percentage)

PARTICIPATION	Methadone Maintenance	Abstinence	Control	Total
No	98	96	98	97
Yes	2	4	2	3
TOTAL	100	100	100	100
n=	93	93	100	286

TABLE IX-15
CLIENT PARTICIPATION IN METHADONE MAINTENANCE
(Percentage)

PARTICIPATION	Methadone Maintenance	Abstinence	Control	Total
No	11	77	76	55
Yes	89	23	24	45
TOTAL	100	100	100	100
n=	93	93	100	286

TABLE IX-16
CLIENT PARTICIPATION IN METHADONE DETOX
(Percentage)

PARTICIPATION	Methadone Maintenance	Abstinence	Control	Total
No	71	18	80	56
Yes	29	82 .	20	44
TOTAL	100	100	100	100
n=	93	· 96	100	289

TABLE IX-17
CLIENT PARTICIPATION IN JOB TRAINING,
REFERRAL, PLACEMENT COUNSELING,
VOCATIONAL REHABILITATION COUNSELING
(Percentage)

PARTICIPATION	Methadone Maintenance	Abstinence	Control	Total
No	95	75	97	89
Yes	5	25	3	11
TOTAL	100	100	100	100
n=	93	93	100	286

TABLE IX-18
DID NTA HELP CLIENT GET A JOB IN THE PAST 2 MONTHS?
(Percentage)

HELP FROM NTA	Methadone Maintenance	Abstinence	Control	Total
Two Months After N NTA				
No	98	91	95	94
Yes	2	9	5	6
Total	100	100	100	100
n=	93	95	100	288
Past Two Months				
No	100	97	97	98
Yes	0	3	3	2
Total	100	100	100	100
n=	92	95	100	287

ficients also were quite low, indicating no useful reduction in the independent variable. Therefore, none of these independent variables explains the behavioral outcomes. Due to the extremely low R^2's, no nonlinear combinations seemed worthwhile.

In view of the very small improvement in R^2 achieved by regrouping clients and decreasing the significance level from .01 to .05, no further multiple regressions seemed warranted.

Services Received by Clients

It is instructive to analyze precisely what services have been received by clients in the NTA program. It will be recalled that nearly all the treatment group clients received either methadone maintenance or methadone detoxification. Now, we will consider what supportive services were received by these clients.[1]

Table IX-12 shows that 43 percent of the maintenance clients and 55 percent of the abstinence clients stated that they had received individual counseling. This surprisingly low percentage could be partially attributable to clients not necessarily perceiving the types of encounters he received with NTA staff as being "individual counseling" per se.

Table IX-13 shows that very few of the clients received group counseling. It is likely that a somewhat higher proportion of the abstinence clients participated in group counseling because some of them were in drug-free programs which emphasize that type of service.

Table IX-14 indicates that chemical treatment (other than methadone) was rarely used in the NTA program. Of course, one would expect that all of the members of the methadone maintenance group would receive methadone maintenance. However, Table IX-15 shows that 11 percent of this group stated that they had not received methadone maintenance. This is probably attributable to their being quickly switched into methadone detoxification upon entering the program; or there may have been confusion on their part as to which entry into NTA they were being questioned about. Of the abstinence

---

[1] Members of the control group reported receiving some services. This is probably because many of them were in treatment for more than one day. It was previously noted that many members of the control groups subsequently re-entered treatment (Table IX-9). Possibly, they mentioned services received during a subsequent NTA experience.

clients, 23 percent claimed that they had received methadone mainte¬ nance. This is undoubtedly attributable, again, to their being switched to methadone maintenance during the course of treatment or confusion as to which entry into NTA they were being questioned about. A similar phenomenon occurred in asking a client whether he participated in methadone detoxification, as shown in Table IX-16.

The lack of client participation in job training, referral, placement counseling, or vocational rehabilitation counseling is indicated in Table IX-17. An extremely small proportion of clients have received this type of assistance. The lack of assistance in obtaining a job is graphically displayed in Table IX-18. An extremely small percentage of these clients received help from NTA in getting a job. Table IX-19 shows essentially that clients engaged in no other treatment activity.

Client Follow-Up

Table IX-20 indicates little contact with NTA after leaving the program; and most of the contact was initiated by the clients, with a visit to the program. Table IX-21 indicates the frequency of client contact. These data raise questions as to why there was so little fol- low-up initiated by program staff. The reason might be that the patient load was so high that staff had little time available to initiate follow-up contacts.

TABLE IX-19
CLIENT'S PARTICIPATION IN OTHER TREATMENT ACTIVITY
(Percentage)

PARTICIPATION	Methadone Maintenance	Abstinence	Control	Total
No	99	97	93	96
Yes	1	3	7	4
TOTAL	100	100	100	100
n=	93	93	100	286

TABLE IX-20
CLIENT CONTACT WITH NTA PROGRAM
AFTER LEAVING TREATMENT
(Percentage)

PARTICIPATION	Methadone Maintenance	Abstinence	Control	Total
No contact	77	75	86	80
Contact by Telephone	0	9	2	4
Contact by Staff Visit	1	0	2	1
Contact by Visit to Program	22	16	10	15
TOTAL	100	100	100	100
n=	93	96	100	289

TABLE IX-21
FREQUENCY OF CLIENT CONTACT WITH NTA
AFTER LEAVING THE PROGRAM
(Percentage)

FREQUENCY	Methadone Maintenance	Abstinence	Control	Total
None	78	75	85	79
Once	5	6	2	5
2 - 3 Times	13	13	4	10
More than 3 Times	4	6	9	6
TOTAL	100	100	100	100
n=	93	96	100	289

Chapter X

CLIENT ATTITUDES AND PERCEPTIONS ABOUT TREATMENT

Client attitudes and perceptions about treatment were not central to this study. Therefore, only rather rudimentary questions were included in the interview instrument concerning these factors. From this viewpoint, this chapter should be regarded as subject to substantial limitations.

Client Readiness to Change or Improve His Life

It is generally recognized that the most favorable condition for bringing about successful behavior change in treatment is the client's readiness to seek assistance for his problems. One hypothesis that could help explain the lack of differences between the treatment and control groups is that there were no differences in the clients' readiness to seek assistance in changing or improving their lives. Some insight into the clients' readiness to seek assistance in changing or improving their lives may be gained by examining the clients' reasons for participating in treatment. These are shown in Table X-1. Although no statistically significant differences appear, these data show that most of the clients in the control and treatment groups voluntarily sought participation in treatment in order to change or improve their drug usage, physical health, mental health, life style, etc. Only 20 percent of all clients were in treatment because of legal coercion; however, no statistically significant differences were found when we compared the percentage of clients in the treatment and control groups who participated involuntarily. Further, the multivariate analyses presented in Chapter IX show that post-treatment behavior is not explained by whether a client's participation is voluntary or forced by legal authorities. However, there is some evidence to support the hypothesis that client readiness may account, at least

145

in part, for the lack of significant differences in the behavior of the different groups.

Treatment Experience at NTA

Another hypothesis that could help explain the lack of statistically significant differences in outcomes among the groups is that clients in the control group benefited from the effects of treatment. That is, although this group did not appear to invest heavily in the treatment process, they, nonetheless, may have been affected by it during the short period they were involved. There is, of course, no hard evidence to support this hypothesis. But it is not an unreasonable one. Not everyone needs the same help or responds in the same way to treatment. There may be many therapeutic pathways through the treatment process.

The manner in which a client can be helped by treatment could be the result of an interplay of several factors:

- The client's interpersonal needs
- The client's strengths and weaknesses
- The client's nontherapeutic resources
- The treatment techniques used to effect change

It is also possible that the amount of time which the client must invest in treatment in order to achieve behavioral change is a function of the interplay of these various factors. All clients, no doubt, had adaptive, coping strengths which served them well in the past. Possibly, a boost from some event during the short-term treatment may have strengthened these coping mechanisms or enhanced the development of new ones. This hypothesis is supported by the "adaptive spiral" process used by Yalom which "refers to the process in which one change in the patient begets changes in his interpersonal environment which begets futher personal change."[1] Thus, perhaps some clients in the control group did benefit from treatment during the limited time they were involved. The impact (in these terms) of the treatment program on clients in the control group is impossible to determine. Consequently, determining the percent of control clients who were helped by the treatment program is also impossible.

---

[1] Irvin D. Yalom, *The Theory and Practice of Group Psychotherapy* (New York: Basic Books, Inc., 1970) .

Nevertheless, investigating the attitudes and perceptions of the clients about their treatment experience provides some idea of whether the clients felt they were helped by the program.

According to Table X-2, 22 percent of the clients in the control group felt they were helped by NTA. Table X-3 shows that 26 percent felt that the time they spent at NTA during the last month in treatment (Table X-4) was adequate to help them "get their thing together." These answers are substantially different from the treatment groups'. Approximately 70 percent of treatment group clients stated that NTA was helpful and that the amount of time spent in treatment during the last month in NTA was adequate.

For the entire sample (including treatment and control groups), client attitudes toward treatment were unrelated to outcomes. The multivariate analyses in Chapter IX found that whether a client stated that NTA helped, that the time spent in treatment during the last month in NTA was adequate, and whether treatment was received after leaving NTA, were unrelated to heroin use, employment, arrests, or incarcerations during the most recent two-month period. Separate multivariate analyses were not conducted for the control group only.

Table X-5, focusing only on the control group, shows the complex relationships between the respondent's answers to questions as to the adequacy of time spent in treatment, whether NTA helped him recover, whether he received treatment after NTA, and how these are related to whether he achieved full recovery. It can only be concluded that there is no clear relationship among these variables. For example, of the 25 control group clients who achieved full recovery, only seven stated that the amount of time spent in NTA was adequate; only three of the 25 re-entered drug treatment after leaving NTA and only seven of the 25 believed that NTA helped in the recovery. One can only conclude that some factors outside of treatment strongly influenced their recovery.

Other evidence regarding the control group's favorable perception of NTA comes from the data elicited from the question as to whether or not the clients would recommend NTA to a friend with a drug problem. Table X-6 shows that 58 percent of the control group would recommend NTA to a friend with a drug problem.[1] This is more than twice the percentage of control group clients who felt that NTA

---

[1] Compared to about 82 percent of the treatment groups.

TABLE X-1

PRINCIPAL REASONS FOR PARTICIPATION IN TREATMENT
(Percentage)

REASONS	Methadone Maintenance	Abstinence	Control	Total
Get Off Drugs	60	59	54	58
Avoid Criminal Activity	1	0	0	0
Improve Physical Health	4	2	3	3
Improve Mental Health	2	1	3	2
Forced by Legal Authority	17	21	21	20
Family or Peer Pressure	1	7	5	4
Could not Support Habit	0	2	1	1
Drug Shortage	2	1	3	2
Desired Change in Life-style	6	2	0	3
Help in Getting a Job	0	1	0	0
Other	7	4	10	7
TOTAL	100	100	100	100
n =	91	94	96	281

TABLE X-2

DID NTA PROGRAM HELP?
(Percentage)

NTA HELPFUL	Methadone Maintenance	Abstinence	Control	Total
No	29	30	78	46
Yes	71	70	22	54
TOTAL	100	100	100	100
n =	93	96	100	289

TABLE X-3

ADEQUACY OF TIME SPENT IN TREATMENT DURING LAST
MONTH
(Percentage)

ADEQUATE TIME SPENT	Methadone Maintenance	Abstinence	Control	Total
No	25	34	74	45
Yes	75	66	26	55
TOTAL	100	100	100	100
n =	93	96	99	288

TABLE X-4

TIME SPENT AT NTA CLINIC DURING LAST MONTH
IN TREATMENT
(Percentage)

TIME SPENT AT NTA	Methadone Maintenance	Abstinence	Control	Total
Less than One Hour	0	0	2	1
One Hour	16	9	43	20
2 - 5 Hours	39	36	39	38
6 -10 Hours	20	30	12	22
11 - 25 Hours	17	15	2	12
Over 25 Hours	8	10	2	7
TOTAL	100	100	100	100
n =	89	88	56	233

TABLE X-5

CLIENT ATTITUDES COMPARED TO POST NTA
TREATMENT AND RECOVERY

(control group only)

Did NTA Help?	Adequate Time Spent in Treatment				Total
	Yes		No		
	Fully Recovered	Not Fully Recovered	Fully Recovered	Not Fully Recovered	
No	4 (1)	7 (0)	14 (1)	52 (13)	77 (15)
Yes	3 (0)	11 (3)	4 (1)	4 (1)	22 (5)
Total	7 (1)	18 (3)	18 (2)	56 (14)	99 (20)

Note: Numbers in parentheses indicate clients who re-entered drug treatment after leaving NTA.

TABLE X-6

WOULD CLIENT RECOMMEND NTA TO A FRIEND
WITH A DRUG PROBLEM?
(Percentage)

RECOMMEND NTA	Methadone Maintenance	Abstinence	Control	Total
No	20	16	42	26
Yes	80	84	58	74
TOTAL	100	100	100	100
n =	92	95	100	287

TABLE X-7

REASON FOR LEAVING NTA
(percentage)

Reason for Leaving	Methadone Maintenance	Abstinence	Control	Total
Did not like it	19	12	29	20
Did not need it	27	18	13	19
Graduated	6	30	4	13
Wanted to use drugs	10	3	9	7
Did not like methadone	13	8	23	15
Went to jail	11	5	5	7
Did not help	2	9	8	7
Left town	5	2	1	3
On the run	3	3	--	2
School/job	--	3	1	1
Family/friend pressure	1	2	--	1
Another non-NTA program	--	--	3	1
Other	3	5	4	4
TOTAL	100	100	100	100
n =	92	98	86	276

TABLE X-8

CHANGES NEEDED IN NTA
(percentage)

Change	Methadone Maintenance	Abstinence	Control	Total
Counseling	(39)	(39)	(31)	(37)
Better counseling	18	17	11	16
More counseling	5	9	2	6
More group counseling	3	3	4	3
More individual couns.	5	2	1	3
More ex-addicts	4	1	1	2
Other complaints & suggestions	4	7	12	7
Methadone	(13)	(14)	(13)	(14)
Less or none	5	7	6	6
More	1	1	--	1
Alternative to	3	--	2	2
More detox	1	2	4	2
Reinstitute take-home program	--	3	--	1
Other comments	3	1	1	2
Other	(48)	(47)	(56)	(49)
Change in program structure/procedures	6	5	--	4
Stricter	2	4	4	3
Better job training/ placement	1	4	5	3
More services	2	3	4	3
Abolish NTA	1	3	--	1
Don't know	19	10	26	17
None	13	14	14	14
Other	4	4	3	4
TOTAL	100	100	100	100

Number of times mentioned: 100   117   81   298

Note: The total number of responses exceed the number of clients in the sample because some respondents indicated more than one change.

helped them. Thus, even though some clients did not feel NTA helped them, they evidently believed it could help others.

Reasons for Terminating Treatment

Despite the fact that clients in the control group left the treatment within five days or less, their leaving did not necessarily mean that their desire for recovery diminished. Possibly they were dissatisfied with the program or simply felt they no longer needed the treatment program. Our data tend to support this assumption. According to Table X-7, only 9 percent of th eclients in the control group said they left because they wanted to use drugs, and only 5 percent left because of incarceration. Most (73 percent) of the clients' reasons for leaving NTA fell into the categories of "didn't like it" (29 percent), "didn't like methadone" (23 percent), "didn't need it" (13 percent), or "didn't help" (8 percent). Taken together, these data suggest that many of the clients in the control group felt they could make changes or improvements in their lives without the assistance of NTA.

Relationship of Attitudes and Perceptions
to Outcomes

The multivariate analyses discussed in Chapter IX considered several variables indicating attitudes and perceptions concerning treatment:

- Was the time spent at NTA adequate?
- Was participation voluntary or forced by legal authorities?
- Did the NTA program help?
- Did anything other than NTA help?
- Would you recommend NTA to a friend with a drug problem?

None of these was correlated with outcomes (heroin use, employment, arrests, or incarcerations). We can only conclude that the clients' attitudes and perceptions, at least as indicated by these measures, are unrelated to outcomes. It was previously noted (in Chapter IX) that outcomes were not correlated with type of treatment services received.

Discussion

Our limited data on the clients' attitudes and perceptions about their NTA treatment experiences show that all types of clients tended to hold favorable attitudes toward the program. The data also suggest that a very limited contact with the program was beneficial to many clients in the control group, although they did not necessarily perceive it as being beneficial. Because there is little evidence on the effects of very short-term treatment, and because our attitudinal data are limited, it is difficult to determine the extent to which limited program contact can account for the lack of differences we found among clients in the treatment and control groups.

Despite these limitations, an analysis of client attitudes and perceptions regarding their treatment experiences appears useful and it could have programmatic implications. The clients did have some ideas on how the treatment programs could be improved in order to effect behavioral changes and to attract clients who need assistance with their drug problems.

Table X-8 shows that 37 percent of the clients responding felt that more and better counseling was very important if NTA is to be more effective in helping people "get their thing together." It was noted previously that many clients apparently retained their commitment to change, even though they quit the program. These data suggest that clients would be more attracted to the program and more likely to remain in treatment if supportive services such as individual counseling, group counseling, and rehabilitative counseling were more available or improved.[1]

Many clients also expressed suspicion and negative attitudes about the role of methadone in the treatment process. Similar attitudes toward methadone and methadone treatment programs were found among detoxification and methadone maintenance clients in another study.[2] In this study, both groups expressed ambivalence about

---

[1] A note of caution in interpreting these findings is appropriate. Some mental health clinicians and researchers have noted that clients may complain about counseling when they can think of nothing else to complain about. There is no way to determine whether this is in fact true in this study; nor has this belief been validated in other studies of which we are aware.

[2] Barry S. Brown, Gloria J. Benn, and Donald R. Jansen, "Methadone Maintenance: Some Client Opinions," *American Journal of Psychiatry*, 132:6, June 1975, pp. 623-6.

methadone. Although they viewed it as capable of helping them and their heroin addiction, they were concerned about possible methadone dependence and about side effecst, both real and imagined.[1] Besides being subject to their own concerns about methadone, clients must contend with the community's concerns and attitudes about methadone being used by treatment programs. The authors of this study concluded that the objective to be sought is "sufficient community tolerance to permit clients to remain in treatment long enough for them to obtain the tools necessary to explore alternatives to the addict lifestyle."[2] They also suggest that the treatment program be sensitive to clients' concerns about methadone and deal with them "through the use of techniques that allow the client to see an end to his reliance on methadone from the time of his entrance into treatment."[3]

Thus, perhaps the drug treatment programs could also improve their ability to effect changes in clients and to become more attractive to clients if they could attend more closely to community and client observations about methadone as a treatment modality. This would require working with the community as well as the clients entering the treatment program.

[1] Ibid., p. 623.
[2] Ibid., p. 626.
[3] Ibid.

Chapter XI

DISCUSSION[1]

This study has raised many issues and tested numerous hypotheses. The results raise questions with respect to some of the common assumptions pertaining to treatment programs.

One is struck first by the very large behavioral change experienced by these clients. However, the data suggest that the effects of treatment cannot be separated from other factors. Moreover, addicts' behavioral change was not only unrelated to presence and type of treatment, but was unrelated to demographic characteristics as well. This absence of differences is little short of baffling.

The "maturing out" hypothesis that has been advanced[2] seems inadequate to explain these findings. In that formulation, the addict is seen as reaching a point at which the rigorous addict life style is felt to be no longer feasible and/or desirable. The addict is forced to explore alternatives to heroin use and all that is involved in maintaining his use of heroin. Whether or not that phenomenon of maturing out exists in fact, it does not appear to fit data from this study, if only because of the limited time frames involved. Addicts were interviewed as little as one year and no more than five years from time of contact with NTA. There were no significant differences in outcomes in terms of time elapsed since leaving NTA.

Three other efforts at explanation may have greater merit. On

---

[1] Much of the discussion in this chapter is drawn from an unpublished paper: Marvin R. Burt, Barry S. Brown, and Robert L. DuPont, "Evaluation of a Large Multi-Modality Drug Treatment Program," (processed).

[2] C. Winick, "Maturing Out of Narcotic Addiction," *Bulletin of Narcotics* 14: 1-7, 1962.

the one hand, forces entirely outside the traditional treatment process may have been at work to help bring about change in addict behavior. The community itself may have changed. Whereas heroin use may have been tolerated in the community in the period preceding addicts' contact with NTA, i.e., in the middle and late 1960's, it may have become increasingly unacceptable as the real dangers of that drug became known. Thus, if he was to remain acceptable to his community, the addict was forced to explore other avenues of behavior. More pointedly, if what was once "cool" became foolish and weak, it may well have become necessary to reassess activity in regard to that substance. Whether or not this describes intellectual and behavioral changes in the decade 1965-1975 in Washington, D.C., is unknown, but two points are worth noting.

First, in a 1972 study conducted among juvenile users and non-users of heroin in the District, it was found that non-users were most likely to relate their non-use of heroin to information that only became available in the early 1970's. The juvenile non-users reported first-hand knowledge of persons who became involved with heroin and whose behavior deteriorated and lives were threatened as a consequence. Since the peak years of heroin use in the District were 1966-1968, this was information simply not available to their elders — the addicts in this study. It suggests, but by no means confirms, a dramatic change in awareness and thinking about heroin by the time the study was undertaken.[1]

A second explanation for the lack of differences between treatment and control groups may lie in the data itself. In this regard, it can be hypothesized that persons who once having made a commitment to seek change, i.e., who enter treatment and then drop out of treatment immediately thereafter, represent a very select group of persons and are improperly cast into a control group. In this formulation, that group would consist, at least largely, of persons who had not quit on their resolve to seek behavioral change, but merely quit on the means to accomplish that change as posed by the treatment program.

Another explanation lies in the role of the criminal justice system's efforts to reduce the supply of illicit drugs and make the

---

[1] Starlett R. Craig and Barry S. Brown, "Comparison of Youthful Heroin Users and Nonusers From One Urban Community," *International Journal of the Addictions*, 10 (1) : 53-64, 1975.

abuser's life style more difficult to maintain. The number of arrests made by the Metropolitan Police Department did not vary markedly during the period in question, but the purity of heroin decreased markedly and the price of heroin increased substantially, making it more difficult for a heroin addict to obtain the drug. Further, strict controls were instituted on the dispensing of methadone and (later) amphetamines.

It seems reasonable to expect these substantial changes in availability, purity, and price of illicit drugs to result in decreased illicit drug taking, and these phenomena probably helped to drive addicts into treatment programs.

In any event, a review of the findings from this study cannot help but raise further questions. One is struck not only by the relatively high rate of prosocial behavioral change taking place within the addict sample surveyed, but also by the fact that change takes place irrespective of the type of treatment initiated and, indeed, irrespective of whether or not treatment is instituted.

The results of this study cause us to re-examine some commonly held assumptions regarding the treatment process. First is the common assumption that it is desirable to keep clients in treatment for extended periods of time. Clients did equally well whether they stayed in treatment one day or five years (or shorter periods of time). Perhaps the client himself is the best judge of how long a period of treatment is sufficient.

The study raises questions with respect to the comparative virtues of methadone maintenance vs. detoxification. Neither modality was found to be superior to the other. Again, perhaps treatment programs should be flexible, as was NTA, with respect to the modality in which the clients should be placed.

There has been a great deal of interest in demographic and background correlates of success in drug treatment. Some studies have produced limited evidence showing that clients with certain characteristics do better in treatment than others. In this study, demographic and background factors failed to explain success in treatment or lack thereof. It is possible that these characteristics may be important in treatments other than methadone maintenance and detoxification. Nearly all the clients shared one characteristic — rather heavy involvement in heroin use. Possibly, if persons who were not heroin addicts were included, some characteristics could be significant; our data neither prove nor disprove this hypothesis.

Chapter XII

CONCLUSIONS

Chapter II specified the following basic issues to be addressed in this study:

- What has happened to former clients who left treatment?
- What influence did treatment seem to have on post-treatment outcomes of former clients?

More recently Robert DuPont, M.D., Director of the National Institute on Drug Abuse, indicated an interest in this study addressing the natural history of drug abuse. This chapter first presents some conclusions regarding the natural history of drug abuse and then answers the research questions.

The discussion of the natural history of drug abuse considers the entire sample; "What has happened to former clients who left treatment?" considers only the two treatment groups. And "What influence did treatment seem to have on post-treatment outcomes of former clients?" compares the treatment and control groups.

Natural History of Drug Abuse

The results of this study provide some insights into the natural history of drug abuse as well as direct answers to the several questions concerned with differential outcomes of different client groups. Of principal interest in this regard are the behavioral changes in these drug abusers from the time shortly before they entered treatment until they were interviewed. Chapter VI described the clients' backgrounds and characteristics, and Chapter VII analyzed their changes in behavior in terms of the various groups of interest.

The behavior of all the respondents (including the control and treatment groups) is shown in Tables XII-1 and XII-2. Substantial reductions in drug taking occurred between the two-month periods

163

TABLE XII-1

DRUG USE
(percentage)

Frequency of Use	2 Months Before NTA	2 Months After NTA	Last 2 Months
Heroin			
Not at all	3	52	64
Occasionally	28	34	29
Daily	69	14	7
Total	100	100	100
n =	289	289	289
Illegal Methadone			
Not at all	64	80	91
Occasionally	32	18	8
Daily	4	2	1
Total	100	100	100
n =	289	289	289
Cocaine			
Not at all	42	70	79
Occasionally	51	30	20
Daily	7	0	1
Total	100	100	100
n =	289	289	289
Amphetamines			
Not at all	72	79	85
Occasionally	21	17	14
Daily	7	4	1
Total	100	100	100
n =	289	289	289

TABLE XII-2

EMPLOYMENT AND CRIMINAL ACTIVITY
(percentage)

Status	2 Months Before NTA	2 Months After NTA	Last 2 Months
Employment			
Paid job	34	37	45
Keeping house, student, job training	5	4	6
Illegal activities	44	38	24
All other activities	17	21	25
Total	100	100	100
n =	289	289	289
Arrests			
Not arrested	76	90	92
Arrested	24	10	8
Total	100	100	100
n =	288	288	288

before entering treatment, after treatment, and before being interviewed (Table XII-1).

Only 7 percent of the respondents used heroin daily compared to 69 percent prior to entering NTA[1] Employment increased (Table XII-2) but this was less dramatic than the decrease in drug taking. Engagement in illegal activities decreased from 44 percent of the respondents to 24 percent during the most recent period. This reduction in reported illegal activities is confirmed by the substantial reduction in the percentage of clients arrested.[2]

These data show drug abusers progressing from frequent use of heroin and other illicit drugs and engagement in other illegal activities to considerably less involvement in illicit drug use and illegal activities. Indeed, Chapter VII showed that 22 percent of the respondents were fully recovered and 58 percent were "partially" or "marginally" recovered by the time they were interviewed.

What Has Happened to Former Clients Who Left Treatment?

This discussion focuses on the three major groups of clients — methadone maintenance, abstinence, and control — ignoring the year in which they left treatment. Subgroups (as well as these major groups) are addressed in Chapter VII.

Three types of behavioral outcomes were investigated:
• Drug use
• Criminal activity
• Socioeconomic productivity

Comparisons were made during three time periods:
• The two-month period immediately prior to entering treatment
• The two-month period immediately after leaving treatment
• The two-month period immediately prior to being interviewed

Drug Use

Heroin use declined dramatically for clients leaving the program. This occurred immediately upon leaving treatment and further improvement had occurred by the time the interviews were conducted. This pattern of immediate involvement followed by further improve-

---

[1] Drug use information was confirmed by urine tests. However, it should be noted that 27 pecent of the urines were positive for preludin.

[2] Arrest information was confirmed by police arrest records.

ment by the time the interviews were conducted occurred for all categories of drugs. While essentially all the respondents were using heroin at least some of the time prior ot entering treatment, 63 to 66 percent stated that they were not using it all during the two-month period prior to being interviewed. Only 4 to 6 percent of the respondents in the two treatment groups admitted to using heroin daily during the two-month period prior to being interviewed. Seventy-two percent of these clients stated that they had been using heroin daily during the two months prior to treatment. Dramatic, statistically significant improvements occurred for both treatment groups; there is no statistically significant difference among the groups. The responses by the former clients were essentially confirmed by urinalysis tests of specimens taken during the interviews.

A substantial statistically significant decline occurred in illegal methadone usage by all treatment groups for all years. Ninety-two percent of the treatment respondents indicated no illegal methadone usage at all during the two-month period prior to being interviewed, while from 31 to 39 percent used it during the two months prior to treatment. There is no statistically significant difference among the groups. In view of the concern over illegal methadone use by persons who don't use other opiates, it is reassuring that *none* of the respondents reported using *only* illicit methadone during the most recent two-month period.

Next to heroin, cocaine was the most popular drug used by these clients during the two-month period prior to entering NTA. Cocaine is not addictive and is rarely a primary drug of abuse. Only 41 to 43 percent of the clients did not use cocaine at all during this preprogram period, but few used it daily (4 to 8 percent). During the two months immediately prior to being interviewed, 77 to 78 percent of the respondents who had been through treatment programs did not use cocaine at all. Hardly any of these individuals used cocaine daily (0 to 3 percent), but a substantial percentage used cocaine occasionally (20 to 22 percent). The decline in use is statistically significant for both treatment groups; there is no statistically significant difference between the groups.

Amphetamines were a relatively less popular drug as compared with heroin or cocaine. All treatment groups reported a reduction in amphetamines used between the two-month period prior to treatment and the two-month period prior to being interviewed.

Barbiturates were a comparatively unpopular drug of abuse among the clients sampled. Few of the clients used barbiturates during the two months prior to entering the program. Nevertheless, there was some improvement among these clients as reflected by the high percentage not using barbiturates at all during the two months prior to being interviewed (93 percent). The improvement realized by the methadone maintenance group is statistically significant but that of the abstinence group is not. However, there are no statistically significant differences between the two groups.

Hallucinogens, dilaudid, minor tranquilizers and other drugs were used very infrequently. The general pattern of reduction in use of drugs previously discussed is also reflected in these. However, none of the improvements in hallucinogen use is statistically significant. For dilaudid, improvements for methadone maintenance and abstinence groups are statistically significant between the period before treatment and the last two months.

The reduction in use of minor tranquilizers is not statistically significant.

The reduction in use of other drugs is statistically significant for both groups.

The respondents were not specifically asked whether they used preludin but whether they used other drugs. In any case, preludin was the drug that most frequently appeared in the urine results; 27 percent of the tests were positive for preludin, indicating widespread abuse of that drug.

Some reduction occurred in marijuana usage between pre- and post-program periods. However, considerable use is indicated. This is hardly surprising in view of the widespread use of marijuana in our society, particularly by persons in the age groups represented in this study. The reduction in marijuana use is statistically significant for the maintenance group, but not for the abstinence group. The difference between the two groups is not statistically significant.

A major concern among methadone programs is the belief that clients may tend to substitute alcohol for heroin. The data do not support this belief. There are only slight changes in drinking behavior. There is no significant difference between pre-treatment and post-treatment drinking behavior or between the two groups.

Another form of substance substitution is increased use of cigarettes after withdrawing from heroin. The responses indicate that this has not occurred. The frequency of cigarette use changed little between the pre-treatment and post-treatment periods. Indeed, there is slight reduction in heavy smoking (i.e., more than one pack each day). The differences are not statistically significant.

Employment

One of the desired results of a drug treatment program is employment or other prosocial activity (e.g., keeping house, going to school, job training). There is a general, but by no means consistent, pattern of improvement in comparing the two-month period prior to treatment with the most recent two-month period.

The abstinence group shows dramatic statistically significant improvement; the percentage of clients having a paid job doubled from 28 to 57 with the methadone maintenance group essentially unchanged. The percentage of abstinence clients who had a paid job or "keeping house, student, or job training" during the last two months was significantly greater than the methadone maintenance group. The abstinence group also experienced a dramatic reduction in illegal activities that was greater than the methadone maintenance group, although that group also showed improvement. Of course, during the period in question, the unemployment rate was increasing substantially. This should affect the results, especially during the most recent period.

A substantial influence on the data could have been exerted by a variety of programs underway in the District of Columbia during these periods including some focusing on the employing of ex-addicts by the U.S. Employment Service, Vocational Rehabilitation, various work-training programs, the Emergency Employment Act and NTA's policy of employing ex-addicts on its staff.

Criminal Behavior

Two measures of criminal behavior are used in this evaluation:
- Frequency of arrests
- Whether or not time was spent in jail

The percentage of clients who were arrested during the two-month period prior to being interviewed was substantially lower than during the two months before treatment, indicating a reduction in criminal behavior as expressed by actual arrests. The reductions are statistically significant for both treatment groups. There is no statistically significant difference between the two groups.

Another indicator of criminal behavior is whether or not a client has spent time in jail during the periods in question. There is improvement, but it is not statistically significant.

What Influence Did Treatment Seem to Have on Post-Treatment Outcomes?

Drug Use

Comparisons were made, in terms of each drug, among the treatment and control groups. No statistically significant differences were found to exist.

During the period 1971-1974, substantial change occurred external to the treatment programs that could help to explain both the substantial decrease in heroin use and the lack of significant differences between the treatment and control groups. Of greatest significance is the substantial decrease in the supply and quality and the rise in the price of heroin. These factors made heroin usage by *all* groups more difficult whether they had received treatment or not.

The substantial reduction in use of illegal methadone by both treatment and control groups during the last two-month period is undoubtedly influenced by the tightening of Federal regulations governing the dispensing of methadone inaugurated late in 1972. Consequently, the supply of illegal methadone in Washington, D.C., was sharply curtailed. This is reflected in data on methadone overdose deaths.

Amphetamine use was severely restricted as the Federal Government initiated a significant policy reducing availability before the most recent time period.

Employment

The abstinence group showed a significantly greater improvement than the control group. Of course, employment is substantially influenced by economic conditions and government programs which may have little relationship to treatment.

Criminal Behavior

There are no statistically significant differences between treatment and control groups in frequency of arrests and whether time was spent in jail.

Multiple Behavioral Outcome Measures

Each respondent was classified (based on his drug use, criminal behavior, and employment) as:

- Fully recovered
- Partially recovered
- Marginally recovered, or
- A failure

As a whole, 22 percent of the respondents were fully recovered, 20 percent were failures and the remaining 58 percent were partially or marginally recovered. Fifty-seven percent achieved either full or partial recovery.

The differences in recovery status among treatment groups are not statistically significant, nor are the differences among the treatment and control groups.

Redefinition of Treatment and Control Groups

The control group was "purified" to include only clients who had entered NTA for one day and did not subsequently re-enter treatment. All other clients were grouped according to the total length of time they remained in treatment, including all entries.

A remarkably consistent pattern of heroin use was shown among all groups. The differences between treatment groups and the control group are not statistically significant.

As in heroin use, the arrest patterns of groups during the most recent two-month period are remarkably similar.

In terms of employment-type activities during the most recent two-month period, the patterns are again generally consistent among the groups; the differences are not statistically significant.

Explanatory Factors

A search was made (Chapter IX) for possible reasons why there are essentially no significant differences in the behavior of former clients sampled among treatment and control groups, and analyses were conducted of factors that might explain outcomes. A considerable number of clients' background and characteristic variables were examined; none of these was significantly different among the groups.

A number of client background, characteristics, and outcome variables (72) were analyzed through factor analysis and multiple regression analyses in attempting to establish relationships among the variables and to determine what variables might explain variance in the dependent (outcome) variables.

The most significant overall finding is that client outcomes are unrelated to any background or characteristic variables included in the study.

Client Attitudes and Perceptions

Chapter X discussed client attitudes and perceptions about treatment. This was not a principal focus of this study; therefore, only rather rudimentary questions were included in the interview instrument, and the results should be regarded with caution.

This analysis shows that there are no significant differences among the treatment and control groups in terms of their personal reasons for participating in treatment. Clients in treatment for more than five days had generally favorable attitudes toward NTA. Approximately 70 percent of the treatment group clients stated that NTA was helpful to them and that the amount of time spent in treatment during their last month in NTA was adequate; 82 percent of them would recommend NTA to a friend with a drug problem.

A substantial percentage of the original control group believed that NTA helped (22 percent) and 20 percent of the clients in the control group subsequently re-entered treatment. Further, 58 percent of control group clients stated that they would recommend NTA to a friend who had a drug problem. Our data tend to show that many of the clients left NTA because they felt they could make changes or improvements in their lives without the help of NTA. However, client attitudes toward treatment were unrelated to outcomes.

The examination of client attitudes and perceptions regarding their treatment experiences suggests there are implications as to how NTA can enhance its ability to attract and effect changes in clients. It appeared that many clients quit not because they changed their commitment to seek change but rather because they questioned the means to achieve that change as offered by the treatment program. Thirty-nine percent of the treatment group and 31 percent of the control group clients responding felt that one of the most important changes needed was more and better counseling. Thus, perhaps clients would be more likely to make an appropriate investment in the treatment process at NTA if the supportive services such as individual counseling, group counseling, rehabilitative counseling, etc., received greater emphasis by the program. Their responses show that few supportive services were received.

A reason that 15 percent of the clients (13 percent of the methadone maintenance group, 8 percent of the abstinence group, and 23 percent of the control group) gave for quitting the program revolved around their suspicious and negative attitudes about methadone's role in the treatment process. This suggests that NTA could improve its ability to retain clients if it could attend more closely to community and client observations about methadone. This would require working with the community as well as the clients entering the treatment programs.

PART II

A FOLLOW-UP STUDY OF FORMER CLIENTS OF NEW YORK CITY'S ADDICTION SERVICES AGENCY

by
Marvin R. Burt
and
Thomas J. Glynn

Chapter I

SUMMARY

We now turn to a study which assesses the experiences of clients who had contact with and/or received treatment from the Addiction Services Agency (ASA) in New York City. The basic questions addressed are those addressed in the first study.

- What happened to former clients who left treatment?
- What influence did treatment seem to have on post-treatment outcomes of former clients?

And the points made in analyzing the first study can be made here too.

Sample Selection

This (New York City) universe of clients was partitioned into three treatment groups and one nontreatment (comparison) group. A sample of 782 clients was drawn from 14 cooperating programs located throughout four boroughs of New York City. These clients were those who had enrolled in or entered one of these treatment programs during the last six months of 1971. The following table shows that this sample was partitioned into those clients who had enrolled in or left[1] a methadone maintenance, ambulatory unit, or therapeutic community treatment program and those who registered at a program but who left within five days ("comparison").

	Number in Sample
Methadone Maintenance	220
Ambulatory Unit	135
Therapeutic Community	204
Comparison	223
Total	782

---

[1] But who remained more than five days after registering.

177

Three types of behavioral outcomes were investigated, as in the case of the first study.

- Drug use
- Criminal activity
- Socioeconomic productivity

Comparisons again were made during three time periods:

- The two-month period immediately prior to entering treatment
- The two-month period immediately after leaving treatment
- The two-month period immediately prior to being interviewed

Measurements were made to determine changes realized by each group comparing the three time periods. The measurements between the experimental and comparison groups were then compared to determine whether the changes appeared to be attributable to the program in question or outside factors.

The sample for each category was randomly selected from the universe of all clients who entered treatment during the study period. The sample respondents were tracked and interviewed, and urine specimens were obtained to validate their responses to questions concerning their use of drugs.

Natural History of Drug Abuse

The results of this (New York) study provide additional insights into the natural history of drug abuse as well as direct answers to the questions asked.

Chapter V in this Part presents detailed data. In summary, and as in the study reported in Part I, the typical client was a black male, twenty-one to twenty-five years old, who had completed the 11th grade. He had used heroin daily for at least two years, had first participated in some type of crime by age eighteen, and was unemployed. Chapter VI analyzes clients' changes in behavior.

The behavior of the respondents (including the comparison and treatment groups) is shown in Tables I-1 and I-2. Substantial reductions in drug taking occurred between the two-month periods before entering treatment, after leaving treatment, and before being interviewed (Table I-1). Only 2 percent of the respondents used

---

[1] Drug use information, as in the Washington study, was confirmed by urine tests.

heroin daily compared to 67 percent prior to entering ASA.[1]

Employment increased (Table I-2) at a rate nearly as dramatic as the decrease in drug taking. There was a substantial reduction in the percentage of clients arrested.[1] This indicates a concomitant reduction in criminal behavior as expressed by actual arrests.

Again we find that drug abusers progressed from frequent use of heroin and other illicit drugs and engagement in other criminal behavior to considerably less involvement in illicit drug use and criminal behavior. By the time they were interviewed, 49 percent of the respondents were fully recovered and 44 percent were "partially" or "marginally" recovered (as defined in Chapter VI, in this Part).

What Has Happened to Former Clients Who Left Treatment?

This discussion focuses on four major groups of clients — methadone maintenance, ambulatory unit, therapeutic community and comparison. These groups are different from those used in the first study.

Three types of behavioral outcomes were investigated:
- Drug use
- Criminal activity
- Socioeconomic productivity

Drug Use

Table I-3 summarizes the results. Again, heroin use declined dramatically for clients leaving the program. This occurred immediately upon leaving treatment and further improvement had occurred by the time the interviews were conducted. Again, this pattern of immediate improvement followed by further improvement by the time the interviews were conducted occurred for most categories of drugs. In no category was there any significant reversion.

While essentially all the respondents were using heroin at least some of the time prior to entering treatment, 79 to 90 percent stated that they were not using it at all during the two-month period prior to being interviewed. Only 2 to 4 percent of the respondents in the three treatment groups admitted to using heroin daily during

---

1 Arrest information was not confirmed.

TABLE I-1

DRUG USE
(percentage)

Frequency of Use	2 Months Before ASA	2 Months After ASA	Last 2 Months
Heroin			
Not At All	19	70	85
Occasionally	14	15	13
Daily	67	15	2
Total	100	100	100
n=	456	451	452
Illegal Methadone			
Not At All	82	90	92
Occasionally	15	9	7
Daily	3	1	1
Total	100	100	100
n=	455	451	451
Cocaine			
Not At All	60	84	86
Occasionally	29	14	13
Daily	11	2	1
Total	100	100	100
n=	456	451	453
Amphetamines			
Not At All	87	96	96
Occasionally	11	4	4
Daily	2	0	0
Total	100	100	100
n=	455	451	451

TABLE I-2
EMPLOYMENT AND CRIMINAL ACTIVITY
(percentage)

Status	2 Months Before ASA	2 Months After ASA	Last 2 Months
Employment			
Employed	23	41	56
Not Employed	77	59	44
Total	100	100	100
n=	451	431	457
Arrests			
Arrested	29	11	5
Not Arrested	71	89	95
Total	100	100	100
n=	444	426	438

TABLE I-3

DRUG USE - ASA
(percentage)

FREQUENCY OF USE	METHADONE MAINTENANCE			AMBULATORY UNIT			THERAPEUTIC COMMUNITY			COMPARISON		
	2 MO. BEFORE ASA	2 MO. AFTER ASA	LAST 2 MO.	2 MO. BEFORE ASA	2 MO. AFTER ASA	LAST 2 MO.	2 MO. BEFORE ASA	2 MO. AFTER ASA	LAST 2 MO.	2 MO. BEFORE ASA	2 MO. AFTER ASA	LAST 2 MO.
Heroin												
Not at all	14	70	86	26	69	79	19	79	90	18	56	81
Occasionally	11	17	10	16	22	18	13	7	8	16	17	18
Daily	75	13	4	58	9	3	68	14	2	66	27	1
Total	100	100	100	100	100	100	100	100	100	100	100	100
n=	111	107	111	108	106	154	154	154	153	83	82	82
Illegal Methadone												
Not at all	73	84	88	87	90	96	87	96	91	81	87	91
Occasionally	23	15	11	12	9	3	12	4	8	13	11	5
Daily	4	1	1	1	1	1	1	0	1	6	2	4
Total	100	100	100	100	100	100	100	100	100	100	100	100
n=	111	107	111	108	108	106	154	154	152	82	82	82
Cocaine												
Not at all	49	78	84	71	84	86	62	90	88	58	78	84
Occasionally	37	19	15	23	15	13	28	10	11	29	16	16
Daily	14	3	1	6	1	1	10	0	1	13	6	0
Total	100	100	100	100	100	100	100	100	100	100	100	100
n=	111	107	112	108	108	106	154	154	153	83	82	82
Amphetamines												
Not at all	86	96	98	89	97	96	84	97	95	92	94	94
Occasionally	12	4	2	8	3	4	15	3	4	5	5	6
Daily	2	0	0	3	0	0	1	0	1	3	1	0
Total	100	100	100	100	100	100	100	100	100	100	100	100
n=	111	107	110	108	108	107	154	154	152	82	82	82

the two-month period prior to being interviewed. Fifty-eight to 75 percent of these clients stated that they had been using heroin daily during the two months prior to treatment. Dramatic, statistically significant improvements occurred for each treatment group; there are no statistically significant differences between any of the groups. The responses by the former clients were essentially confirmed by urinalysis tests of specimens taken during the interviews.

A substantial statistically significant decline occurred in illegal methadone usage by all treatment groups. Four to 12 percent of the treatment respondents indicated usage of illegal methadone during the two-month period prior to being interviewed, while from 13 to 27 percent used it during the two months prior to treatment. There are no statistically significant differences between any of the groups.

Next to heroin (and excluding marijuana, alcohol, and cigarettes), cocaine was the most popular drug used by these clients during the two-month period prior to entering ASA. Cocaine is not addictive and is rarely a primary drug of abuse. Forty-nine to 71 percent of the clients did not use cocaine at all during this pre-program period, although 6 to 14 percent used it daily. During the two months immediately prior to being interviewed, 84 to 88 percent of the respondents who had been through treatment programs did not use cocaine at all. Few of the remaining individuals used cocaine daily (1 percent), although a larger percentage used cocaine occasionally (11 to 15 percent). The decline in use is statistically significant for two of the three treatment groups; there is a statistically significant difference between the ambulatory unit and methadone maintenance groups.

Barbiturates were a relatively less popular drug as compared with heroin or cocaine. All treatment groups reported a statistically significant reduction in barbiturates used between the two-month period prior to treatment and the two-month period prior to being interviewed.

Amphetamines were a comparatively unpopular drug of abuse among the clients sampled. Few of the clients used amphetamines during the two months prior to entering the program. Nevertheless, there was some improvement for each of the groups as reflected by the high percentage not using amphetamines at all during the two months immediately before the interview (95 to 98 percent). The improvements realized within both the methadone maintenance and the therapeutic community groups are statistically significant, but the improvement within the ambulatory unit group is not. However, there are no statistically significant differences between any of the groups.

Hallucinogens and other drugs were used very infrequently. The general pattern of reduction in use of drugs previously discussed is also reflected in these. The improvements in hallucinogen use were statistically significant for both the ambulatory unit and therapeutic community groups and, once again following the usage pattern of other drugs, there were no statistically significant differences between any of the groups.

However, regarding other drugs, while not differing significantly from the above pattern, there was some tendency toward increased usage after treatment. In the two months prior to entering the ASA program 94 to 98 percent of the treatment group clients reported that they did not use other drugs. During the two months prior to being interviewed 89 to 99 percent reported not using other drugs. The only statistically significant differences in other drug usage between these two time periods was between the methadone maintenance and therapeutic community groups.

Since the number of clients responding to the "use of other drugs" item is lower than the number of clients responding to items regarding specific drugs and the reported usage percentages both before and after are quite low, the results obtained should not be viewed with alarm. They do indicate, however, that there should be careful monitoring of other drug substitution after treatment.

Statistically significant reductions occurred in marijuana usage between pre- and post-program periods for all groups. Nevertheless, considerable post-treatment use is indicated. This is hardly surprising in view of the widespread use of marijuana in our society, particularly by persons in the age groups represented in this study.

A major concern among methadone programs is the belief that clients may tend to substitute alcohol for heroin. The data do not support this belief. There are only slight changes in drinking behavior for the methadone maintenance group. There are, however, statistically significant increases between pre-treatment and posttreatment in the occasional use of alcohol for ambulatory unit clients and a similar, though statistically non-significant, pattern for therapeutic community clients.

Another form of substance substitution may be an increased use of cigarettes after withdrawing from heroin. The responses indicate that this has not occurred. Indeed, there was a statistically significant reduction in the frequency of cigarette use for all treatment groups between the pre-treatment and post-treatment periods.

Employment

As regards the Washington study in Part I, Table I-4 shows a general, statistically significant pattern of improvement in employment comparing the two-month period prior to treatment with the most recent two-month period.

For each treatment group, the number of clients employed in the two months prior to being interviewed was twice as much or more than during the two months prior to entering treatment. Statistically, this improvement is highly significant for each treatment group, as well as between the therapeutic community and methadone maintenance groups. Although employment increases were significant for both of these groups, the therapeutic community clients quadrupled their employment rate (17 vs. 66 percent) between the two periods while the methadone maintenance clients doubled theirs (26 vs. 50 percent).

Of course, during the period in question, the unemployment rate was increasing substantially. This should affect the results, especially during the most recent period. The fact that the employment rate for each of the treatment groups continued to improve during this period further dramatizes the reported increases.

Criminal Behavior

As in the case of the Washington study, the percentage of clients who were arrested during the two-month period prior to being interviewed was substantially less than during the two months before treatment, indicating a reduction in criminal behavior as expressed by actual arrests (Table I-4). The reductions are statistically significant for each treatment group. There is no statistically significant difference between any of the groups.

Using the indicator of whether or not a client has spent time in jail during the periods in question, here also there are statistically significant improvements for each of the groups and no significant differences between any of the groups.

TABLE I-4
EMPLOYMENT AND CRIMINAL ACTIVITY
(percentage)

STATUS	METHADONE MAINTENANCE			AMBULATORY UNIT			THERAPEUTIC COMMUNITY			COMPARISON		
	2 MO. BEFORE ASA	2 MO. AFTER ASA	LAST 2 MO.	2 MO. BEFORE ASA	2 MO. AFTER ASA	LAST 2 MO.	2 MO. BEFORE ASA	2 MO. AFTER ASA	LAST 2 MO.	2 MO. BEFORE ASA	2 MO. AFTER ASA	LAST 2 MO.
Employed												
Yes	26	39	50	21	41	52	17	46	66	31	35	51
No	74	61	50	79	59	48	83	54	34	69	65	49
Total	100	100	100	100	100	100	100	100	100	100	100	100
n=	109	94	112	107	106	108	152	152	154	83	79	83
Arrested												
Yes	32	12	7	23	10	1	33	7	5	28	16	6
No	68	88	93	77	90	99	67	93	95	72	84	94
Total	100	100	100	100	100	100	100	100	100	100	100	100
n=	110	92	105	102	105	102	149	150	151	83	79	80
Incarcerated												
Yes	18	13	6	12	8	3	29	3	3	21	6	4
No	82	87	94	88	92	97	71	97	97	79	94	96
Total	100	100	100	100	100	100	100	100	100	100	100	100
n=	109	95	94	99	106	98	150	151	147	81	79	75

What Influence Did Treatment Seem to Have on Post-Treatment Outcomes?

Drug Use

Comparisons were made, in terms of each drug, between each of the treatment groups and the comparison group. No statistically significant differences were found to exist between the periods two months before treatment and the two immediately prior to the interview.

The reduction in use of illegal methadone by both treatment and comparison groups during the last two-month period was undoubtedly influenced by the tightening of Federal regulations governing the dispensing of methadone inaugurated late in 1972.

Amphetamine use was severely restricted as the Federal Government initiated a significant policy reducing availability before the most recent time period.

Employment

The therapeutic community group showed a significantly greater improvement than the comparison group. As previously noted, employment is influenced by economic conditions and government programs which may have little relationship to treatment.

Criminal Behavior

There are no statistically significant differences between treatment and comparison groups in frequency of arrests and whether time was spent in jail.

Multiple Behavioral Outcome Measures

As a whole, 49 percent of the respondents were fully recovered, 7 percent were failures and the remaining 44 percent were partially or marginally recovered. Eighty-two percent achieved either full or partial recovery.

There are statistically significant differences in recovery status in only one area — between the therapeutic community group and the control and methadone maintenance groups with regard to the number of their clients who were classified as fully recovered. The therapeutic community group reported significantly higher numbers of fully recovered clients, but these results must be viewed with caution as explained in Chapter VI. There are no significant differences between the treatment and comparison groups.

Redefinition of Treatment and Comparison Groups (Chapter VII)

The comparison groups were "purified" to include only clients who had entered ASA for 1 to 5 days and did not subsequently re-enter treatment. All other clients were grouped according to the total length of time they remained in treatment, including all entries.

Little relationship was found between total time spent in treatment and the *amount* of behavioral change realized by the clients. The major exception was that clients in treatment for more than 364 days realized a higher employment rate than other clients (except those in treatment 6-14 days) .

Explanatory Factors (Chapter VIII)

A number of client background and characteristic variables were examined. F-tests indicated that age, marital status, and age of first heroin use were significantly different among the groups; these and a number of other client background characteristics and outcome variables were analyzed through multiple regression analyses in an attempt to determine what variables might explain variance in the dependent (outcome) variables.

Again client outcomes are unrelated to any background or characteristic variables included in the study.

Discussion (Chapter IX)

One is struck, again, by the very large behavioral changes. However, the data suggest that the effects of treatment cannot be separated from other factors. Moreover, clients' behavioral change was not only essentially unrelated to presence and type of treatment, but also was unrelated to demographic and background characteristics as well. This absence of differences is little short of baffling.

Chapter IX discusses several possible interpretations of this phenomenon. Forces entirely outside the traditional treatment process may be at work to help bring about change in addict behavior. The community may have changed; or, as heroin use may have been tolerated in the community in the period preceding addicts' contact with ASA, it may have become increasingly unacceptable as the real dangers of the drug became known. Thus, if the addict were to remain acceptable to his community, he was forced to explore other avenues of behavior. Whether or not this describes the intellectual and behavioral changes in the decade 1965 to 1975 in New York City is unknown.

A different explanation for the lack of differences between treatment and comparison groups may lie in the data. In this regard, we can hypothesize that persons having made a commitment to seek change, i.e., who enter treatment and then drop out of treatment immediately thereafter, represent a very select group of persons who are improperly cast into a comparison group. In this formulation, that group would consist, at least partly, of persons who had not given up their decision to seek behavioral change, but merely quit on the means to accomplish that change as posed by the treatment program.

Another explanation could lie in the criminal justice system's efforts to reduce the supply of illicit drugs and make the abuser's lifestyle more difficult to maintain. An accompanying decrease in the purity of heroin and an increase in price would make it more difficult for an addict to obtain the drug. However, no data are available from New York City prior to 1973. Therefore, we do not know to what extent this occurred. Strict controls on the dispensing of methadone were instituted late in 1972. Later, amphetamines were also put under strict controls.

We continue to re-examine commonly-held assumptions. First, again, is the common assumption that it is desirable to keep clients in treatment for extended periods of time. Little relationship was found between the amount of time clients spent in treatment and the amount of behavioral change realized. Perhaps the client is the best judge of how long a period of treatment is sufficient.

This particular study raises questions with respect to the comparative virtues of methadone maintenance, ambulatory, and residential therapeutic community programs. No modality was found to be clearly superior to the others, although the residential therapeutic communities produced slightly better outcomes than the other modalities. Again, perhaps treatment programs should be flexible, with respect to the modality in which the clients should be placed.

Again, in study II, demographic and background factors failed to explain success in treatment or lack thereof.

Chapter II

INTRODUCTION

This study was conducted for the National Institute on Drug Abuse by Burt Associates, Incorporated, under Contract No. 271-76-4405. Its purpose was to conduct an analysis of data on former clients of the Addiction Services Agency (ASA) programs in New York City to determine their post-treatment functioning.

Chapter III of this report describes the ASA programs, Chapter IV, and Chapter IV of Part I, describe the methodology used, Chapter V presents a profile of clients upon entering ASA, Chapter VI measures the change in behavior comparing the period before treatment to the period after treatment, and Chapter VII presents an analysis of different client groupings. In Chapter VIII, searches are made for factors which might explain the results. Discussion of the results and implications of them is presented in Chapter VIII and Chapter IX contains conclusions.

Chapter III

DESCRIPTION OF THE ADDICTION SERVICES AGENCY DURING THE TIME PERIODS UNDER STUDY

Background

Scope of the Problem

Estimates of the magnitude of drug addiction in New York City have varied markedly. These numerous estimates have not been subjected to reliable epidemiologic verification. A 1972 estimate indicated a figure of 150,000 addicts, or roughly 1.9 percent of the total New York City population of 7,902,050.[1] Other estimates, however, have ranged from 50,000 to 700,000 addicts.[2]

In 1970 there were at least 972 narcotic-related deaths in New York City.[3] Nearly 23% of these deaths occurred in Manhattan's Central Harlem and the Bronx's Mott Haven and Morrisania sections. These areas, however, account for less than 9% of New York City's total population. Heroin was the leading cause of death for males aged 15-34 when all sections of the City were considered.

A 1973 study of addicts in the Bedford-Stuyvesant section of Brooklyn reported that 83% of the sampled addicts had been arrested after the onset of addiction.[4] In 1972, 45% of all suspects admitted to the City's prisons were classified as addicts. The Police Commissioner

---

[1] Finney, G. S., *Drugs: Administering Catastrophe.* Washington, D.C.: Drug Abuse Council, 1975.

[2] Ibid.

[3] City of New York "Comprehensive Plan for the Control of Drug Abuse and Addiction," 1972.

[4] Newman, R., "Arrest Histories Before and After Admission to a Methadone Maintenance Treatment Program," unpublished, 1973.

193

estimated that, in 1971, heroin addicts were responsible for nearly half of all crimes against property committed in the City.[1]

Treatment Programs

In 1971 there were four major groupings (by sponsor) of drug treatment programs in New York City. The first two sponsors were agencies of the City government and treated the majority of addicts.

(1)   Addiction Services Agency (ASA) — The ASA is an organizational element of the NYC Human Resources Administration. In 1971, the primary focus of the programs run directly by ASA and those run by its delegates was on a drug-free regimen. During the latter phases of the current study, the drug abuse treatment element of the Health Services Administration (see [2] below) came under ASA and with this, a greater emphasis upon methadone maintenance.

(2)   Health Services Administration (HSA) — HSA is a department of the City government. The abuse treatment program was located in the Health Department (an organizational element of HSA) but was transferred during the course of this study to ASA. Since the primary thrust of HSA programs involved methadone maintenance, this modality became an important part of ASA.

(3)   Beth Israel Medical Center (Morris J. Bernstein Institute) — Beth Israel operated two separate methadone based treatment programs for heroin addiction. One offered a short-term, in-patient detoxification program and the other, methadone maintenance treatment.

(4)   Numerous private treatment programs which received funds from both public (i.e., federal, state and/or local) and private sources. These programs utilized a number of different modalities.

A brief description of ASA's (including HSA) development follows.[2]

[1] Leslie, A. C., "A Benefit/Cost Analysis of New York City's Heroin Addiction Problems and Programs — 1971," Office of Program Analysis, Health Services Administration, 1971.

[2] This brief description of ASA's development relies heavily on a report prepared by William A. Diaz and Stephen M. David, "The New York City Addiction Services Agency — A Political History 1965-72," New York: Institute for Social Research, Fordham University, 1972.

Development of ASA

Prior to 1965, drug programs in New York City were accorded a relatviely minor role in the City Department of Health. Drug abuse and addiction, however, became an issue in the mayoralty campaign of 1965. As a result of campaign pledges, the new mayor, John V. Lindsay, established an Office of the Coordinator of Addiction Programs (OCAP), in early 1966. The creation of this office was followed two months later by the passage of a statewide bill establishing a Narcotic Addiction Control Commission (NACC). The role of this commission was the development of a massive statewide treatment program for drug addicts.

In the fall of 1967, OCAP became the Addiction Services Agency (ASA) and was made part of the City's Human Resources Administration (previously, OCAP had been an independent agency in the Office of the Mayor). Funding for ASA was provided by the City, the State (under NACC funding) and OEO.

During this time, ASA began moving away from direct operations to a program-by-contract basis, a process that was completed in late 1971. This contractual relationship included Phoenix House, a city-wide network of drug-free therapeutic communities begun by OCAP in 1967. The role of ASA became one of quality control and result assessment.

Philosophical Base

Through 1971, ASA and ASA delegates operated a multi-modal program employing a wide range of treatment strategies (see Table II-1). Each program combined a treatment effort with counseling services (drug counseling, vocational counseling). Provisions were also included to deal with clients who were ill or pregnant. The client population is shown below.

	August 1971		
	% Enrolled	No. Enrolled	No. of Programs
Total City-Wide	100.0	18,072	235
Methadone Maintenance	55.1	9,958	92
Drug-Free	44.9	8,114	143

The philosophy of the programs (including the HSA component of ASA) included:

- An equal reliance on drug-free strategies and methadone maintenance
- Use of ex-addict counselors in all treatment strategies
- Clear and limited program goals
  - cessation of illegal drug use
  - cessation of participation in illegal activities
  - participation in jobs, education, job training
- Retention in treatment
- Minimal waiting lists

TABLE III-1
ASA AND ASA-DELEGATES TREATMENT MODALITIES[1]

Drug Detoxification
Drug Information/Education
Community Activities, Recreation
Alternative Programs (personal growth groups, training
    in vocational skills)
Brief Counseling (Drop-in Centers)
Out-Patient Short-term Psychotherapy
Family Therapy
Out-Patient Psychotherapy (Long-Term)
Out-Patient Group Therapy (Traditional)
Out-Patient Group Therapy (Heavy Encounter)
Day Care (Informal — Light Therapy)
Religious Groups (Non-Residential)
Day Care (Structured-Therapeutic)
Day/Night Ward
Religious Programs (Residential)
Halfway Houses
Therapeutic Communities (Light Encounter)
Therapeutic Communities (Heavy Encounter)
Out-Patient Methadone to Abstinence
Out-Patient Methadone Maintenance
Cyclazocine Programs (Narcotic Antagonist)

----

[1] This table is taken from the Pittel-Hare referral system; each modality on this list was not necessarily available through ASA at the time of this study.

In-Patient Psychiatric Evaluation or Hospital Care
Alcohol Detoxification
In-Patient Methadone to Abstinence
Alcohol After-Care (group sessions, counseling, support)

Treatment Model

Admission to a particular program was determined by a potential client's score on an instrument utilized in the Pittel-Hare Referral System. This system operates on the

> . . . central premise . . . that successful treatment outcome of drug abusers (rehabilitation) depends on a proper matching of client needs with a treatment program geared to meet those needs. The client's needs are ascertained through administration of an exhaustive questionnaire (either read to the client or used as the basis for a semi-structured interview). Based on the responses, a drug score, social stake score and a prognostic index are compiled. The Pittel-Hare theory reflects a belief that a greater amount of intervention in a client's life is required for someone with a high drug score and a low social stake score. Hence, a residential treatment center would be contraindicated for a youthful drug abuser who was not addicted and came from a reasonably stable family (Whiting, 1974, p. 3-4).[1]

A client's score on the Pittel-Hare would generally enable either him or his counselor to choose within a range of several modalities. The range of modalities to which a client might be referred is reflected in Table III-1.

Central Referral Unit (CRU)

The majority of new clients reported to CRU. A large number, however, did not go through this Unit because they had entered a program directly; ASA did not require CRU processing in order for a client to enter treatment. CRU operated on an appointment-only basis, although appointments could usually be made for the same or next day. The first CRU was opened in Manhattan in 1971; two additional offices were opened later in Brooklyn and in the Bronx. Each unit administered the Pittel-Hare instrument to each client and made referrals to the appropriate treatment modality; the Brooklyn unit also provided health screening. These facilities were funded by OEO.

---

[1] Whiting, A. "Review of a CRU Retention Study," Research Department Addiction Services Agency, 1974.

Treatment Modalities

The three modalities reviewed in this study are methadone maintenance, therapeutic community, and ambulatory unit (outpatient,
drug-free). There were no uniform treatment procedures established
for each of these modalities by ASA. Thus, it is not possible to describe a consistent approach followed by all the programs in any
modality. Each program tended to function in a relatively unique
manner in response to the varied clientele, communities, and administrative structure present in New York City during the time of
the study. The following discussion briefly describes each program
for which information was available, as it was during 1970-71.

Therapeutic Communities

Four residential therapeutic communities were included in the
sample. Phoenix House was a classical therapeutic community in the
Synanon/Daytop model. It accepted clients from a variety of sources
(including the criminal justice system) who were detoxified. There
were no demographic or drug-of-abuse qualifications for entry, although the clients were predominantly heroin abusers. It was a 24
hour residential program, operating as a closed heterogeneous, hier-
archical, tribal society. The minimum time required for satisfactory
completion of the program was two years and there were sanctions
against leaving. The treatment regimen featured a fundamental re-
wards system through step-by-step progression through a series of
jobs and an emphasis on honesty and disclosure. Group meetings
were held frequently and group encounter therapy sessions three
times per week. Phoenix House followed the classical Synanon/Day-
top belief in a non-professional approach and was staffed by ex-addicts. In contrast to Synanon, it believed in re-entry — moving people back into the society outside of the therapeutic community. Phoenix House had a strong educational program. It operated its own
public school and a tutorial program. Some clients who were sufficiently advanced in the program attended high school outside of
the facility. Following an initial six-month period, families of residents were involved.

Samaritan House followed a more contemporary model than Phoenix House and was considerably more psychologically and profes-
sionally oriented. The program's induction phase featured psychol-
ogical testing and preliminary evaluation. Based on a type of thera-

peutic community model, client progress was developmental, based on step-by-step progression through a series of jobs and increasing personal responsibility. Clients participated in individual counseling, group encounters, seminars, and recreational activities. The program had a strong residential education program providing classwork, tutoring, and educational placement. Parents were requested to become actively involved in the program.

Information on Veritas is limited. However, it was a traditional therapeutic community apparently operated along the lines of Phoenix House.

Project Return was a residential treatment program for adolescent and young adult heroin addicts. The clients had to be detoxified prior to entry into the program. Treatment content was similar to the traditional therapeutic community model, but the methods reportedly were less punitive. The length of time required to complete the program was an average of 13 months. The clinical staff were all ex-addicts. The program had an extensive educational and tutorial program. Parents were involved through weekly parent group meetings.

Ambulatory Programs

Seven ambulatory programs were included in the sample.[1] The "bulk" of Fort Greene's clients were heroin addicts. Based on the concept of self-help, treatment goals were to help addicts achieve attitude changes, self-discipline, reunion with their families, and independence from social service agencies. Services consisted mainly of group and individual therapy, recreation activities, work sessions, and job referral. The clinical staff was composed entirely of ex-addicts.

Project Revive admitted persons who were less than 22 years old, whose behavior marked them as "drug-prone," who were beginning to experiment with drugs, or who had a history of use but were not "hard-core" users. Revive sought to achieve positive attitudinal and behavioral changes through group encounters, individual counseling, tutoring, vocational counseling and placement, education in Puerto Rican and Black culture and history, recreational activities, and pro-

---

[1] No descriptive information is available from ASA on three of these programs: ARTC, The Family, and Flushing Youth Center.

gressively demanding work assignments and responsibilities. One-half of the clinical staff were ex-addicts.

ESPADA admitted drug users or experimenters, drug-prone and/or acting out teenagers and their families. The majority of clients were heroin users. The program provided regular group therapy sessions, individual counseling and weekly parent groups. A psychologist was available on a consultant basis, but all counselors were paraprofessionals. Classes were held in remedial education and centered around math and verbal skills in preparing clients for the G.E.D. exam.

Genesis II postulated that there is a set of behaviors and attitudes which characterizes the life of a drug user and that new patterns of behaviors can be established through counseling. The program provided group and individual counseling, recreational activities and encounters. G.E.D. preparatory courses were offered four nights a week. Urinalysis tests were performed two to three times per week. All staff except the Director were ex-addicts.

Methadone Maintenance

No descriptive information on the methadone maintenance programs is available from ASA. The programs were: ARTC, Bronx State, and Downstate.

Criminal Justice System

A firm relationship was established between ASA and the criminal justice system. ASA or ASA delegates handled the clients who were referred by the courts or New York City Department of Corrections (although this latter department is empowered to detoxify offenders without referral). In 1971, LEAA began funding a Court Referral Project whereby individuals who had been arrested, and who were substance abusers, could be identified, interviewed, and, where appropriate, recommended for placement in a community-based treatment program in lieu of prosecution and incarceration.

A second effort carried out in conjunction with the criminal justice system was the Rikers Island Counseling and Referral Project. Begun in early 1972, it was designed to provide essential counseling services to sentenced adults and adolescents who have a history of drug abuse or addiction.

Chapter IV

METHODOLOGY

Sample

· The sample encompassed 14 cooperating programs located throughout four boroughs in New York City. These included three methadone maintenance programs (ARTC, Bronx State, Downstate), four therapeutic communities (Phoenix House, Project Return, Samaritan House, and Veritas), and seven ambulatory counseling programs (ARTC, Fort Green, Genesis II, Revive, ESPADA, The Family and Flushing Youth Center). The 14 treatment programs were identified and selected by the Addiction Services Agency. Some treatment programs saw fit not to participate. Thus, the resulting sample must be considered as being biased by self-selection. Further, the 14 programs can in no way be considered as representing the universe of each type of program, nor the universe of ASA clients. A sample of 782 clients was drawn from the 14 programs who enrolled or entered ASA treatment programs during the last six months of 1971. Interviewing was conducted during the period August 6, 1974 through April 30, 1975. It should be noted that approximately 28 percent of the clients sampled were either graduates or still in treatment.

The table below indicates the total sample for each modality, and the number and percentage of sample clients successfully interviewed.

	Methadone Maintenance	Therapeutic Community	Ambulatory Unit	Total
Total sample (number)	273	290	219	782
Number dead	19	5	3	27
Number interviewed	142	185	135	462
Percent of total sample interviewed	52	64	62	59*

* The percentage becomes 63 if the number dead is added to the number interviewed.

The methodology encompassed comparing the pre- and post-treatment behavior of these clients during three two-month periods:

- The period two months before entering treatment
- Two months after leaving treatment
- Two months before being interviewed

Client behaviors were measured in terms of frequency of drug use, criminal behavior, and employment or other prosocial activities.[1]

Limitations

Several limitations, some of which have already been mentioned, must be borne in mind in interpreting the results of this study. First, there is the bias introduced by permitting the programs to select themselves. Thus, these results can in no way be assumed to be representative of either the modalities in question or of ASA as a whole. Secondly, substantial bias is introduced because the data in this report represent completed interviews on only 59 percent of the clients sampled. Further bias is introduced by the frequently encountered problem of incomplete responses to interview questions. Thus, the "n's" fluctuate substantially between questions. Third, the responses on arrests, incarcerations, and criminal activity have not been validated, nor have the data on employment been validated. However, data on current drug use were found to be generally consistent with urinalysis tests on specimens taken during the interview. Fourth, approximately 28 percent of the sample consisted of clients who were either graduates or in treatment. One would expect that clients in a program would be less "at risk" than those not in a program and one would hope that graduates would be less likely to have undesirable outcomes than persons who had not graduated. Further, the sample was purposively selected so that clients in treatment for varying lengths of time are represented. This has the effect of skewing the sample considerably toward clients with longer lengths of time in treatment as compared to random sampling without consideration of time spent in treatment.

_____

[1] A description of the procedures actually used in finding the clients and conducting the interviews may be found in the following reports: Macro Systems, Inc., "Three-Year Follow-Up Study of Addiction Services Agency Drug Program Clients: Phase II" and "Three-Year Follow-Up Study of ASA Drug Program Clients: Phase III" (New York: Macro Systems, Inc., 1975)

Characteristics of Interviewed and Non-Interviewed Clients

Because only 59 percent of the sample was interviewed, serious questions are raised as to how representative the interviewed clients are of the total sample. Unfortunately, little is known of the characteristics and backgrounds of the sample clients who were not interviewed. This discussion considers those variables for which data are available on the non-interviewed clients.

Table IV-1 shows that the clients interviewed tended to be younger than those who were not interviewed. For example, 20 percent of those interviewed were less than 21 years of age, while only 10 percent of those not interviewed were this young. The differences are statistically significant ($< .05$).

Table IV-2 compares the characteristics in terms of sex, race, and ethnicity. The sex distributions are only slightly different and the difference in distributions is not statistically significant. For races however, the distributions are substantially different among those interviewed and those not interviewed. While both groups contain approximately the same proportion of blacks, they are quite different with respect to whites and "other."[1]

With respect to ethnicity, there are again statistically significant differences among those interviewed and not interviewed. The clients interviewed contain a substantially higher proportion of Puerto Ricans than those not interviewed.

The educational attainment of the two groups is shown in Table IV-3. The differences between the two groups are statistically significant both for highest grade completed and whether the client is a high school graduate or has obtained a G.E.D.

As indicated in Table IV-4, there are no significant differences among the two groups with respect to marital status.

These differences in characteristics would be of interest principally in the event that it was found that the characteristics in question helped to explain outcomes. However, it will be demonstrated in Chapter IV that none of these characteistics contributed significantly to explaining outcomes of clients. Therefore, although significant differences were found among clients interviewed vs. clients not interviewed, there is no evidence that these differences act to bias the

---

[1] It is by no means clear why there are so many persons of "other" races included in the sample. ASA data indicate that only about 1 percent of their clients are of "other" races. We therefore suspect that this category is in error.

TABLE IV-1

CHARACTERISTICS OF INTERVIEWED AND NON-INTERVIEWED CLIENTS:
AGE OF INTERVIEWEE
(percentage)

AGE	INTERVIEWED	NOT INTERVIEWED	TOTAL
< 18	3	1	2
18-20	17	9	14
21-25	40	37	39
26-30	22	25	23
31-36	10	18	13
>36	8	10	9
TOTAL	100	100	100
n =	457	308	765

SIGNIFICANT TEST

$x^2 = 40.4$ df = 5   p = <.005

TABLE IV-2

CHARACTERISTICS OF INTERVIEWED AND NON-INTERVIEWED CLIENTS:
SEX, RACE, AND ETHNICITY
(percentage)

CHARACTERISTIC	INTERVIEWED	NOT INTERVIEWED	TOTAL
Sex			
Male	78	76	77
Female	22	24	23
Total	100	100	100
n =	457	321	778
Race			
Black	50	46	49
White	44	22	35
Other	6	32	16
Total	100	100	100
n =	142	115	257
Ethnicity			
Puerto Rican	75	57	67
Other	25	43	33
Total	100	100	100
n =	142	115	257

SIGNIFICANT TESTS

Variable	x^2	DF	SIGNIFICANCE
Race	99.2	2	<.001
Ethnicity	18.7	2	<.001

TABLE IV-3

CHARACTERISTICS OF INTERVIEWED AND NON-INTERVIEWED CLIENTS:
EDUCATIONAL ATTAINMENT
(percentage)

VARIABLE	INTERVIEWED	NOT INTERVIEWED	TOTAL
Highest Grade Completed			
< 9	6	11	8
9	14	16	14
10	20	19	20
11	27	23	26
12[a]	23	26	24
> 12	10	5	8
Total	100	100	100
n =	456	247	703
H.S. Graduate or GED			
High school	25	29	26
GED	17	2	12
Neither	58	69	62
Total	100	100	100
n =	454	234	688

SIGNIFICANT TESTS

Variable	X^2	DF	Significance
Highest Grade Completed	11.7	5	.04
H.S. Graduate or GED	34.0	2	< .001

[a]It should be noted that completion of the twelfth grade
may not necessarily entail graduation from high school.

TABLE IV-4

CHARACTERISTICS OF INTERVIEWED AND NON-INTERVIEWED CLIENTS:
MARITAL STATUS
(percentage)

MARITAL STATUS	INTERVIEWED	NOT INTERVIEWED	TOTAL
Single	65	68	66
Married	16	18	16
Separated	15	11	14
Divorced/Widowed	4	3	4
Total	100	100	100
n =	456	274	730

results. This analysis has not been helpful in attempting to assess the extent to which the lack of data on 41 percent of the sample acts to bias the results.

We can only conclude that the interview responses can in no way be assumed to be representative of the total sample. Therefore, any interpretation of the results must be regarded with great caution.

Evaluation Criteria

The evaluation criteria employed in this study were the same as those employed in the Washington study.[1] The criteria of effectiveness focus on the changes in behaviors in the four categories as measured before and after the program. The time periods also are similar to the Washington study periods:

- The two-month period immediately prior to entering ASA treatment
- The two-month period immediately after leaving treatment
- The period two months immediately prior to being interviewed

---

[1]
- Frequency of heroin usage before the program compared to that after the program
- Frequency of other drug usage before the program compared to that after the program
- Amount of criminal activity before the program compared to that after the program
- Employment before the program compared to that after the program

Chapter V

PROFILE OF CLIENTS UPON ENTERING ASA

What type of person entered these ASA programs? Random samples (stratified by length of time in treatment, and graduation and current program status) were drawn of clients entering each of the 14 programs specified in Chapter IV. This chapter presents a composite of the characteristics upon entering treatment of the sampled clients who were interviewed, and detailed statistical analyses of the data are given in later chapters.

Client Characteristics

Table V-1 shows that the majority of the clients were male (78 percent), black (50 percent), and less than twenty-six years old (60 percent).

Backgrounds

Table V-2 depicts the backgrounds of these clients. Eighty-four percent of the clients had fathers who worked regularly, and 40 percent had mothers who worked regularly. Forty-one percent of the clients responding had a father and mother who had completed the twelfth grade. Thirty-three percent of the clients had completed the twelfth grade.[1]

---

[1] A large number of the respondents indicated "don't know" when asked the highest grade completed by each parent (26 percent for mothers, 49 percent for fathers).

TABLE V-1

CLIENT CHARACTERISTICS
(percentage)

Sex (n=457)

Male	78
Female	22

Race (n=457)

Black	50
White	44
Other	6

Age (n=457)

Less than 18	3
18-20	17
21-25	40
26-30	22
31-36	10
Over 36	8

TABLE V-2

CLIENT BACKGROUNDS
(percentage)

Both Parents Living At Home When
Client Was Youth (n=457)

Yes	54
No	46

Parents' Work History (n=396)	Mother	Father
Never Worked	35	4
Worked Occasionally	25	12
Worked Regularly	40	84

Educational Level Attained By Clients' Parents	(n=335) Mother	(=261) Father
< 7 Grade	15	20
7-9 Grade	16	16
10-11 Grade	29	28
12 Grade	31	24
> 12 Grade	9	12

Highest Grade Completed (n=456)

< 9	Grade	6
9	Grade	14
10	Grade	20
11	Grade	27
12	Grade	23
12	Grade	10

Client Status Upon Entering ASA

Table V-3 depicts client status upon entering ASA as recorded by the questionnaire responses.

Only 21 percent of the clients were living alone; 97 percent of the clients indicated that their health status was "excellent" or "good." Sixty-seven percent of the clients had been incarcerated. Eighty-one percent of the clients entered treatment voluntarily.

Table V-4 shows the age of the clients when they first participated in each type of crime. Virtually all had participated in a drug-related crime, 76 percent of them before age eighteen (28 percent before age fourteen). Data shown on other types of crimes are not interpretable due to the low "n's" caused by missing data (i.e., incomplete interviews).

Client Behavior During the Two Months Immediately Prior to Entering ASA

Table V-5 shows that during the two-month period immediately prior to entering ASA, 81 percent of the clients used heroin at least occasionally and 67 percent used it daily. Forty percent of the clients also used cocaine at least occasionally and marijuana was used by 54 percent. Barbiturates were used at least occasionally by 26 percent of the clients, but use of the remaining drugs in Table V-5 was relatively infrequent.

TABLE V-3

CLIENT STATUS UPON ENTERING ASA
(percentage)

Living Arrangement (n=456)

Alone	21
With Someone Else	79
Excellent	68
Good	29
Fair	3
Poor	0

Incarceration Status (n=447)

Never Incarcerated	33
Incarcerated One or More Times	67

Type of Participation (n=390)

Voluntary	81
Forced by Legal Authorities	19

[1] General Health Status 2 Months Before (n=341)

According to Table V-6, 29 percent of the clients were arrested and 21 percent incarcerated during this two-month period. Table V-7 shows that only 23 percent of the clients were employed. Table V-8 indicates their primary non-job related activities. As indicated in the footnote in Table V-8, these data are not entirely consistent with Table V-7; nor is the small percentage indicating engagement in illegal activities consistent with the percentage arrested or incarcerated indicated in Table V-6.

----

[1] Self-assessment

TABLE V-4
AGE OF CLIENT WHEN FIRST PARTICIPATED IN CRIME
(percentage)

Type of Crime	Never Involved	Age when First Involved						Total
		13 or Less	14-15	16-17	18-19	20-25	Over 25	
Drug Related (n=450)	3	28	26	22	12	7	2	100
Property* (n=295)	2	15	18	32	16	13	4	100
Violent* (n=130)	4	2	9	24	29	27	5	100
Victimless* (n=27)	19	4	7	15	33	18	4	100
Other* (n=49)	8	0	14	23	16	20	19	100

*These data should be viewed with considerable caution due to the low "n's" attributable to missing data.

TABLE V-5
FREQUENCY OF DRUG USE - TWO MONTH PERIOD
PRIOR TO ENTERING ASA
(percentage)

Drugs	Frequency of Use			Total	N
	Not at All	Occasionally	Daily		
Heroin	19	14	67	100	456
Illegal Methadone	82	15	3	100	455
Cocaine	60	29	11	100	456
Amphetamines	87	11	2	100	455
Barbiturates	74	20	6	100	455
Hallucinogens	89	10	1	100	454
Marijuana	46	33	21	100	456
Other Drugs	97	2	1	100	368

TABLE V-6

ARRESTS AND INCARCERATIONS — TWO-MONTH PERIOD
PRIOR TO ENTERING ASA
(percentage)

Arrests
Not Arrested	71
Arrested	29
Total	100
n=	444

Incarcerations
Not Incarcerated	79
Incarcerated	21
Total	100
n=	439

TABLE V-7

EMPLOYMENT TWO MONTHS PRIOR
TO ENTERING ASA[1]
(percentage)

Employed	Percent
Yes	23
No	77
Total	100
n=	451

[1] Caution should be exercised in interpreting this table — see explanatory footnote, Table V-8.

TABLE V-8

PRIMARY NON-JOB RELATED ACTIVITY TWO MONTHS PRIOR TO ENTERING ASA[1]
(percentage)

Activity	Percent
Housewife	1
Student	7
Drug Program	2
Using Drugs	38
Illegal Activities	10
Hanging Out	33
Other	9
Total	100
n=	387

----

[1] Caution should be exercised in interpreting this table. The item asked "(While out of work and not looking for a job, or receiving job training), how did you spend most of your time?" Those responding, in Table V-7, that they were employed during this two-month period, should not have replied to the item cited in this table. This was not the case — 13% of methadone maintenance, 2% of ambulatory, 10% of therapeutic community, and 7% of control respondents replied "yes" on Table V-7 and *also* responded to Table V-8. These respondents may not have been employed for the full two-month period and thus may have been responding for their activities in the partial period. Data are not available to either support or deny this supposition.

Chapter VI

EFFECTIVENESS — CHANGE IN BEHAVIOR

This chapter addresses the evaluation criteria discussed in the previous chapter, and applies them to our research questions:

- What happened to former clients who left treatment?
- What influence did treatment seem to have on post-treatment outcomes of former clients?

To show what happened to clients in terms of the behavioral elements defined and then to compare their behavior with that of individuals in the comparison group, F, t and Chi-square tests (as appropriate) were performed (for the tables contained in this chapter). These were not significant at the .05 level, except in the instances specifically noted, but complete results of these tests are contained in Appendix B.

Comparison of Methadone Maintenance, Residential Therapeutic Community, Ambulatory, and Comparison Groups

T tests were performed on: (1) the differences between behavior two months before entering ASA and two months after leaving for each group; (2) the differences between behavior two months before entering ASA and two months before being intervewed; (3) comparing the differences in behavioral changes in (1) and (2) for each of the three groups (correcting probabilities for degrees of freedom). F tests were performed among groups. Statistically significant results (p < .05) are reported in the text.

Heroin Use

Table VI-1 shows that heroin use declined dramatically for clients leaving the program. This occurred immediately upon leaving treatment and further improvement occurred by the time the interviews were conducted. While 74 to 86 percent of the clients were using heroin at least some of the time prior to entering treatment,[1] 79 to 90 percent stated that they were not using it at all during the two-month period prior to being interviewed. Only 2 to 4 percent of the clients in any of the three treatment groups admitted to using heroin daily during the two months prior to being interviewed. Dramatic, statistically significant improvement occurred for all treatment groups.

Statistically significant improvements also were achieved by the clients who had not received treatment (i.e., left within five days of acceptance). The methadone maintenance and therapeutic community groups achieved greater reduction in heroin use than the comparison group by the period two months after leaving treatment. However, by the two-month period prior to the interviews, there were no statistically significant differences.[2]

The responses by the former clients, as indicated in Table VI-1, were essentially confirmed by urinalysis tests of specimens taken during the interviews.[3]

Illegal Methadone Usage

Statistically significant declines in illegal methadone usage are shown (Table VI-2) for only the methadone maintenance and therapeutic community treatment groups by the period two months after leaving treatment. By the most recent period, however, all but the ambulatory unit experienced statistically significant reductions in use. Eighty-eight to 96 percent of each group indicated no illegal methadone usage during the two-month period immediately prior to being interviewed, while 73 to 87 percent did not use it during

---

[1] It is surprising that 14 percent of methadone maintenance clients stated that they did not use heroin at all prior to entering treatment. This could be attributable to: (1) they misrepresented the use of heroin at intake in order to get methadone; (2) they lied to the interviewer; (3) they were confused as to the time period in question; etc.

[2] None of the t tests are significant among groups but the F test is significant — this is probably an aberration and will be ignored.

[3] Urine test results were available for 319 of the 432 clients responding to the question regarding heroin use during the two-month period prior to the interview. Of these 319 clients, 303 (95 percent) gave answers that were consistent with the urine test results.

TABLE VI-1

HEROIN USE
(percentage)

FREQUENCY OF USE	METHADONE MAINTENANCE			AMBULATORY UNIT			THERAPEUTIC COMMUNITY			COMPARISON		
	2 MO. BEFORE ASA	2 MO. AFTER ASA	LAST 2 MO.	2 MO. BEFORE ASA	2 MO. AFTER ASA	LAST 2 MO.	2 MO. BEFORE ASA	2 MO. AFTER ASA	LAST 2 MO.	2 MO. BEFORE ASA	2 MO. AFTER ASA	LAST 2 MO.
NOT AT ALL	14	70	86	26	69	79	19	79	90	18	56	81
OCCASIONALLY	11	17	10	16	22	18	13	7	8	16	17	18
DAILY	75	13	4	58	9	3	68	14	2	66	27	1
TOTAL	100	100	100	100	100	100	100	100	100	100	100	100
N =	111	107	111	108	108	106	154	154	153	83	82	82

SIGNIFICANT TESTS

VARIABLE DESCRIPTION	GROUP	F-TEST	T-TEST	DF	SIGNIFICANCE
2 before vs 2 after	Comparison	--	6.2	81	<.001
	Ambulatory Unit	--	10.6	107	<.001
	Methadone Maintenance	--	12.7	106	<.001
	Therapeutic Community	--	15.3	153	<.001
	Comparison vs Methadone Maint.	--	-2.8	187	.031
	Comparison vs Therapeutic Commun.	--	-3.1	234	.014
	Among Groups	4.4	--	3	.005
2 before vs last 2	Comparison	--	13.6	81	<.001
	Ambulatory Unit	--	13.3	105	<.001
	Methadone Maintenance	--	18.9	109	<.001
	Therapeutic Community	--	20.9	152	<.001
	Among Groups	2.8	--	3	.041

the months immediately prior to treatment.

The comparison group showed no significant reduction in use until the most recent period. There are no statistically significant differences in improvement between the treatment groups and the comparison group.

It has already been noted that a reduction in use of illegal methadone by both treatment and comparison groups during the last two-month period was influenced by the tightening of Federal regulations inaugurated late in 1972. The supply of illegal methadone in New York City should have been sharply curtailed; however, unfortunately, respondents in New York were not asked about use of legal methadone.

Cocaine

Next to heroin, as in Washington, cocaine was the most popular drug used by respondents during the two-month period immediately prior to entering the ASA program. Table VI-3 shows that 49 to 71 percent of the clients did not use cocaine during this preprogram period; only a few used it daily (6 to 14 percent). During the two months immediately prior to being interviewed, 84 to 88 percent of the respondents who had been through treatment programs did not use cocaine. Few of these individuals used cocaine daily (1 percent) but a substantial percentage used cocaine occasionally (11 to 15 percent).

As with heroin, all the groups show substantial statistically significant reductions in usage, but the reduction for the methadone maintenance group was significantly greater than that for the ambulatory group; there are no statistically significant differences in reductions in usage among the other groups.

Amphetamines

Amphetamines were a less popular drug (Table VI-4) than heroin or cocaine. All treatment groups reported a reduction in amphetamine usage between the two-month period prior to treatment and the two months prior to being interviewed. However, the reduction for the ambulatory unit group was not statistically significant during the most recent period.

The comparison group realized no statistically significant improvement. However, there are no statistically significant differences be-

TABLE VI-2

ILLEGAL METHADONE USE
(percentage)

FREQUENCY OF USE	METHADONE MAINTENANCE			AMBULATORY UNIT			THERAPEUTIC COMMUNITY			COMPARISON		
	2 MO. BEFORE ASA	2 MO. AFTER ASA	LAST 2 MO.	2 MO. BEFORE ASA	2 MO. AFTER ASA	LAST 2 MO.	2 MO. BEFORE ASA	2 MO. AFTER ASA	LAST 2 MO.	2 MO. BEFORE ASA	2 MO. AFTER ASA	LAST 2 MO.
NOT AT ALL	73	84	88	87	90	96	87	96	91	81	87	91
OCCASIONALLY	23	15	11	12	9	3	12	4	8	13	11	5
DAILY	4	1	1	1	1	1	1	0	1	6	2	4
TOTAL	100	100	100	100	100	100	100	100	100	100	100	100
n =	111	107	111	108	108	106	154	154	152	82	82	82

SIGNIFICANT TESTS

VARIABLE DESCRIPTION	GROUP	T-TEST	DF	SIGNIFICANCE
2 before vs 2 after	Methadone Maintenance	2.6	106	.012
	Therapeutic Community	3.4	153	<.001
2 before vs last 2	Comparison	2.2	80	.032
	Ambulatory Unit	2.2	105	.028
	Methadone Maintenance	3.2	109	.002

TABLE VI-3

COCAINE USE
(percentage)

FREQUENCY OF USE	METHADONE MAINTENANCE			AMBULATORY UNIT			THERAPEUTIC COMMUNITY			COMPARISON		
	2 MO. BEFORE ASA	2 MO. AFTER ASA	LAST 2 MO.	2 MO. BEFORE ASA	2 MO. AFTER ASA	LAST 2 MO.	2 MO. BEFORE ASA	2 MO. AFTER ASA	LAST 2 MO.	2 MO. BEFORE ASA	2 MO. AFTER ASA	LAST 2 MO.
NOT AT ALL	49	78	84	71	84	86	62	90	88	58	78	84
OCCASIONALLY	37	19	15	23	15	13	28	10	11	29	16	16
DAILY	14	3	1	6	1	1	10	0	1	13	6	0
TOTAL	100	100	100	100	100	100	100	100	100	100	100	100
n =	111	107	112	108	108	106	154	154	153	83	82	82

SIGNIFICANT TESTS

VARIABLE DESCRIPTION	GROUP	F-TEST	T-TEST	DF	SIGNIFICANCE
2 before vs 2 after	Comparison	--	3.2	81	.003
	Ambulatory Unit	--	3.2	107	.002
	Methadone Maintenance	--	6.2	106	< .001
	Therapeutic Community	--	7.2	153	< .001
	Among Groups	3.3	--	3	.021
2 before vs last 2	Comparison	--	4.9	81	< .001
	Ambulatory Unit	--	3.7	105	< .001
	Methadone Maintenance	--	7.7	110	< .001
	Therapeutic Community	--	6.0	152	< .001
	Ambulatory vs Methadone Maint.	--	-3.3	215	.007
	Among Groups	3.1	--	3	.026

TABLE VI-4

AMPHETAMINE USE
(percentage)

FREQUENCY OF USE	METHADONE MAINTENANCE			AMBULATORY UNIT			THERAPEUTIC COMMUNITY			COMPARISON		
	2 MO. BEFORE ASA	2 MO. AFTER ASA	LAST 2 MO.	2 MO. BEFORE ASA	2 MO. AFTER ASA	LAST 2 MO.	2 MO. BEFORE ASA	2 MO. AFTER ASA	LAST 2 MO.	2 MO. BEFORE ASA	2 MO. AFTER ASA	LAST 2 MO.
NOT AT ALL	86	96	98	89	97	96	84	97	95	92	94	94
OCCASIONALLY	12	4	2	8	3	4	15	3	4	5	5	6
DAILY	2	0	0	3	0	0	1	0	1	3	1	0
TOTAL	100	100	100	100	100	100	100	100	100	100	100	100
N =	111	107	110	108	108	107	154	154	152	82	82	82

SIGNIFICANT TESTS

VARIABLE DESCRIPTION	GROUP	T-TEST	DF	SIGNIFICANCE
2 before vs 2 after	Ambulatory Unit Therapeutic Community	2.3 3.7	107 153	.027 <.001
2 before vs last 2	Methadone Maintenance Therapeutic Community	3.1 2.9	108 151	.003 .004

tween the treatment and comparison groups. It has already been noted that a significant policy was initiated by the Federal Government prior to the most recent two-month period which considerably restricted the availability of amphetamines.

Barbiturates

According to Table VI-5, 68 to 76 percent of the clients did not use barbiturates during the two months immediately prior to entering the program. There are statistically significant improvements for all three treatment groups and the comparison group.

There are no statistically significant differences in improvement between the treatment and comparison groups.

Hallucinogens

Table VI-6 indicates infrequent use of the hallucinogens. Only the improvements for ambulatory units and therapeutic communities are statistically significant. The improvement for the comparison group is not statistically significant, and there are no statistically significant differences in improvement between the treatment and comparison groups.

Other Drugs

Use of other drugs was infrequent (Table VI-7). None of the changes in "other" drug usage is statistically significant.

Marijuana

Table VI-8 shows a general reduction in marijuana usage among the periods in question, although considerable use is indicated. This is hardly surprising in view of the widespread use of marijuana in our society, particularly by persons in the age groups represented in the sample. Reductions in marijuana use are statistically significant for all groups. The therapeutic community group experienced significantly greater reduction in usage than the comparison and methadone maintenance groups comparing the period of two months after treatment with two months before.

However, the therapeutic community clients increased their frequency of use thereafter, and by the two-month period prior to the interview, there are no statistically significant differences in the

TABLE VI-5

BARBITURATE USE
(percentage)

FREQUENCY OF USE	METHADONE MAINTENANCE			AMBULATORY UNIT			THERAPEUTIC COMMUNITY			COMPARISON		
	2 MO. BEFORE ASA	2 MO. AFTER ASA	LAST 2 MO.	2 MO. BEFORE ASA	2 MO. AFTER ASA	LAST 2 MO.	2 MO. BEFORE ASA	2 MO. AFTER ASA	LAST 2 MO.	2 MO. BEFORE ASA	2 MO. AFTER ASA	LAST 2 MO.
NOT AT ALL	68	86	89	76	94	94	75	94	95	80	87	94
OCCASIONALLY	24	9	10	17	5	6	21	5	5	16	11	5
DAILY	8	5	1	7	1	0	4	1	0	4	2	1
TOTAL	100	100	100	100	100	100	100	100	100	100	100	100
N =	111	107	110	108	108	107	154	154	152	82	82	82

SIGNIFICANT TESTS

VARIABLE DESCRIPTION	GROUP	T-TEST	DF	SIGNIFICANCE
2 before vs 2 after	Ambulatory Unit	4.5	107	<.001
	Methadone Maintenance	3.4	106	<.001
	Therapeutic Community	5.1	153	<.001
2 before vs last 2	Comparison	2.7	81	.008
	Ambulatory Unit	4.3	106	<.001
	Methadone Maintenance	4.6	108	<.001
	Therapeutic Community	5.1	151	<.001

TABLE VI -6

HALLUCINOGEN USE
(percentage)

FREQUENCY OF USE	METHADONE MAINTENANCE			AMBULATORY UNIT			THERAPEUTIC COMMUNITY			COMPARISON		
	2 MO. BEFORE ASA	2 MO. AFTER ASA	LAST 2 MO.	2 MO. BEFORE ASA	2 MO. AFTER ASA	LAST 2 MO.	2 MO. BEFORE ASA	2 MO. AFTER ASA	LAST 2 MO.	2 MO. BEFORE ASA	2 MO. AFTER ASA	LAST 2 MO.
NOT AT ALL	90	97	95	87	97	96	88	97	96	90	93	96
OCCASIONALLY	9	3	5	10	3	4	12	3	4	10	6	4
DAILY	1	0	0	3	0	0	0	0	0	0	1	0
TOTAL	100	100	100	100	100	100	100	100	100	100	100	100
N =	111	107	111	108	108	106	154	154	152	81	82	82

SIGNIFICANT TESTS

VARIABLE DESCRIPTION	GROUP	T-TEST	DF	SIGNIFICANCE
2 before vs 2 after	Ambulatory Unit	2.7	107	.009
	Therapeutic Community	3.6	153	<.001
2 before vs last 2	Ambulatory Unit	2.3	105	.024
	Therapeutic Community	2.7	151	.008

TABLE VI-7

OTHER DRUG USE
(percentage)

FREQUENCY OF USE	METHADONE MAINTENANCE			AMBULATORY UNIT			THERAPEUTIC COMMUNITY			COMPARISON		
	2 MO. BEFORE ASA	2 MO. AFTER ASA	LAST 2 MO.	2 MO. BEFORE ASA	2 MO. AFTER ASA	LAST 2 MO.	2 MO. BEFORE ASA	2 MO. AFTER ASA	LAST 2 MO.	2 MO. BEFORE ASA	2 MO. AFTER ASA	LAST 2 MO.
NOT AT ALL	98	97	89	94	99	93	98	98	99	97	99	96
OCCASIONALLY	2	1	3	6	0	0	1	0	1	2	1	0
DAILY	0	2	8	0	1	7	1	2	0	1	0	4
TOTAL	100	100	100	100	100	100	100	100	100	100	100	100
N =	105	102	103	78	74	75	114	118	116	71	72	70

SIGNIFICANT TESTS

VARIABLE DESCRIPTION	GROUP	T-TEST	DF	SIGNIFICANCE
2 before vs last 2	Therapeutic Community vs Meth. Maint.	3.1	211	.014

TABLE VI-8

MARIJUANA USE
(percentage)

FREQUENCY OF USE	METHADONE MAINTENANCE			AMBULATORY UNIT			THERAPEUTIC COMMUNITY			COMPARISON		
	2 MO. BEFORE ASA	2 MO. AFTER ASA	LAST 2 MO.	2 MO. BEFORE ASA	2 MO. AFTER ASA	LAST 2 MO.	2 MO. BEFORE ASA	2 MO. AFTER ASA	LAST 2 MO.	2 MO. BEFORE ASA	2 MO. AFTER ASA	LAST 2 MO.
NOT AT ALL	47	63	55	51	70	59	42	72	61	43	58	58
OCCASIONALLY	40	31	38	25	22	35	31	23	31	40	32	35
DAILY	13	6	7	24	8	6	27	5	8	17	10	7
TOTAL	100	100	100	100	100	100	100	100	100	100	100	100
n =	111	107	111	108	107	106	154	154	154	83	82	83

SIGNIFICANT TESTS

VARIABLE DESCRIPTION	GROUP	F-TEST	T-TEST	DF	SIGNIFICANCE
2 before vs 2 after	Comparison	--	2.8	81	.007
	Ambulatory Unit	--	4.3	107	<.001
	Methadone Maintenance	--	4.0	106	<.001
	Therapeutic Community	--	8.0	153	<.001
	Comparison vs Therapeutic Commun.	--	3.0	234	.017
	Therapeutic Commun. vs Meth.Maint.	--	3.3	259	.008
	Among Groups	5.1	--	3	.002
2 before vs last 2	Comparison	--	2.4	82	.019
	Ambulatory Unit	--	3.4	105	.002
	Methadone Maintenance	--	2.0	109	.049
	Therapeutic Community	--	5.0	153	<.001

changes in marijuana usage between the three types of treatment or between the treatment and comparison groups.

Alcohol Use

A major concern among methadone programs is the belief that clients may tend to substitute alcohol for heroin. Table VI-9 does not support this belief. The ambulatory group realized a statistically significant increase in drinking. There was little change in the percentage of clients drinking daily, but a substantial increase in occasional drinking. There are slight changes for the other groups in drinking behavior after treatment compared to before treatment, but these are not statistically significant. These groups realized a reduction in daily drinking and a substantial increase in the percentage of clients drinking occasionally.

There are no statistically significant differences in drinking behavior among the three types of treatment groups or between the treatment and comparison groups.

Cigarette Use

Table VI-10 does not support the belief in increased use of cigarettes after withdrawing from heroin. Although only the ambulatory and therapeutic community groups realized significant reductions by the period two months after leaving ASA, all the groups experienced statistically significant reductions in cigarette use between the pretreatment period and most recent period.

Again, there are no statistically significant differences between the treatment modalities or between the treatment and comparison groups.

Employment

Table VI-11 shows that there is a general increase in client employment when one compares the two-month period prior to treatment with the most recent two-month period.[1] The therapeutic community group showed the most dramatic improvement; the percent-

_____

[1] It would be interesting to know how many of these former clients were employed by the drug treatment programs; unfortunately this information was not collected.

TABLE VI-9
ALCOHOL USE
(percentage)

FREQUENCY OF USE	METHADONE MAINTENANCE			AMBULATORY UNIT			THERAPEUTIC COMMUNITY			COMPARISON		
	2 MO. BEFORE ASA	2 MO. AFTER ASA	LAST 2 MO.	2 MO. BEFORE ASA	2 MO. AFTER ASA	LAST 2 MO.	2 MO. BEFORE ASA	2 MO. AFTER ASA	LAST 2 MO.	2 MO. BEFORE ASA	2 MO. AFTER ASA	LAST 2 MO.
RARELY	29	36	31	59	45	37	47	32	22	38	46	29
OCCASIONALLY	47	37	50	30	44	51	34	53	67	47	39	64
DAILY	24	27	19	11	11	12	19	15	11	15	15	7
TOTAL	100	100	100	100	100	100	100	100	100	100	100	100
N =	91	83	95	92	91	94	129	133	134	68	72	75

SIGNIFICANT TESTS

VARIABLE DESCRIPTION	GROUP	T-TEST	DF	SIGNIFICANCE
2 before vs last 2	Ambulatory Unit	-2.6	85	.012

age of clients having a paid job increased from 17 to 66. The improvements for all groups are statistically significant. The improvement for the residential therapeutic community group is significantly greater than that for the methadone maintenance and comparison groups.

It is of interest to know whether clients who were not employed were engaged in other prosocial activities — keeping house, being a student, or being in job training. Unfortunately, as indicated in Chapter V, the responses to questions about activities other than employment were ambiguous. Because these data are distorted, they are not presented.

Criminal Behavior

Table VI-12 shows that the percentage of clients who were arrested during the two-month period prior to being interviewed was substantially less than during the two months before treatment. The percentage of clients who were arrested varied between 1 and 7 percent during the most recent period in contrast to 23 to 33 percent during the period before treatment. This indicates a very substantial reduction in criminal behavior as expressed by actual arrests. These reductions are statistically significant.

There are no statistically significant differences between types of treatment or treatment and comparison groups.

Taking as an indicator of criminal behavior whether or not a client has spent time in jail, Table VI-13 shows statistically significant improvements only for the therapeutic community and comparison groups by the period two months after leaving ASA. However, by the most recent period, all groups shows statistically significant improvement.

Again, there are no statistically significant differences between the types of treatment or between treatment and comparison groups.

As already pointed out, consistency is not necessarily expected among arrests and incarcerations during a two-month period.

Summary

Table VI-14 summarizes this discussion by presenting for each behavioral outcome measure whether:
  • Significant improvements were realized in any of the treat-

TABLE VI-10

CIGARETTE USE
(percentage)

FREQUENCY OF USE	METHADONE MAINTENANCE			AMBULATORY UNIT			THERAPEUTIC COMMUNITY			COMPARISON		
	2 MO. BEFORE ASA	2 MO. AFTER ASA	LAST 2 MO.	2 MO. BEFORE ASA	2 MO. AFTER ASA	LAST 2 MO.	2 MO. BEFORE ASA	2 MO. AFTER ASA	LAST 2 MO.	2 MO. BEFORE ASA	2 MO. AFTER ASA	LAST 2 MO.
RARELY	7	12	3	7	12	6	9	12	5	14	13	5
≤1 PACK PER DAY	51	51	60	54	56	51	48	59	65	50	57	68
1.5-2 PACKS PER DAY	27	24	27	29	23	35	25	22	23	18	21	18
>2 PACKS PER DAY	15	13	10	10	9	8	18	7	7	18	9	9
TOTAL	100	100	100	100	100	100	100	100	100	100	100	100
N =	108	93	101	102	100	93	149	148	142	78	76	76

SIGNIFICANT TESTS

VARIABLE DESCRIPTION	GROUP	T-TEST	DF	SIGNIFICANCE
2 before vs 2 after	Ambulatory	2.1	99	.035
	Therapeutic Community	4.1	142	<.001
2 before vs last 2	Ambulatory	18.3	101	<.001
	Methadone Maintenance	18.4	107	<.001
	Therapeutic Community	22.3	148	<.001
	Comparison	13.8	77	<.001

TABLE VI-11

EMPLOYMENT STATUS
(percentage)

EMPLOYED	METHADONE MAINTENANCE			AMBULATORY UNIT			THERAPEUTIC COMMUNITY			COMPARISON		
	2 MO. BEFORE ASA	2 MO. AFTER ASA	LAST 2 MO.	2 MO. BEFORE ASA	2 MO. AFTER ASA	LAST 2 MO.	2 MO. BEFORE ASA	2 MO. AFTER ASA	LAST 2 MO.	2 MO. BEFORE ASA	2 MO. AFTER ASA	LAST 2 MO.
YES	26	39	50	21	41	52	17	46	66	31	35	51
NO	74	61	50	79	59	48	83	54	34	69	65	49
TOTAL	100	100	100	100	100	100	100	100	100	100	100	100
n =	109	94	112	107	106	108	152	152	154	83	79	83

SIGNIFICANT TESTS

VARIABLE DESCRIPTION	GROUP	F-TEST	T-TEST	DF	SIGNIFICANCE
2 before vs 2 after	Ambulatory	--	3.8	105	<.001
	Methadone Maintenance	--	2.2	92	.028
	Therapeutic Community	--	5.4	151	<.001
	Comparison vs Therapeutic Commun.	--	-3.3	229	.008
	Among Groups	4.8	--	3	.003
2 before vs past 2	Comparison	--	2.7	82	.009
	Ambulatory	--	5.9	106	<.001
	Methadone Maintenance	--	4.1	108	<.001
	Therapeutic Community	--	9.0	152	<.001
	Comparison vs Therapeutic Commun.	--	-3.5	234	.004
	Therapeutic Commun. vs Meth. Maint.	--	-3.4	260	.006
	Among Groups	6.5	--	3	<.001

TABLE VI-12

ARRESTS--TWO MONTH PERIODS
(percentage)

ARRESTED	METHADONE MAINTENANCE			AMBULATORY UNIT			THERAPEUTIC COMMUNITY			COMPARISON		
	2 MO. BEFORE ASA	2 MO. AFTER ASA	LAST 2 MO.	2 MO. BEFORE ASA	2 MO. AFTER ASA	LAST 2 MO.	2 MO. BEFORE ASA	2 MO. AFTER ASA	LAST 2 MO.	2 MO. BEFORE ASA	2 MO. AFTER ASA	LAST 2 MO.
NO	68	88	93	77	90	99	67	93	95	72	84	94
YES	32	12	7	23	10	1	33	7	5	28	16	6
TOTAL	100	100	100	100	100	100	100	100	100	100	100	100
N =	110	92	105	102	105	100	149	150	151	83	79	80

SIGNIFICANT TESTS

VARIABLE DESCRIPTION	GROUP	x^2	DF	SIGNIFICANCE
2 before vs 2 after	Methadone Maintenance	10.1	1	.002
	Ambulatory	5.6	1	.012
	Therapeutic Community	28.6	1	<.001
2 before vs 2 after	Comparison	11.7	1	<.001
	Methadone Maintenance	20.0	1	<.001
	Ambulatory	23.1	1	<.001
	Therapeutic Community	37.6	1	<.001

TABLE VI -13

INCARCERATIONS--TWO MONTH PERIODS
(percentage)

TIME SPENT IN JAIL	METHADONE MAINTENANCE			AMBULATORY UNIT			THERAPEUTIC COMMUNITY			COMPARISON		
	2 MO. BEFORE ASA	2 MO. AFTER ASA	LAST 2 MO.	2 MO. BEFORE ASA	2 MO. AFTER ASA	LAST 2 MO.	2 MO. BEFORE ASA	2 MO. AFTER ASA	LAST 2 MO.	2 MO. BEFORE ASA	2 MO. AFTER ASA	LAST 2 MO.
NO	82	87	94	88	92	97	71	97	97	79	94	96
YES	18	13	6	12	8	3	29	3	3	21	6	4
TOTAL	100	100	100	100	100	100	100	100	100	100	100	100
N =	109	95	94	99	106	98	150	151	147	81	79	75

SIGNIFICANT TESTS

VARIABLE DESCRIPTION	GROUP	x^2	DF	SIGNIFICANCE
2 before vs 2 after	Therapeutic Community	36.7	1	<.001
	Comparison	6.1	1	.011
2 before vs last 2	Methadone Maintenance	5.4	1	.02
	Ambulatory	4.5	1	.04
	Therapeutic Community	35.6	1	<.001
	Comparison	8.6	1	.003

TABLE VI-14
SUMMARY OF BEHAVIORAL OUTCOMES

Behavioral Outcome Measure	Significant Improvement in any of the Treatment Groups; Most Recent 2 Months Compared to 2 Months Before Treatment?	Significant Difference Between any two of the Treatment Groups?	Significant Differences Between any of the Treatment Groups and the Comparison Group?	Significant Differences Among all Treatment Groups and the Comparison Group?
Drug Use				
Heroin	Yes	No	No	Yes[1]
Illegal Methadone	Yes	No	No	No
Cocaine	Yes	Yes	No	Yes
Amphetamines	Yes	No	No	No
Barbiturates	Yes	No	No	No
Hallucinogens	Yes	No	No	No
Other Drugs	No	Yes	No	No
Marijuana	Yes	No	No	No
Alcohol	Yes	No	No	No
Cigarettes	Yes	No	No	No
Employment	Yes	Yes	Yes	Yes
Criminal Activity				
Arrests	Yes	No	No	No
Incarcerations	Yes	No	No	No

---

[1] There were no significant differences between any of the Treatment Groups or between any of the Treatment Groups and the Comparison Group (t-test); a significant difference among the groups, however, was obtained at the .04 level (F-test). This is probably a statistical aberration and will be ignored.

TABLE VI-15

EXTENT OF RECOVERY
(percentage)

EXTENT OF RECOVERY	METHADONE MAINTENANCE	AMBULATORY UNIT	THERAPEUTIC COMMUNITY	CONTROL	TOTAL
Fully	42	47	58	42	49
Partially	36	33	29	40	33
Marginally	12	13	7	11	11
Failure	10	7	6	7	7
TOTAL	100	100	100	100	100
n =	112	108	154	83	457

SIGNIFICANT TESTS

VARIABLE DESCRIPTION	GROUP	x^2	DF	SIGNIFICANCE
Therapeutic Community vs Control	Fully Recovered	5.095	1	.03
Therapeutic Community vs Methadone Maintenance	Fully Recovered	6.403	1	.02

ment modalities comparing the most recent two-month period with the two-month period immediately prior to treatment

- There are significant differences between any two of the treatment modalities
- There are significant differences between any of the treatment modalities and the comparison group
- There are significant differences among all treatment groups and the comparison group

Multiple Behavioral Outcomes

Table VI-15 indicates the behavioral outcomes, expressed in terms of extent of recovery, achieved by each of the four groups. The category "Partial" includes all four Partial categories and "Marginal" includes all three Marginal categories discussed in Part I.

The therapeutic community group experienced a higher rate of full recovery than the other groups. Chi-square tests were run on 24 variations of the distributions; only two were significant at the .05 level: therapuetic community vs. comparison and therapeutic community vs. methadone maintenance (using "fully recovered" vs. the other three categories of recovery). It should be noted that one would expect that one of the 24 tests would be significant by chance; and the differences between therapeutic community and other groups in terms of full or partial recovery vs. marginal recovery or failure are not statistically significant. Thus, these comparative results should be viewed with caution.

As a whole, 49 percent of the respondents were fully recovered, 7 percent were failures, and the remaining 44 percent were partially or marginally recovered. Eighty-two percent achieved either full or partial recovery.

Chapter VII

ANALYSIS OF DIFFERENT CLIENT GROUPINGS

The definition of the comparison group in this study was, necessarily, rather arbitrary. It consisted of clients who had left treatment within five days of entry. However, as will be noted in Chapter VIII, 42 percent of the comparison group members subsequently re-entered treatment. Thus, the comparison group was not as "pure" as one would like.

In view of this "contamination" of the comparison group, a different type of grouping seemed to be of interest. Because of comparison group contamination, a purer comparison group was established consisting of clients who never received more than five days of treatment.[1]

Relationships between total time in treatment and outcomes are analyzed by partitioning clients receiving more than five days of treatment into groups depending upon *total* length of time spent in treatment. Thus, if a client entered treatment once for ten days and a second time for 50 days, his total time in treatment would be 60 days. Groupings were determined by first examining frequency distributions and then forming groups having no less than 30 clients.[2]

Formally stated, the following hypothesis is tested:
- There is no difference in behavioral change realized between groups differentiated by length of time in treatment

Table VII-1 shows status in terms of the major outcome variables for clients grouped by *total* time in treatment. We conclude that there is little relationship between total time spent in treatment and

---

[1] We sought to limit the new comparison group to persons with no more than one day of treatment, but five days had to be used in order to obtain at least 30 individuals.

[2] This criterion was violated for the 6-14 day group (where 28 are included).

TABLE VII-1

CLIENT OUTCOMES BY TOTAL DAYS IN TREATMENT
(Percentage)

VARIABLE	TOTAL TIME IN TREATMENT														
	2 BEFORE					2 AFTER					PAST 2				
	<6 DAYS	6-14 DAYS	15-120 DAYS	121-364 DAYS	>364 DAYS	<6 DAYS	6-14 DAYS	15-120 DAYS	121-364 DAYS	>364 DAYS	<6 DAYS	6-14 DAYS	15-120 DAYS	121-364 DAYS	>364 DAYS
HEROIN USE															
Never	22	36	18	19	19	67	64	56	68	74	72	82	85	90	85
Occasionally	13	28	8	13	15	17.	11	18	18	13	28	14	14	7	12
Daily	65	36	74	68	66	16	25	26	14	13	0	4	1	3	3
TOTAL	100	100	100	100	100	100	100	100	100	100	100	100	100	100	100
n =	37	28	61	83	198	36	28	61	83	196	36	28	59	83	197
COCAINE USE															
Never	57	64	54	66	61	78	79	79	84	86	83	82	88	87	85
Occasionally	27	29	38	25	28	17	14	20	15	13	17	14	12	12	14
Daily	16	7	8	9	11	5	7	1	1	1	0	4	0	1	'1
TOTAL	100	100	100	100	100	100	100	100	100	100	100	100	100	100	100
n =	37	28	61	83	198	36	28	61	83	196	36	28	59	83	197
AMPHETAMINE USE															
Never	92	93	85	86	86	94	96	97	96	96	92	100	98	96	95
Occasionally	6	7	15	14	11	6	4	3	4	4	8	0	2	3	5
Daily	2	0	0	0	3	0	0	0	0	0	0	0	0	1	0
TOTAL	100	100	100	100	100	100	100	100	100	100	100	100	100	100	100
n =	36	28	61	83	198	36	28	61	83	196	36	28	59	83	196
BARBITURATE USE															
Never	80	78	70	77	72	86	93	93	89	90	92	100	96	95	91
Occasionally	17	18	23	18	19	14	4	5	7	8	8	0	2	5	9
Daily	3	4	7	5	9	0	3	2	4	2	0	0	2	0	0
TOTAL	100	100	100	100	100	100	100	100	100	100	100	100	100	100	100
n =	36	28	61	83	198	36	28	61	83	196	36	28	60	83	196
ARRESTED?															
Yes	16	44	41	20	28	8	8	14	7	13	3	4	2	10	5
No	84	56	59	80	72	92	92	86	93	87	97	96	98	90	95
TOTAL	100	100	100	100	100	100	100	100	100	100	100	100	100	100	100
n =	37	27	59	80	194	36	25	58	81	192	36	25	60	80	189
INCARCERATED?															
Yes	17	35	25	14	21	3	7	7	5	10	3	4	0	8	4
No	83	65	75	86	79	97	93	93	95	90	97	96	100	92	96
TOTAL	100	100	100	100	100	100	100	100	100	100	100	100	100	100	100
n =	36	26	59	77	193	35	27	58	82	191	33	24	58	77	183
EMPLOYED?															
Yes	24	25	24	24	21	42	33	30	28	49	54	64	39	45	66
No	76	75	76	76	79	58	67	70	72	51	46	36	61	55	34
TOTAL	100	100	100	100	100	100	100	100	100	100	100	100	100	100	100
n =	37	28	59	82	195	36	27	56	82	194	37	28	61	83	198

Table continued on next page

TABLE VII-1 (continued)

SIGNIFICANT TESTS [1]/

Variable Description	Group	T Test[2]/	F Test	x^2 Test	DF	Significance
Heroin						
2 Before vs 2 After	6-14 vs >364 days	-3.4			222	.01
2 Before vs 2 After	All		3.6		398	.004
2 Before vs Past 2	All		2.6		397	.02
Arrested						
2 Before vs Past 2	<6 vs 6-14 days			-12.0	1	< .001
2 Before vs Past 2	<6 vs 15-120 days			- 8.5	1	.01
2 Before vs Past 2	6-14 vs 121-364 days			28.4	1	< .001
2 Before vs Past 2	6-14 vs >364 days			4.5	1	.05
2 Before vs Past 2	15-120 vs 121-364 days			51.9	1	< .001
2 Before vs Past 2	15-120 vs >364 days			6.4	1	.02
2 Before vs Past 2	121-364 vs >364 days			- 7.9	1	.01
Incarcerated						
2 Before vs Past 2	<6 vs 6-14 days			- 4.0	1	.05
2 Before vs Past 2	6-14 vs 121-364 days			28.2	1	< .001
2 Before vs Past 2	15-120 vs 121-364 days			36.8	1	< .001
2 Before vs Past 2	121-364 vs >364 days			- 6.2	1	.02
Employment						
2 Before vs Past 2	6 vs >364 days			- 4.3	1	.05
2 Before vs Past 2	15-120 vs >364 days			-11.1	1	< .001
2 Before vs Past 2	121-364 vs >364 days			-23.5	1	< .001

---

[1]For difference among time-in-treatment groups.

[2]Probabilities corrected for degrees of freedom.

TABLE VII -2
CLIENTS WITH POST-ASA TREATMENT COMPARED TO
CLIENTS WITH NO POST-ASA TREATMENT
(PERCENTAGE)

VARIABLE	POST-ASA TREATMENT?					
	2 BEFORE		2 AFTER		PAST 2	
	YES	NO	YES	NO	YES	NO
HEROIN USE						
NEVER	15	22	53	77	84	85
OCCASIONALLY	13	15	17	14	12	13
DAILY	72	63	30	9	4	2
TOTAL	100	100	100	100	100	100
N =	123	290	122	290	122	286
COCAINE USE						
NEVER	63	61	78	86	86	87
OCCASIONALLY	27	28	19	12	12	12
DAILY	10	11	3	2	2	1
TOTAL	100	100	100	100	100	100
N =	123	290	122	290	122	287
AMPHETAMINE USE						
NEVER	89	86	92	98	93	97
OCCASIONALLY	9	13	7	2	4	3
DAILY	2	1	1	0	3	0
TOTAL	100	100	100	100	100	100
N =	122	290	122	290	122	285
BARBITURATE USE						
NEVER	75	74	84	94	88	96
OCCASIONALLY	18	20	11	5	10	4
DAILY	7	6	5	1	2	0
TOTAL	100	100	100	100	100	100
N =	122	290	122	290	121	286
ARRESTED?						
YES	33	28	21	6	12	2
NO	67	72	79	94	88	98
TOTAL	100	100	100	100	100	100
N =	120	281	120	284	118	281
INCARCERATED?						
YES	24	19	14	4	7	3
NO	76	81	86	96	93	97
TOTAL	100	100	100	100	100	100
N =	119	279	119	287	114	270
EMPLOYED?						
YES	27	22	32	46	48	60
NO	73	78	68	54	52	40
TOTAL	100	100	100	100	100	100
N =	122	287	123	286	123	290

TABLE VII-2 (continued)

SIGNIFICANT TESTS

Variable Description	Group	T Test	F Test	X^2 Test	DF	Significance
Hallucinogens						
2 Before vs 2 After	1 vs 2	-2.4			409	.016
Barbiturates						
2 Before vs 2 After	1 vs 2	-2.7			410	.007
Heroin						
2 Before vs 2 After	1 vs 2	-2.8			410	.006
Employment						
2 Before vs 2 After	1 vs 2	-2.9			406	.005
2 Before vs Past 2	1 vs 2	-2.7			408	.008
2 Before vs Past 2	1 vs 2			13.2	1	<.001

TABLE VII-3
CLIENT BEHAVIOR BY NUMBER OF TREATMENT EPISODES

VARIABLE	NUMBER OF TREATMENT EPISODES											
	2 BEFORE				2 AFTER				PAST 2			
	1	2	3	>3	1	2	3	>3	1	2	3	>3
HEROIN USE												
NEVER	19	18	22	21	74	71	58	52	84	87	84	82
OCCASIONALLY	14	13	16	7	14	15	16	22	14	12	9	14
DAILY	67	69	62	72	12	14	26	26	2	1	7	4
TOTAL	100	100	100	100	100	100	100	100	100	100	100	100
N =	246	137	45	28	244	137	43	27	244	135	45	28
COCAINE USE												
NEVER	61	57	67	61	88	79	75	85	86	81	96	82
OCCASIONALLY	28	31	27	25	10	20	23	7	13	18	4	14
DAILY	11	12	6	14	2	1	2	8	1	1	0	4
TOTAL	100	100	100	100	100	100	100	100	100	100	100	100
N =	246	137	45	·28	244	137	43	27	245	133	45	28
AMPHETAMINE USE												
NEVER	87	85	93	93	98	94	93	100	96	95	100	93
OCCASIONALLY	11	14	5	3	2	6	7	0	4	4	0	7
DAILY	2	1	2	4	0	0	0	0	0	1	0	0
TOTAL	100	100	100	100	100	100	100	100	100	100	100	100
N =	245	137	45	28	244	137	43	27	245	133	45	28
BARBITURATE USE												
NEVER	74	75	78	72	94	88	86	82	95	92	96	79
OCCASIONALLY	21	20	18	7	5	10	9	11	5	8	4	14
DAILY	5	5	4	21	1	2	5	7	0	0	0	7
TOTAL	100	100	100	100	100	100	100	100	100	100	100	100
N =	245	137	45	28	244	137	43	27	245	133	45	28
ARRESTED?												
YES	26	31	33	39	7	13	15	23	3	4	10	15
NO	74	69	67	61	93	87	85	77	97	96	90	85
TOTAL	100	100	100	100	100	100	100	100	100	100	100	100
N =	239	134	43	28	231	128	41	26	240	129	42	27
INCARCERATED?												
YES	19	23	24	22	4	10	12	12	2	3	12	9
NO	81	77	76	78	96	90	88	88	98	97	88	91
TOTAL	100	100	100	100	100	100	100	100	100	100	100	100
N =	239	132	41	27	234	130	41	26	230	120	41	23
EMPLOYED?												
YES	21	23	31	22	41	43	54	19	55	58	60	50
NO	79	77	69	78	59	57	46	81	45	42	40	50
TOTAL	100	100	100	100	100	100	100	100	100	100	100	100
N =	245	137	42	27	234	136	41	26	247	137	45	28

the *amount* of behavioral change realized. The changes in drug use between the period before entering ASA and the most recent period are not significantly different between any two of the groups.[1] Chi-square tests indicate as many instances where groups with shorter treatments experienced significantly greater changes in arrests and incarcerations (compared to groups with longer stays) than conversely. However, clients in treatment for more than 364 days realized significantly greater improvement in employment than other groups (except those with 6-14 days treatment); no significant differences exist among other groups.

Post-ASA Treatment

Another hypothesis is that clients who received drug treatment after leaving ASA in 1971 are likely to experience different behavioral outcomes. Table VII-2 indicates, not surprisingly, that clients who did not re-enter treatment after leaving ASA in 1971 tended to experience greater favorable behavioral changes during the period after leaving treatment than other clients. However, by the time the interviews were conducted, there were no significant differences in the amount of behavioral change experienced between the two types of clients with the exception of employment; clients with no post-ASA treatment were significantly more likely to be employed.

Number of Treatment Episodes

Another hypothesis is that client behavioral outcomes are related to the number of treatment episodes. Table VII-3 shows no consistently different patterns in terms of *either* amount of behavioral change realized by each group or their status during the most recent period.

---

[1] The F test was significant at the .02 level. However, none of the t tests were significant at the .05 level with probabilities corrected for degrees of freedom.

Chapter VIII

A SEARCH FOR EXPLANATORY FACTORS

We analyze again possible reasons why no consistent patterns are found in the behavior of former clients (New York) sampled among treatment and comparison groups and we search for factors that might explain outcomes. First, the backgrounds and characteristics of the clients are examined to determine whether there are significant differences among groups. Possible differences in the comparison group and the treatment groups are examined in terms of subsequent treatment and type of participation in ASA. Third, possible interpretations are analyzed through multivariate analyses. Finally, a limited analysis is made of the services actually received by the clients.

Sex

Table VIII-1 shows that the percentage of respondents who are male varies between 73 and 82 percent among the groups. These differences are not significant.

Race

Table VIII-2 shows that the percentage of clients who are black varies from 49 to 54, white clients from 41 to 47, and clients of other races from 3 to 9. These differences are not significant.

Age

The age distributions among the various groups are quite different. Table VII-3 shows these differences in the distributions. They are significantly different among groups. Especially evident are significant differences between the ages of methadone maintenance

TABLE VIII-1

SEX
(percentage)

SEX OF CLIENT	METHADONE MAINTENANCE	AMBULATORY UNIT	THERAPEUTIC COMMUNITY	COMPARISON
Male	82	73	78	80
Female	18	27	22	20
TOTAL	100	100	100	100
n =	112	108	154	83

TABLE VIII-2

RACE
(percentage)

RACE OF CLIENT	METHADONE MAINTENANCE	AMBULATORY UNIT	THERAPEUTIC COMMUNITY	COMPARISON
Black	.49	49	50	54
White	44	42	47	41
Other	7	9	3	5
TOTAL	100	100	100	100
n =	112	108	154	83

TABLE VIII-3

AGE
(percetange)

AGE OF CLIENT	METHADONE MAINTENANCE	AMBULATORY UNIT	THERAPEUTIC COMMUNITY	COMPARISON
< 18	1	6	4	1
18-20	1	22	27	15
21-25	27	39	46	48
26-30	36	24	14	16
31-36	17	4	6	13
> 36	18	5	3	7
TOTAL	100	100	100	100
n =	112	108	154	83

SIGNIFICANT TESTS

VARIABLE DESCRIPTION	GROUP	x^2	F-TEST	T-TEST	DF	SIGNIFICANCE
Age of Client	Among Groups	93.143	--	--	15	<.001
	Among Groups	--	30.096	--	3	<.001
	Comparison vs Meth. Maint.	--	--	-4.436	193	<.001
	Comparison vs Therap. Comm.	--	--	3.678	235	.002
	Ambulatory vs Meth. Maint.	--	--	-6.569	218	<.001
	Meth. Maint. vs Therap. Comm.	--	--	9.581	264	<.001

TABLE VIII-4

HIGHEST GRADE COMPLETED
(percentage)

HIGHEST GRADE COMPLETED	METHADONE MAINTENANCE	AMBULATORY UNIT	THERAPEUTIC COMMUNITY	COMPARISON
< 9	14	6	3	4
9	8	15	14	19
10	18	16	22	25
11	24	29	30	24
12	26	26	21	18
> 12	10	8	10	10
TOTAL	100	100	100	100
n =	112	108	154	83

TABLE VIII-5

MARITAL STATUS
(percentage)

MARITAL STATUS	METHADONE MAINTENANCE	AMBULATORY UNIT	THERAPEUTIC COMMUNITY	COMPARISON
Single	53	79	70	54
Married	21	8	16	18
Separated	20	11	10	22
Divorced	5	2	4	5
Widowed	1	0	0	1
TOTAL	100	100	100	100
n =	111	108	154	83

SIGNIFICANT TESTS

VARIABLE DESCRIPTION	GROUP	x^2	F-TEST	T-TEST	DF	SIGNIFICANCE
Marital Status	Among Groups	--	6.827	--	3	<.001
	Comparison vs Ambulatory	—	--	3.479	189	.004
	Ambulatory vs Meth. Maint.	--	—	-3.678	217	.002
	Meth. Maint. vs Therap. Comm.	—	—	2.847	263	.029

TABLE VIII-6

LIVING WITH SOMEONE
(percentage)

LIVING WITH SOMEONE	METHADONE MAINTENANCE	AMBULATORY UNIT	THERAPEUTIC COMMUNITY	COMPARISON
No	21	17	22	27
Yes	79	83	78	73
TOTAL	100	100	100	100
n =	112	107	154	83

TABLE VIII-7

AGE FIRST USED HEROIN
(percentage)

AGE	METHADONE MAINTENANCE	AMBULATORY UNIT	THERAPEUTIC COMMUNITY	COMPARISON
<14	6	12	18	14
14-15	9	19	28	23
16-17	28	31	28	25
18-19	23	14	17	13
> 19	34	24	9	25
TOTAL	100	100	100	100
n =	111	91	149	78

SIGNIFICANT TESTS

VARIABLE DESCRIPTION	GROUP	x^2	F-TEST	T-TEST	DF	SIGNIFICANCE
Age First Used Heroin	Among Ages	41.8	--	--	12	<.001
	Meth. Maint. vs Therap. Comm.	—	—	5.847	258	<.001
	Among Groups	—	9.5	—	3	<.001

clients and each of the other groups, with the tendency for methadone maintenance clients to be older. The multivariate analysis (discussed later in this chapter), however, shows no significant relationship between age and outcome.

Highest Grade Completed

Table VIII-4 shows roughly similar distributions in highest grade completed among each of the groups. Here also, multivariate analysis indicates no significant relationship between highest grade completed and outcome.

Marital Status

According to Table VIII-5, the percentage of clients who are unmarried (i.e., single, divorced or widowed), differs among each of the groups, varying from 59 to 81 percent. The differences are statistically significant among the groups and between ambulatory unit clients and comparison and methadone maintenance and therapeutic community clients. Once again, multivariate analysis indicates no significant relationship between marital status and outcome.

Living with Someone

Living with someone is believed to be a measure of stability in the individual's lifestyle. The percentage of clients in this category, shown in Table VIII-6, varies only from 73 to 83 percent and the differences are not statistically significant.

Age First Used Heroin

The earlier the age when an individual first uses heroin, the more he is believed to have adopted heroin use as a long-term lifestyle. Table VIII-7 presents the distribution of ages at which the respondents first used heroin. There are differences in the patterns among the groups with statistically significant differences being found among both ages and groups and between methadone maintenance and therapeutic community clients. Most evident is the tendency of methadone maintenance clients to begin heroin use at a later age than clients in other groups, although multivariate analysis uncovered no significant relationship between age of first heroin use and outcome.

Treatment Prior to Entering ASA

Table VIII-8 shows that there are some differences in terms of the percentage of respondents who had been in a drug treatment program prior to entering ASA. The percentage ranges from 21 to 39 with the comparison group at 33. There are statistically significant differences among the groups and between ambulatory unit and methadone maintenance and therapeutic community clients; multivariate analysis does not indicate a significant relationship between prior treatment and outcome.

Treatment After ASA

Another hypothesis that could explain the lack of consistent patterns in the differences in effectiveness among the groups would be that members of the comparison groups obtained treatment subsequent to their leaving the ASA. Table VIII-9 shows that 42 percent of the comparison group entered treatment subsequent to ASA, compared to 21 to 46 percent of the treatment groups. These differences are statistically significant with regard to comparison among the groups, and between ambulatory units and therapeutic communities and methadone maintenance groups.

These data raise serious questions regarding the adequacy of the comparison group. Later in this chapter we employ extensive multiple regression to determine whether drug treatment after leaving ASA explains outcomes. In Chapter VII, the comparison group was purified to include only persons who never received more than five days of drug treatment.

Type of Participation ·

It is generally believed that a person whose participation in a drug treatment program has been forced by legal authorities is less likely to be successful than one who·participates voluntarily. Thus, one hypothesis that could help explain the lack of consistent patterns of difference between the treatment and comparison groups, is that there are differences in the type of participation. Table VIII-10, in contradistinction to the results of the Washington study, shows that some of these differences are statistically significant, but that these differences do not consistently vary with regard to the comparison group. That is, while there is a significant difference between the comparison and methadone maintenance groups, there are also sig-

TABLE VIII-8

DRUG TREATMENT BEFORE ASA
(percentage)

TREATMENT PRIOR TO ASA	METHADONE MAINTENANCE	AMBULATORY UNIT	THERAPEUTIC COMMUNITY	COMPARISON
No	61	79	66	67
Yes	39	21	34	33
TOTAL	100	100	100	100
n =	109	108	148	81

SIGNIFICANT TESTS

VARIABLE DESCRIPTION	GROUP	X^2	F-TEST	T-TEST	DF	SIGNIFICANCE
Drug Treatment Before ASA	Pre-ASA Treat. vs no Pre-ASA Treatment.	8.739	—	––	3	.03
	Ambulatory vs Meth. Maint.	7.61	—	—	1	< .01
	Ambulatory vs Therap. Comm	4.219	––	—	1	< .025

TABLE VIII-9

DRUG TREATMENT AFTER LEAVING ASA
(percentage)

TREATMENT AFTER ASA	METHADONE MAINTENANCE	AMBULATORY UNIT	THERAPEUTIC COMMUNITY	COMPARISON
Yes	46	21	21	42
No	54	79	79	58
TOTAL	100	100	100	100
n =	85	102	149	77

SIGNIFICANT TESTS

VARIABLE DESCRIPTION	GROUP	x^2	F-TEST	T-TEST	DF	SIGNIFICANCE
Drug Treatment	Post-ASA Treat. vs No Post-ASA Treat.	25.5	--	--	3	< .001
	Meth. Maint. vs Ambulatory	12.5	--	--	1	< .001
	Meth. Maint. vs Therap. Comm.	15.1	--	--	1	< .001
	Therap. Comm. vs Comparison	9.9	--	--	1	< .01
	Ambulatory vs Comparison	8.3	--	--	1	< .01

TABLE VIII-10

TYPE OF PARTICIPATION IN ASA
(percentage)

PARTICIPATION IN ASA	METHADONE MAINTENANCE	AMBULATORY UNIT	THERAPEUTIC COMMUNITY	COMPARISON
Voluntary	93	84	71	73
Forced	7	16	29	27
TOTAL	100	100	100	100
n =	105	101	140	44

SIGNIFICANT TESTS

VARIABLE DESCRIPTION	GROUP	x^2	F-TEST	T-TEST	DF	SIGNIFICANCE
Type of Participation in ASA	Among Groups	21.1	—	--	3	<.001
	Meth. Maint. vs Therap. Comm.	17.18	—	--	1	<.001
	Meth. Maint. vs Comparison	10.05	--	--	1	<.01
	Ambulatory vs Therap. Comm.	4.64	--	--	1	<.05

nificant differences between the therapeutic community group and the ambulatory and methadone maintenance groups. In addition, multivariate analysis does not indicate any significant relationship between type of participation and outcome.

Multivariate Analysis

Thus far, the behavior of the treatment and control groups in this study has been analyzed in terms of a single variable at a time. Now, this analysis attempts to determine to what extent various independent variables of interest "explain" outcomes (dependent variables).

The following independent variables are considered:
- Sex
- Race
- Age
- Highest grade completed
- Marital status
- Living with someone
- Caretakers' work history
- Heroin use 2 months before entering ASA
- Prior drug treatment
- Voluntary vs. involuntary participation
- Major source of income 2 months before entering ASA (job; other)
- Number of associates using drugs 2 months before entering ASA
- Number of associates using drugs 2 months after leaving ASA
- Number of associates using drugs past 2 months
- Job 2 months before entering ASA (yes; no)
- Job 2 months after leaving ASA (yes; no)

The following dependent variables are considered:
- Heroin use past 2 months
- Major source of income past 2 months (job; other)
- Job held past 2 months

The dependent variable "arrests past 2 months" was not used because the extremely small number of individuals arrested would distort the results.

Missing data can cause substantial problems in conducting multivariate analyses. Therefore, we rejected all variables from consideration that had more than 15 percent of the observations missing (i.e., no response to the interview question). This resulted in the following variables' being rejected:

- Type of services received
- Most helpful activity
- Number of times incarcerated

Table VIII-11 shows the independent and dependent variables included in each of the stepwise multiple regressions. An X indicates the variable was included. Only two of the squared multiple correlation coefficients exceed 0.27; both of these are for the ambulatory group.

The second regression run for the ambulatory group shows a R^2 of 0.46, indicating that 46 percent of the variance in major source of income (job; other) is explained by the independent variables. However, 32 percent of the variance is explained by one independent variable: whether the client held a job during the period two months after leaving treatment. No other variable explains more than 4 percent of the variance, and the combined explanatory power of the seven additional independent variables with the highest correlation coefficients with the dependent variable is only 14 percent (including colinearity). The first regression run for ambulatory clients showed only a slight correlation (0.1) between this independent variable and the dependent variable: heroin use past two months.

The third regression run for the ambulatory group shows a R^2 of 0.43. However, 28 percent of the variance in the dependent variable, whether a job was held in the past two months, is explained by the same independent variable as in the previous regression run (i.e., whether the client held a job during the two-month period after leaving ASA). No other independent variable explains more than 4 percent, and the combined explanatory power of the eight additional independent variables with the highest correlation coefficients with the dependent variable is only 15 percent (including colinearity).

This relationship seems rather obvious: that an individual who was employed during the period two months after leaving treatment is more likely to be employed during the two-month period prior to the interview than one who was not so employed. However, it does not hold for clients outside of ambulatory programs. We can find no reasonable explanation for why this relationship applies only to the ambulatory group.

This independent variable explained only the following percentage of the variance in other regression runs:

TABLE VIII-11

STEPWISE MULTIPLE REGRESSIONS

| | REGRESSION RUN | | | | | | | | |
| | AMBULATORY | | | METH. MAINT. | | | R T C | | |
Independent Variables	1	2	3	4	5	6	7	8	9
Black	X	X	X	X	X	X	X	X	X
White	X	X	X	X	X	X	X	X	X
Other race	X	X	X	X	X	X	X	X	X
Married	X	X	X	X	X	X	X	X	X
Living with someone	X	X	X	X	X	X	X	X	X
Father worked	X	X	X	X	X	X	X	X	X
Mother worked	X	X	X	X	X	X	X	X	X
Prior drug program	X	X	X	X	X	X	X	X	X
Incarcerated, past 2 mo.	X	X	X	X	X	X	X	X	X
Incarcerated after leaving ASA	X	X	X	X	X	X	X	X	X
Major source of income 2 mo. before (job, other)	X	X	X	X	X	X	X	X	X
Major source of income 2 mo. after (job, other)	X	X	X	X	X	X	X	X	X
Number of associates using drugs, 2 mo. before	X	X	X	X	X	X	X	X	X
Number of associates using drugs, 2 mo. after	X	X	X	X	X	X	X	X	X
Number of associates using drugs, past 2 mo.	X	X	X	X	X	X	X	X	X
Job 2 mo. before entering ASA	X	X	X	X	X	X	X	X	X
Job 2 mo. after leaving ASA	X	X	X	X	X	X	X	X	X
Voluntary vs involuntary participation	X	X	X	X	X	X	X	X	X
Age	X	X	X	X	X	X	X	X	X
Sex	X	X	X	X	X	X	X	X	X
Highest grade completed	X	X	X	X	X	X	X	X	X
Heroin use 2 mo. before entering ASA	X	X	X	X	X	X	X	X	X
Dependent Variables									
Heroin use past 2 mo.	X			X			X		
Major source of income past 2 mo. (job, other)		X			X			X	
Job held past 2 mo.			X			X			X
Multiple Correlation Squared (R^2)	.27	.46	.43	.20	.27	.24	.14	.25	.24

TABLE VIII-12

CLIENT PARTICIPATION IN INDIVIDUAL COUNSELING
(percentage)

PARTICIPATION	METHADONE MAINTENANCE	AMBULATORY UNIT	THERAPEUTIC COMMUNITY	COMPARISON
No	13	7	10	27
Yes	87	93	90	73
TOTAL	100	100	100	100
n =	92	87	125	37

TABLE VIII-13

CLIENT PARTICIPATION IN GROUP COUNSELING
(percentage)

PARTICIPATION	METHADONE MAINTENANCE	AMBULATORY UNIT	THERAPEUTIC COMMUNITY	COMPARISON
No	49	6	3	15
Yes	51	94	97	85
TOTAL	100	100	100	100
n =	72	95	140	40

Regression Run	Group	Percentage Variance
4	Methadone Maintenance	3
5	Methadone Maintenance	2
6	Methadone Maintenance	2
7	RTC	0
8	RTC	0
9	RTC	0

Services Received by Clients

It would be instructive to analyze precisely what supportive services have been received by clients in the ASA program. Data were collected concerning such services as individual and group counseling, vocational rehabilitation, job counseling, methadone maintenance and detoxification, and treatment with drugs besides methadone. The percentage of respondents in each of these seven service categories was, however, low; only the individual and group counseling categories represented 75 percent of the sample or more, with the other services ranging from 23 to 52 percent respondent representation.

Since such low response rates may yield spurious data, only the individual and group counseling services will be discussed below.

Table VIII-12 shows that 87 percent of methadone maintenance, 90 percent of therapeutic community, and 93 percent of ambulatory unit respondents stated that they had received individual counseling.[1] The fact that some clients did not indicate that they had received such counseling could be partially attributable to those clients not necessarily perceiving the types of encounters received with ASA staff as being "individual counseling" per se. Others may have simply not been counseled.

Table VIII-13 indicates sharp differences among the treatment groups in the number of respondents who reported participating in group counseling. While nearly all ambulatory unit and therapeutic community respondents participated (94 and 97 percent, respec-

---

[1] Members of the control group reported receiving some services. This is probably because many of them were in treatment for more than one day. It was previously noted that many members of the control groups subsequently re-entered treatment (Table VIII-9). Possibly they mentioned services received during a subsequent ASA experience.

tively), just over half (51 percent) of the methadone maintenance respondents did so. Such variation in service participation may be attributed to differing emphasis in types of services offered in particular treatment modalities.

Chapter IX

DISCUSSION

Very large behavioral changes were experienced by these New York City clients. But the data presented here suggest that the effects of treatment cannot be separated from other factors. And, as also in the case of the Washington study, addicts' behavioral change was not only unrelated to type of treatment but was unrelated to demographic and background characteristics as well. This absence of differences is, again, surprising. The Winick maturing-out hypothesis that has been advanced[1] could possibly explain these findings. Addicts were interviewed more than three years after leaving the program. However, because there are no measurements taken, say one or two years after leaving treatment, there is no way to test this hypothesis.

We have already noted three other efforts at explanation. Forces entirely outside the traditional treatment process may have been at work to help bring about change in addict behavior. The community may have changed. Heroin use may have become increasingly unacceptable as the real dangers of that drug became known. If the addict was to remain acceptable to his community, he obviously was forced to explore other avenues of behavior. It may well have become necessary to reassess activity in regard to heroin. Whether or not the intellectual and behavioral changes in New York City in the decade 1965-1975 are explained by this analysis we cannot be sure.

We can repeat here our hypothesis that persons who once having made a commitment to seek change, i.e., who enter treatment and then drop out of treatment immediately thereafter, might be improperly cast into a comparison group. In this formulation, as already noted, that group would consist, at least largely, of persons

---

[1] Winick, C. P. "Maturing Out of Narcotic Addiction." *Bull. Narc.* 14, 1-7, 1962.

who had not quit on their resolve to seek behavioral change, but merely quit on the means to accomplish that change as posed by the treatment program.

We note, finally, the role of the criminal justice system's efforts in reducing the supply of illicit drugs and in making the abuser's lifestyle more difficult to maintain. An accompanying decrease in the purity of heroin and increase in price would make it more difficult for an addict to obtain the drug. However, no data are available for New York City prior to 1973. Therefore, we do not know to what extent this occurred; strict controls on the dispensing of methadone were instituted late in 1972. Later, amphetamines were also put under strict controls.

The results of this study, as well as of the Washington study, cause us to re-examine commonly held assumptions regarding the treatment process. No relationship was found between the amount of time clients spent in treatment and the *amount* of behavioral change realized; however, clients in treatment for more than 364 days realized a significantly higher employment rate than other clients (except those in treatment 6-14 days). Perhaps, the client himself is the best judge of how long a period of treatment is sufficient.

We have raised questions, then, with respect to the comparative virtues of methadone maintenance, ambulatory, and residential therapeutic community programs. No modality was found to be clearly superior to the others, although the residential therapeutic community clients had slightly better outcomes than other modalities. Again, perhaps treatment programs should be flexible with respect to the modality in which the clients are placed.

There has been a great deal of interest in demographic and background correlates of success in drug treatment. Some studies have produced limited evidence showing that clients with certain characteristics do better in treatment than others. In this study, demographic and background factors failed to explain success in treatment or lack thereof.[1]

---

[1] Pre-treatment employment explained 28-32 percent of the variance in post-treatment employment for ambulatory clients, but did not explain post-treatment employment for other clients.

Chapter X

CONCLUSIONS

Natural History of Drug Abuse

We have shown that there were behavioral changes in these drug abusers from the time shortly before they entered treatment until they were interviewed. Chapter V in Part II described the New York City clients' backgrounds and characteristics and Chapter VI analyzed their changes in behavior in terms of the various groups of interest.

The behavior of all the New York respondents (including the comparison and treatment groups) is shown in Tables X-1 and X-2. Substantial reductions in drug-taking occurred between the two-month periods before entering treatment, after treatment, and before being interviewed (Table X-1).

Only 2 percent of the respondents used heroin daily during the two months preceding treatment compared to 67 percent prior to entering ASA.[1] Employment increased (Table X-2) although this was somewhat less dramatic than the decrease in drug taking. There was also a substantial reduction in the percentage of clients arrested;[2] this carries with it the implication of a decrease in illegal activities.

These data, like the Washington data, show drug abusers progressing from frequent use of heroin and other illicit drugs and engagement in other illegal activities to considerably less involvement in illicit drug use and illegal activities. Chapter VII showed that 49 percent of the respondents were fully recovered and 44 per-

---

[1] Drug use information was confirmed by urine tests.
[2] Arrest information was not confirmed.

269

TABLE X-1
DRUG USE
(percentage)

Frequency of Use	2 Months Before ASA	2 Months After ASA	Last 2 Months
Heroin			
Not At All	19	70	85
Occasionally	14	15	13
Daily	67	15	2
Total	100	100	100
n=	456	451	452
Illegal Methadone			
Not At All	82	90	92
Occasionally	15	9	7
Daily	3	1	1
Total	100	100	100
n=	455	451	451
Cocaine			
Not At All	60	84	86
Occasionally	29	14	13
Daily	11	2	1
Total	100	100	100
n=	456	451	453
Amphetamines			
Not At All	87	96	96
Occasionally	11	4	4
Daily	2	. 0	0
Total	100	100	100
n=	455	451	451

TABLE X-2
EMPLOYMENT AND CRIMINAL ACTIVITY
(percentage)

Status	2 Months Before ASA	2 Months After ASA	Last 2 Months
Employment			
Employed	23	41	56
Not Employed	77	59	44
Total	100	100	100
n=	451	431	457
Arrests			
Arrested	29	11	5
Not Arrested	71	89	95
Total	100	100	100
n=	444	426	438

cent were partially or marginally recovered by the time they were interviewed.

What Has Happened to Former Clients

Our three major groups of clients in treatment[1] — methadone maintenance, ambulatory unit and therapeutic community — have been studied in Part II. Subgroups (as well as these major groups) are addressed in Chapter VI, Part II.

Drug Use

Heroin use declined dramatically for clients leaving the program. The pattern of immediate improvement followed by further improvement by the time the interviews were conducted occurred for most categories of drugs. In no category was there any significant reversion. Approximately 80 percent of the respondents were using heroin at least some of the time prior to entering treatment, but 79 to 90 percent stated that they were not using it at all during the two-month period prior to being interviewed. Only 2 to 4 percent of the respondents in the three treatment groups admitted using heroin daily during the two-month period prior to being interviewed. Fifty-eight to 75 percent of these clients stated that they had been using heroin daily during the two months prior to treatment. Statistically significant improvements occurred for each treatment group and there are no statistically significant differences between any of the groups. Urinalysis tests of specimens taken during the interviews confirmed the responses of the former clients.

Likewise, a decline occurred in illegal methadone usage by all treatment groups. Four to 12 percent of the treatment respondents indicated usage of illegal methadone during the two-month period prior to being interviewed, while from 13 to 27 percent used it during the two months prior to treatment. There are no statistically significant differences between any of the groups.

Next to heroin (and excluding marijuana, alcohol, and cigarettes), cocaine was the most popular drug used by these clients during the two-month period prior to entering ASA. Forty-nine to 71 percent

---

[1] It should be noted that 27 of the 782 clients in the sample died. Nineteen of these were former methadone maintenance clients, 5 therapeutic community clients and three ambulatory clients. However, methadone maintenance clients tended to be older.

of the clients did not use cocaine at all during this preprogram period, although 6 to 14 percent used it daily. During the two months immediately prior to being interviewed 84 to 88 percent of the respondents who had been through treatment programs did not use cocaine at all. Few of the remaining individuals used cocaine daily (1 percent), although a larger percentage used cocaine occasionally (11 to 15 percent). The decline in use is statistically significant for two of the three treatment groups; there is a statistically significant difference between the ambulatory unit and methadone maintenance groups.

Barbiturates were a relatively less popular drug as compared with heroin or cocaine. All treatment groups reported a statistically significant reduction in barbiturates used between the two-month period prior to treatment and the two-month period prior to being interviewed.

Amphetamines were a comparativley unpopular drug of abuse among the clients sampled. Few of the clients used amphetamines during the two months prior to entering the program. Nevertheless, there was some improvement for each of the groups as reflected by the high percentage not using amphetamines at all during the two months immediately before the interviews — 95 to 98 percent. The improvements realized by both the methadone maintenance and the therapeutic community groups are statistically significant but the improvement in the ambulatory unit group is not. However, there are no statistically significant differences between any of the groups.

Hallucinogens and other drugs were used very infrequently. The general patterns of reduction in use of drugs is also reflected in use of these substances. The improvements in hallucinogen use were statistically significant for both the ambulatory unit and therapeutic community groups and, once again following the usage pattern of other drugs, there were no statistically significant differences between any of the groups.

However, regarding other drugs, while not differing significantly from the above pattern, there was some tendency toward increased usage after treatment. In the two months prior to entering the ASA program 94 to 98 percent of the treatment group clients reported that they did not use other drugs. During the two months prior to being interviewed 89 to 99 percent reported not using other drugs. The only statistically significant difference in other drug usage between these two time periods was between the methadone maintenance and therapeutic community groups, in which the methadone maintenance group reported using other drugs more often.

Since the number of clients responding to the "use of other drugs" item is lower than the number of clients responding to items regarding specific drugs and the reported usage percentages both before and after are quite low, the results obtained should not be viewed with alarm. It does indicate, however, that there should be careful monitoring of other drug substitution after treatment.

Statistically significant reductions occurred in marijuana usage between pre- and post-treatment periods for all groups. Nevertheless, considerable post-program use is indicated. This is hardly surprising in view of the widespread use of marijuana in our society, particularly by persons in the age groups represented in this study.

The data do not support the belief that clients may tend to substitute alcohol for heroin. There are only slight changes in drinking behavior for the methadone maintenance group. There are, however, statistically significant increases between pre-treatment and post-treatment in the occasional use of alcohol for ambulatory unit clients and a similar, though statistically non-significant, pattern for therapeutic community clients.

Increased use of cigarettes has not occurred. Indeed, there was a statistically significant reduction in the frequency of cigarette use for all treatment groups between the pre-treatment and post-treatment periods.

Employment

As regards employment of ex-clients, there is a general, statistically significant pattern of improvement in this regard, comparing the two-month period prior to treatment with the most recent two-month period.

For each treatment group, the number of clients employed in the two months prior to being interviewed was twice as much or more than during the two months prior to entering treatment. Statistically, this improvement is highly significant for each treatment group, as well as between the therapeutic community and methadone maintenance groups. Although employment increases were significant for both of these groups, the therapeutic community clients quadrupled their employment rate (17 vs. 66 percent) between the two periods while the methadone maintenance clients doubled theirs (26 vs. 50 percent).[1]

---

[1] It is not known to what extent the programs employed their clients.

Of course, during the period in question, the unemployment rate was increasing substantially. This should affect the results, especially during the most recent period. The fact that the employment rate for each of the treatment groups continued to improve during this period further dramatizes the reported increases.

Criminal Behavior

There was a reduction in criminal behavior as expressed by actual arrests. The reductions are statistically significant for each treatment group. There is no statistically significant difference between any of the groups.

As regards the question of whether clients spent time in jail during the periods in question, there are statistically significant improvements for each of the groups and no significant differences between any of the groups.

What Influence Did Treatment Seem to Have on Post-Treatment Outcomes?

Drug Use

No statistically significant differences were found to exist between the periods two months before treatment and the two immediately prior to the interview between the treatment groups and the comparison group.

The reduction in use of illegal methadone by both treatment and comparison groups during the last two-month period is undoubtedly influenced by the tightening of Federal regulations governing the dispensing of methadone inaugurated late in 1972.

Amphetamine use was severely restricted as the Federal Government initiated a significant policy reducing availability before the most recent time period covered in this study.

Employment

The therapeutic community group showed a significantly greater improvement than the comparison group.

Criminal Behavior

As in the case of the Washington study, there are no statistically significant differences between treatment and comparison groups in frequency of arrests and whether time was spent in jail.

Multiple Behavioral Outcome Measures

As a whole, 49 percent of the respondents were fully recovered, 7 percent were failures and the remaining 44 percent were partially or marginally recovered. Eighty-two percent achieved either full or partial recovery.

There are statistically significant differences in recovery status in only one area — between the therapeutic community group and the comparison and methadone maintenance groups with regard to the number of their clients who were classified as fully recovered. The therapeutic community group reported significantly higher numbers of fully recovered clients, but these results must be viewed with caution.[1] There are no significant differences between the treatment and control groups.

Redefinition of Treatment and Comparison Groups

The comparison group was "purified" to include only clients who had entered ASA for 1 to 5 days and did not subsequently re-enter treatment. All other clients were grouped according to the total length of time they remained in treatment, including all entries.

Little relationship was found between total time spent in treatment and the amount of behavioral change realized.

Explanatory Factors

A search was made (Chapter VIII) for possible reasons as to why there are essentially no consistent patterns in the behavior of former clients sampled among treatment and comparison groups, and an analysis was conducted of factors that might explain outcomes. A number of clients' background and characteristic variables were examined. F tests indicated that age, marital status, and age of first heroin use were significantly different among the groups; these and a number of other client background characteristics and outcome variables were analyzed through multiple regression analyses in attempting to determine what variables might explain variance in the dependent (outcome) variables.

---

[1] One would expect that one of the tests would be statistically significant by chance; and the differences between therapeutic community and other groups in terms of full or partial recovery vs. marginal recovery or failure are not statistically significant.

Again, in the New York City study as in the Washington study, the overall finding is that the client outcomes are unrelated to background or characteristic variables included in the study.

The results of this study caused us to re-examine some commonly held assumptions such as its being desirable to keep clients in treatment for extended periods of time. No relationship was found between the amount of time clients spent in treatment and the amount of behavioral change realized. Perhaps the client is the best judge of how long a period of treatment is sufficient.

The study raises questions with respect to the comparative virtues of methadone maintenance, ambulatory, and residential therapeutic community programs. No modality was found to be clearly superior to the others, although the residential therapeutic communities produced slightly better outcomes than other modalities. Again, perhaps treatment programs should be flexible, with respect to the modality in which the client should be placed.

There had been a great deal of interest in demographic and background correlates of success in drug treatment. Some studies have produced limited evidence showing that clients with certain characteristics do better in treatment than others. In this study, demographic and background factors failed to explain success in treatment or lack thereof.[1]

---

[1] With the exception of pre-treatment employment of ambulatory clients, as previously noted.

PART III

A FOLLOW-UP STUDY OF FORMER CLIENTS OF DRUG TREATMENT PROGRAMS IN WASHINGTON, D.C. AND NEW YORK CITY

by
Marvin R. Burt
and
Thomas J. Glynn

Chapter I

INTRODUCTION

Several major limitations should be noted in interpreting and comparing the results of the two follow-up studies presented. First, the NTA sample was drawn randomly from the universe of NTA clients, stratified by modality and the year in which the client left treatment. Thus, the sample is representative of all clients within each cell irrespective of the NTA clinic at which the client was treated and (except for the comparison group) the length of time spent in treatment. Few clients of drug free programs are included because NTA had few such clients; such persons are commonly treated by programs outside of NTA. In contrast, the ASA sample is stratified, not only by modality, but also by the length of time clients spent in ASA treatment. Thus, 27 percent of the former ASA clients interviewed were graduates or still in treatment; an additional 26 percent were in continuous treatment for over 12 months. The NTA sample contained few graduates or persons in treatment and few persons in continuous treatment for more than one year. One would expect that clients in a program would be less "at risk" than those not in a program and one would hope that graduates would be less likely to have undesirable outcomes than persons who have not graduated.

Second, the NTA follow-up data include only responses from 81 percent of the sample, while the ASA data include only 59 percent of that sample. In both cases, there may therefore be some bias, probably more for the ASA data because of the lower response rate. And one cannot conclude that the interview responses are representative of the entire sample.

Third, bias may be introduced by incomplete responses to interview questions. The "n's" in the ASA data fluctuate substantially between questions; this is not a problem in the NTA data.

Fourth, there is the issue of the validity of the responses. In both studies, urine samples obtained from respondents were tested for the presence of drugs and the results compared to responses to questions concerning current drug use.[1] These comparisons showed a high degree of validity in both studies. Responses to questions about arrests and incarcerations were compared to police records for the NTA sample; this showed a high degree of validity. Such a comparison was not made for the ASA sample. Employment or school status was not validated for either sample.

It is interesting to note that of the NTA clients' urine tests, 27 percent were positive for preludin, 26 percent for morphine or quinine, and 17 percent for methadone. These clients were also tested for cocaine, codeine, amphetamines and barbiturates; only 1-2 percent of the urines were positive for each of these drugs. For ASA clients, 20 percent were positive for morphine or quinine and 39 percent for methadone.[2] Cocaine was detected in 2 percent of the urines as were barbiturates. The urines were not tested for any other drugs.

In Chapter II, of Part III, profiles of the clients upon entering treatment are presented; Chapter III compares the client behaviors during the periods before and after treatment. Chapter IV searches for factors which might explain the results. Discussion of the results is presented in Chapter V, and Chapter VI presents implications for treatment and research.

----

[1] These tests showed that 88 percent of the NTA respondents and 95 percent of the ASA respondents gave answers that were consistent with the test results regarding the presence of morphine or quinine.

[2] Of the 90 ASA respondents whose urine tests were positive for methadone, 48 were in legitimate methadone programs at the time the specimen was taken. Thus, 13 percent of the urines taken reflected use of illegal methadone, while 8 percent of the respondents stated that they used illegal methadone.

Chapter II

PROFILE OF CLIENTS UPON ENTERING TREATMENT

What types of persons are included in the respective samples? As indicated in Parts I and II, data on NTA encompasses random samples of clients who left NTA during the three-year period from 1971-1973 while the ASA sample represents clients who left programs during 1971. Here we present a composite of the characteristics upon entering treatment of the sample clients who were interviewed.

Client Characteristics

Table II-1 shows that the NTA clients were typically male (82 percent), black (86 percent) and relatively young (21 to 25). The ASA sample had a roughly similar proportion of males (78 percent), but a sharply different racial distribution (50 percent black). With respect to age, clients under the age of eighteen were purposefully excluded from the NTA sample and thus only ASA has clients in their sample less than eighteen years of age. However, while the differences in the age distributions are not substantial, the ASA sample has a somewhat higher proportion of older clients (40 percent are over the age 25 compared to 32 percent for NTA).

Backgrounds

Table II-2 depicts the backgrounds of these clients. Comparable data are not available for all of these variables. Thus, data were not

TABLE II-1

CLIENT CHARACTERISTICS
(percentage)

	NTA (n=289)	ASA (n=457)
Sex		
Male	82	78
Female	18	22
Race		
Black	86	50
White	14	44
Other	––	6
Age		
Less than 18	0	3
18-20	26	17
21-25	42	40
26-30	20	22
31-36	5	10
Over 36	7	8

TABLE II-2

CLIENT BACKGROUNDS–NTA
(percentage)

Birthplace (n=151) *	
Washington, D.C.	59
Other	41
Client Caretakers Until Age 15 (n=289)	
Parents	89
Other	11
Caretakers' Work History (n=288)	
Never worked	3
Worked occasionally	15
Worked regularly	82
Educational Level Attained by Clients' Parents (n=289)	
Grades 1-8	18
Grade 9	11
Grade 10	11
Grade 11	11
Grade 12	28
Above grade 12	21

Illegal Drug Use by Clients' Family (n=288)

No	89
Yes	11

Highest Grade Completed (n=288)

Grades 1-8	6
Grade 9	7
Grade 10	25
Grade 11	22
Grade 12	33
Above grade 12	7

Veteran Status (n=233) *

Not a veteran	89
Veteran	11

Mental Health Treatment Prior to First Entry (n=227) *

Never treated	95
Treated	5

CLIENT BACKGROUNDS—ASA

Both Parents Living At Home When
Client Was Youth (n=457)

Yes	54
No	46

Parents' Work History (n=396)	Mother	Father
Never Worked	35	4
Worked Occasionally	25	12
Worked Regularly	40	84

Educational Level Attained By Clients' Parents

	(n=335) Mother	(n=261) Father
Grades 1-6	15	20
Grades 7-9	16	16
Grades 10-11	29	28
Grade 12	32	24
Above Grade 12	9	12

Highest Grade Completed (n=456)

Grades 1-8	6
Grade 9	14
Grade 10	20
Grade 11	27
Grade 12	23
Above Grade 12	10

*Source: CCI Files

collected from ASA on birthplace, client caretakers until age 15, illegal drug use by client's family, veteran status, and mental health treatment prior to first entry. The data on education level attained by clients' parents are not comparable because the NTA data consider the mother and father together while the ASA data separate them. The patterns appear to be roughly similar, but again they are not precisely comparable. NTA clients showed a somewhat higher level of educational attainment than the ASA clients; 40 percent completed at least the twelfth grade compared to 33 percent for the ASA clients.

Client Status Upon Entering Treatment

Table II-3 shows that little data are available on these variables from the ASA. In terms of type of participation, a higher proportion of the NTA clients were forced into participation by legal authorities (26 compared to 19 percent). Table II-4 shows the age of the clients when they first participated in each type of crime. The ASA clients showed a marked pattern of beginning drug use at a substantially earlier age than the NTA clients. For example, 28 percent of them reported that they had first participated in a drug-related crime before age 14 compared to 4 percent of the NTA clients. Nearly all the clients in both samples had at some time participated in drug-related crimes. For the other four categories of crime, the ASA data show extremely low "n's" caused by incomplete interviews. Therefore, those data should be regarded with considerable caution. The incomplete data available seem to indicate a higher proportion of ASA clients being involved in property crimes. Fifty-two percent of the NTA clients participated in a property crime, 24 percent before age eighteen; this compares with 98 percent of the ASA clients participating in such crimes, and 65 percent before age eighteen.

TABLE II-3
CLIENT STATUS UPON ENTERING NTA
(percentage)

Living Arrangement (n=208) *

Alone	13
Spouse	14
Parents	35
Other relatives	11
Friends	19
Institution (hospital, halfway house, etc.)	7
No stable arrangement and other	1

Number of Dependents (n=162) *

None	49
One	22
Two	20
Three or more	9

General Health Status[1] (n=183) *

Excellent	23
Good	53
Fair	20
Poor	4

Duration of Daily Heroin Use (n=162) *

No days	1
16-180 days	3
181-365 days	7
1-2 years	22
Over 2 years	67

Daily Heroin Use (in dollars) (n=106) *

Less than $6	13
$6-40	42
$41-100	31
$101-150	10
More than $150	4

Time Incarcerated (n=198) *

Never	60
1-5 days	3
6 days - 1 year	15
1-2 years	7
2-4 years	4

*Source: CCI Files

[1] Physician's assessment following physical examination.

CLIENT STATUS UPON ENTERING ASA
(percentage)

4-10 years	9
More than 10 years	2
Type of Participation (n=286)	
Voluntary	74
Forced by legal authorities	26
Living arrangement (n=456)	
Alone	21
With someone else	79
[1]General Health Status 2 Months Before (n=341)	
Excellent	68
Good	29
Fair	3
Poor	0
Incarceration status (n=447)	
Never incarcerated	33
Incarcerated one or more times	67
Type of participation (n=390)	
Voluntary	81
Forced by legal authorities	19

*Client Behavior During the Two Months
Immediately Prior to Entering Treatment*

Table II-5 shows that during the two-month period immediately prior to entering NTA, nearly all the clients used heroin at least occasionally and 69 percent used it daily. While the ASA clients showed nearly as heavy daily use as those in NTA, 19 percent of them did not use it at all and only proportionately half as many used it occasionally. NTA clients also showed more use of illegal methadone, cocaine, amphetamines, marijuana and alcohol. ASA clients showed somewhat greater use of barbiturates.

According to Table II-6, a slightly higher proportion of ASA clients were arrested during the two-month period prior to treatment and a higher proportion were incarcerated. Tables II-7 and II-8 show that a higher proportion of NTA clients (34 compared to 23 percent) had engaged in prosocial activities such as having a paid job or keeping house. Unfortunately, it is hazardous to compare data

[1] Self-assessment

TABLE II-4

AGE OF CLIENT WHEN FIRST PARTICIPATED IN CRIME
(percentage)
NTA

Type of Crime*	Never Involved	Age when First Involved					
		13 or less	14-15	16-17	18-19	20-25	Over 25
Drug Related	2	4	20	30	23	19	2
Property	48	6	8	10	13	11	4
Violent	73	1	1	5	7	11	2
Victimless	69	1	3	5	6	13	3
Other	96	0	0	1	1	2	0

*n=288 for all rows

ASA

Type of Crime	Never Involved	Age When First Involved					
		13 or less	14-15	16-17	18-19	20-25	Over 25
Drug Related (n=450)	3	28	26	22	12	7	2
Property** (n=295)	2	15	18	32	16	13	4
Violent** (n=130)	4	2	9	24	29	27	5
Victimless** (n=27)	19	4	7	15	33	18	4
Other** (n=49)	8	0	14	23	16	20	19

**These data should be viewed with considerable caution due to
the low "n's" attributable to missing data.

TABLE II-5

FREQUENCY OF DRUG USE - TWO MONTH PERIOD PRIOR TO ENTERING TREATMENT
(percentage)

Drug	Frequency of Use-NTA				Frequency of Use-ASA			
	Not At All	Occasionally	Daily	N	Not At All	Occasionally	Daily	N
Heroin	3	28	69	289	19	14	67	456
Illegal Methadone	64	32	4	289	82	15	3	455
Cocaine	42	51	7	289	60	29	11	456
Amphetamines	72	21	7	289	87	11	2	455
Barbiturates	82	16	2	289	74	20	6	455
Hallucinogens	87	12	1	289	89	10	1	454
Dilaudid	86	11	3	289	--	--	--	--
Minor Tranquilizers	90	9	1	289	--	--	--	--
Other Drugs	91	8	1	289	97	2	1	368
Marijuana	26	43	31	289	46	33	21	456
Alcohol	36	54	10	289	--	--	--	--
Cigarettes	12	53	35	289	--	--	--	--

on engagement in other activities, as noted in the footnote to Table II-8. Further, it should be noted that the ASA data on illegal activities are probably understated as they are quite inconsistent with the data on Table II-6. Taken at face value, the illegal activities data show a much higher level of engagement in illegal activities for the NTA clients.

TABLE II-6
ARRESTS AND INCARCERATIONS — TWO-MONTH PERIOD PRIOR TO ENTERING TREATMENT
(percentage)

	NTA	ASA
Arrests	(n=288)	(n=444)
Not arrested	76	71
Arrested	24	29
	NTA	ASA
Incarcerations	(n=287)	(n=439)
Not incarcerated	87	79
Incarcerated	13	21

TABLE II-7
EMPLOYMENT — TWO-MONTH PERIOD PRIOR TO ENTERING TREATMENT
(percentage)

NTA

Status	Percent
Paid job	34
Keeping house	5
Student, job training	0
Illegal activities	43
All other activities	18
Total	100
n=	289

ASA

Status	Percent
Paid job	23
No paid job	77
Total	100
n=	451

TABLE II-8
PRIMARY NON-JOB RELATED ACTIVITY TWO MONTHS
PRIOR TO ENTERING ASA[1]

Activity	Percent
Housewife	1
Student	7
Drug Program	2
Using Drugs	38
Illegal Activities	10
Hanging Out	33
Other	9
Total	100
n=	387

[1] Caution should be exercised in interpreting this table. The item asked "(While out of work and not looking for a job, or receiving job training) how did you spend most of your time?" Those responding, in Table II-7, that they were employed during this two-month period should not have replied to the item cited in this table. This was not the case — 13% of methadone maintenance, 2% of ambulatory, 10% of therapeutic community, and 7% of comparison respondents replied "yes" on Table II-8. These respondents may not have been employed for the full two-month period and thus may have been responding for their activities in the partial period. Data are not available to either support or deny this supposition.

Chapter III

EFFECTIVENESS – CHANGE IN BEHAVIOR

This chapter addresses each of the evaluation criteria presented. For each evaluation criterion, the research questions initially posed are answered.[1]

For each effectiveness measure, we showed what happened to both NTA and ASA clients in terms of the behavioral elements defined. There was, however, a lack of comparability between the ASA and NTA samples, response rates, etc., and therefore the comparisons must be viewed with considerable caution.

This chapter discusses only the behavioral changes associated with participation in an NTA or ASA program. Therefore, neither the NTA nor the ASA comparison groups are considered in this analysis; comparisons are made only between NTA and ASA clients who have participated in a treatment modality for six days or more. Few differences in effectiveness exist among treatment modalities within NTA or ASA, and only one of the modalities (methadone maintenance) is comparable between NTA and ASA. For these reasons (and to simplify comparisons between NTA and ASA), treatment modalities (methadone maintenance and abstinence in the NTA; methadone maintenance, ambulatory unit, and therapeutic community in the ASA) are not considered individually in the tables.

Comparison of NTA and ASA
Treatment Outcomes

Heroin Use

Table III-1 shows that heroin use declined dramatically for both

---

[1] • What happened to former clients who left treatment?
   • What influence did treatment seem to have on post-treatment outcomes of former clients?

TABLE III-1

DRUG USE
(percentage)

Frequency of Use	NTA			ASA		
	2 Months Before	2 Months After	Last 2 Months	2 Months Before	2 Months After	Last 2 Months
Heroin						
Not at all	2	55	65	20	73	86
Occasionally	26	33	30	13	15	11
Daily	72	12	5	67	12	3
Total	100	100	100	100	100	100
n=	189	189	189	373	369	370
Illegal Methadone						
Not at all	65	83	92	83	91	92
Occasionally	32	15	7	15	8	7
Daily	3	2	1	2	1	1
Total	100	100	100	100	100	100
n=	189	189	189	373	369	369
Cocaine						
Not at all	42	72	78	61	85	86
Occasionally	52	27	20	29	14	13
Daily	6	1	2	10	1	1
Total	100	100	100	100	100	100
n=	189	189	189	373	369	371
Amphetamines						
Not at all	75	80	86	86	97	97
Occasionally	18	16	13	12	3	3
Daily	7	4	1	2	0	0
Total	100	100	100	100	100	100
n=	189	189	189.	373	369	369

NTA and ASA clients leaving the programs. This improvement, which was statistically significant for each treatment modality in both programs, occurred immediately upon leaving treatment and further improvement occurred by the time the interviews were conducted.

Illegal Methadone

Use of illegal methadone, as indicated by Table III-1, followed the same pattern of improvement as that noted above for heroin. This improvement was more dramatic for the NTA program, where both treatment modalities showed statistically significant improvement. The ASA program, with a considerably larger percentage of clients indicating non-use of illegal methadone before treatment, consequently had less room for improvement. Nevertheless, two of the three ASA treatment groups showed statistically significant improvement when the period two months prior to treatment was compared with the period two months preceding the interview.

Cocaine

Next to heroin, cocaine was the most popular drug used by respondents during the two-month period immediately prior to entering either the NTA or the ASA program. Once again, Table III-1 depicts a similar pattern of improvement for both program groups — improvement immediately after treatment followed by further improvement just prior to the interview. As with heroin, the improvement reported in each treatment modality in the NTA and ASA programs was statistically significant.

Amphetamines

Table III-1 shows that amphetamines were a less popular drug than heroin or cocaine for clients in both treatment programs. Here again, a similar improvement pattern is noted, as well as the continued pattern of ASA clients reporting initially lower drug-use percentages than NTA clients. This high percentage of initial non-users results in an asymptotic curve which precludes continued significant improvement by all but a few of these programs' clients. The percentage improvements for both NTA and ASA clients were, however, similar; improvements were statistically significant for both NTA treatment modalities and for two of the three ASA treatment modalities.

It should be noted that a significant policy was initiated by the federal government prior to the most recent two-month period which considerably restricted the availability of amphetamines and reduced their potential for abuse.

Barbiturates

As indicated by Table III-2, barbiturates were a comparatively unpopular drug of abuse among the clients in both treatment programs. Although the same improvement trend may be observed for both NTA and ASA clients, the pattern of initially lower drug use by ASA clients noted above is reversed with this case. Nevertheless the NTA and ASA programs showed an identical percentage of non-users in the most recent period. Statistically significant improvement was reported for one of the two NTA treatment modalities and for each of the ASA treatment modalities.

Hallucinogens

Use of hallucinogens was limited, as shown in Table III-2. The percentage of NTA clients using these drugs increased slightly between the pre-treatment period and the most recent period. There were, however, no statistically significant changes between any of the NTA treatment modalities. The ASA clients followed a pattern of hallucinogen use similar to that of the NTA clients. The ASA group, however, experienced somewhat greater improvement, as indicated by the statistically significant decrease in use for two of the three ASA treatment modalities.

Marijuana

Table III-2 shows some reductions in marijuana usage among the periods in question, although considerable use is indicated. This is hardly surprising in view of the widespread use of marijuana in our society, particularly by persons in the age groups represented in the samples. The previously observed improvement pattern is somewhat disrupted here, particularly among ASA clients. Clients in this program showed a reduction in use during the period just after leaving treatment, but reported an increase in their occasional use of marijuana for the period two months prior to being interviewed. Nevertheless, both groups indicated that their use of this substance was

TABLE III-2

DRUG USE
(percentage)

Frequency of Use	N T A			A S A		
	2 Months Before	2 Months After	Last 2 Months	2 Months Before	2 Months After	Last 2 Months
Barbiturates						
Not at all	85	89	93	73	92	93
Occasionally	12	10	5	21	6	7
Daily	3	1	2	6	2	0
Total	100	100	100	100	100	100
n =	189	189	189	373	369	369
Hallucinogens						
Not at all	89	94	93	89	97	96
Occasionally	10	6	7	10	3	4
Daily	1	0	0	1	0	0
Total	100	100	100	100	100	100
n =	189	189	189	373	369	369
Marijuana						
Not at all	27	35	36	46	69	59
Occasionally	43	41	37	32	25	34
Daily	30	24	27	22	6	7
Total	100	100	100	100	100	100
n =	189	189	189	373	369	369
Other Drugs[1]						
Not at all	94	97	98	97	98	94
Occasionally	5	3	2	3	0	1
Daily	1	0	0	0	2	5
Total	100	100	100	100	100	100
n =	189	189	189	373	369	369

[1]Comparability of NTA-ASA data regarding use of other drugs is limited; dilaudid, minor tranquilizers, and legal methadone were not categorized as "other drugs" in the NTA study while they were, if mentioned, so categorized in the ASA study. The NTA study dealt separately with these drugs—see Table V-3.

less in the most recent period than prior to treatment; this reduction in use was statistically significant for one of the NTA treatment modalities and for each of the ASA treatment modalities.

Other Drugs

The data indicating use of "other drugs" in Table III-2 present a somewhat ambiguous picture as pointed out in footnote 1 to that table. While there is value in studying the use of "other drugs" reported by the NTA and ASA clients separately, comparison of the two programs in this regard is made difficult because several drugs are included in the ASA category that are dealt with separately in the NTA analysis.

In viewing each program's report of "other drug" use separately, NTA clients show the pattern of improvement noted for the majority of drugs cited above; statistically significant improvements occurred for both treatment modalities. ASA clients differed in their improvement pattern. One treatment modality reported increased usage, one initially improved and then reverted and another reported essentially no difference. No statistically significant reductions were reported for treatment modalities in the ASA program, although it must be reemphasized that with such high initial percentages of non-use, statistically significant improvement is quite difficult.

Legal Methadone, Dilaudid, and Minor Tranquilizers

Table III-3 presents data concerning three drug categories which were included in the NTA, but not in the ASA analysis. There is comparatively little use in each category, although a statistically significant reduction in dilaudid use between the period prior to treatment and the most recent period was reported by both NTA treatment modalities.

Alcohol Use[1]

A major concern among methadone programs is the belief that clients may tend to substitute alcohol for heroin. Table III-4 does

---

[1] It should be noted that the frequency of use categories for the ASA and NTA programs differ. This should not substantially affect the results, although the difference tends to deflate the ASA "occasionally" data.

TABLE III-3

DRUG USE
(percentage)

Frequency of Use	N T A[1]		
	2 Months Before	2 Months After	Last 2 Months
Legal Methadone			
Not at all	85	95	92
Occasionally	4	1	2
Daily	11	4	6
Total	100	100	100
n =	189	189	189
Dilaudid			
Not at all	86	92	93
Occasionally	11	7	6
Daily	3	1	1
Total	100	100	100
n =	189	189	189
Minor Tranquilizers			
Not at all	94	94	95
Occasionally	4	6	4
Daily	2	0	1
Total	100	100	100
n =	189	189	189

[1] No separate data were compiled for these drugs in the ASA study.

[2] Some private physicians were making methadone available on prescription during the period two moths before entering treatment.

TABLE III-4

DRUG USE
(percentage)

Frequency of Use	N T A		
	2 Months Before	2 Months After	Last 2 Months
Alcohol			
Not at all	37	40	39
Occasionally	54	52	53
Daily	9	8	8
Total	100	100	100
n =	189	189	189
Cigarettes			
Not at all	12	12	12
1 pack or less/day	53	60	63
More than 1 pack/day	35	28	25
Total	100	100	100
n =	189	189	189
Frequency of Use	A S A		
	2 Months Before	2 Months After	Last 2 Months
Alcohol			
Rarely	45	37	29
Occasionally	37	46	57
Daily	18	17	14
Total	100	100	100
n =	312	307	323
Cigarettes			
Rarely	8	12	5
1 pack or less per day	50	56	59
1.5-2 packs per day	27	23	28
2 packs per day	15	9	8
Total	100	100	100
n =	359	341	336

TABLE III-5

EMPLOYMENT
(percentage)

Program	Status	2 Months Before	2 Months After	Last 2 Months
NTA	Paid job	33	37	48
	Keeping house, student, job training	5	4	6
	Illegal activities	46	38	24
	All other activities	16	21	22
	Total	100	100	100
	n=	189	189	189
ASA[1]	Employed	21	43	57
	Not employed	79	57	43
	Total	100	100	100
	n=	368	352	374

[1]Other types of activities are not shown for reasons explained in Part II. Further, the ASA data are not comparable to the NTA data.

not confirm this belief. Alcohol use among NTA clients is essentially unchanged among the three time periods. No statistically significant differences were reported for either of the NTA treatment modalities.

The ASA clients indicated increased use of alcohol between the period prior to treatment and the most recent period. However, this increase was strictly in the occasional use of alcohol; reported daily use of this substance declined slightly between the periods in question. A statistically significant increase in alcohol use was recorded for only one of the three ASA treatment modalities.

Cigarette Use[1]

Another form of substance substitution has been suggested to be increased use of cigarettes after withdrawing from heroin. The data obtained do not support this belief. As shown in Table III-4 a pattern of diminished use of cigarettes was indicated for both NTA and ASA clients. This reduction in use did not take the form of refraining from smoking cigarettes at all, but rather was observed in a reduced amount of heavy smoking. This reduction was statistically significant for each of the ASA treatment modalities.

Employment

Employment is an important outcome measure for the success of drug treatment. Table III-5 indicates that the improvement pattern noted in drug use is also evident with regard to employment status. More NTA and ASA clients were employed immediately after treatment than before and a still greater number were employed in the most recent period. This improvement is especially dramatic for ASA clients; statistically significant differences between the period prior to treatment and the most recent period were recorded for each treatment modality. Since other status categories were used in the NTA analysis, statistical tests were not run exclusively on employment for clients in that program.

Using employment combined with other prosocial activities (keeping house, student, job training) compared to all other activities,

---

[1] It should be noted that the frequency of use categories for the ASA and NTA programs differs. This should not substantially affect the results, although it may account for the presence of statistically significant results in the ASA program and the lack of them in the NTA program.

TABLE III-6

ARRESTS
(percentage)

Status	NTA			ASA		
	2 Months Before	2 Months After	Last 2 Months	2 Months Before	2 Months After	Last 2 Months
Arrested	25	11	9	30	9	4
Not Arrested	75	89	91	70	91	96
Total	100	100	100	100	100	100
n=	188	188	188	361	347	358

statistically significant improvements were realized for the abstinence group, but not the methadone maintenance group at NTA.

Criminal Behavior

Two measures of criminal behavior were used in this study:
- Frequency of arrests
- Whether or not time had been spent in jail

Table III-6 shows that the percentage of NTA and ASA clients who were arrested during the two-month period prior to being interviewed was substantially less than during the two months before treatment. These reductions are statistically significant for each treatment modality in both NTA and ASA. Additionally, the trend toward improvement immediately after treatment followed by further improvement in the most recent period is observed in this category of behavior also.

Another indicator of criminal behavior is whether or not a client has spent time in jail during the periods in question. Table III-7 indicates that while ASA clients reported substantial reductions in incarcerations between these periods, the percentage of NTA clients incarcerated during the same time span did not change. ASA clients followed the improvement pattern noted above; NTA clients improved slightly (but insignificantly) immediately after treatment and then reverted to their original incarceration percentage in the most recent period. The ASA clients' reductions are statistically significant for each treatment modality.

Summary[1]

Table III-8 summarizes this discussion of the NTA and ASA treatment programs by presenting for each behavioral outcome measure whether:
- Significant improvements were realized in any of the treatment modalities within each program, comparing the most recent two-month period with the two-month period immediately prior to treatment

---

[1] As may be noted, this table summarizes not only the behavioral changes discussed in this chapter but also those changes that occurred between and among treatment and comparison groups. These summaries are arranged in one table for greater ease of comparison. Specific results may be reviewed in Parts I and II.

TABLE III-7

INCARCERATIONS
(percentage)

Status	NTA			ASA		
	2 Months Before	2 Months After	Last 2 Months	2 Months Before	2 Months After	Last 2 Months
Incarcerated	12	9	12	21	7	4
Not Incarcerated	88	91	88	79	93	96
Total	100	100	100	100	100	100
n=	188	188	188	358	352	339

- There are significant differences between any two of the treatment modalities in each of the programs
- There are significant differences between any of the treatment modalities and the comparison group in each of the programs
- There are significant differences among any of the treatment groups and the comparison group in each of the programs

Multiple Behavioral Outcomes

As in the reports in Parts I and II, our analysis focused for a good deal of the time on one behavior at a time. Now, we address again multiple behavioral outcomes expressed in terms of each respondent's:

- Drug use
- Arrests and incarcerations
- Employment

We define a fully recovered person as one who during the most recent two-month period was:

- Using no illicit drug (except marijuana)
- Not arrested or incarcerated
- Either employed, keeping house, in school or in job (vocational) training[1]

A respondent is defined as a program failure if, during the most recent two-month period, he:

- Used an illicit drug daily, or
- Was incarcerated

Between these two extremes of success and failure are several types of partial and marginal success. The following matrix defines nine mutually exclusive and collectively exhaustive categories ranging from success to failure.[2]

---

[1] Unfortunately, the questionnaire used in interviewing ASA clients did not permit tabulation of respondents who were in vocational training or males "keeping house"; these activities should also be considered as prosocial activities.

[2] This is a modification of categories suggested by Barry S. Brown, "The Role of Research in a Narcotics Treatment Program," *Drug Forum*, Vol. 3 (2), Winter, 1974, and G. E. Vaillant, "A Twelve-Year Follow-up of New York City Addicts: Vol. I, The Relation of Treatment to Outcome," *American Journal of Psychiatry*, 122: 727-736, 1966.

TABLE III-8

SUMMARY OF BEHAVIORAL OUTCOMES

Behavioral Outcome Measure	Significant Improvement in any of the Treatment Groups; Most Recent 2 Months Compared to 2 Months Before Treatment?		Significant Difference Between any two of the Treatment Groups?		Significant Differences Between any of the Treatment Groups and Comparison Group?		Significant Differences Among all Treatment Groups and the Comparison Group?	
Drug Use	ASA	NTA	ASA	NTA	ASA	NTA	ASA	NTA
Heroin	Yes	Yes	No	No	No	No	Yes[1]	No
Illegal Methadone	Yes	Yes	No	No	No	No	No	No
Cocaine	Yes	Yes	Yes	No	No	No	Yes	No
Amphetamines	Yes	Yes	No	No	No	No	No	No
Barbiturates	Yes	Yes	No	No	No	No	No	No
Hallucinogens	Yes	Yes	No	No	No	No	No	No
Other Drugs[2]	No	Yes	Yes	Yes	No	No	No	No
Marijuana	Yes	No	No	No	No	No	No	No
Alcohol	Yes	No	No	No	No	No	No	No
Cigarettes	Yes	No	No	No	No	No	No	No
Employment[3]	Yes	Yes	Yes	No	Yes	No	Yes	Yes
Criminal Activity								
Arrests	Yes	Yes	No	No	No	No	No	No
Incarcerations	Yes	No	No	No	No	No	No	No

[1]There were no significant differences between any of the Treatment Groups or between any of the Treatment Groups and the Comparison Group (t-test); a significant difference among the groups, however, was obtained at the .04 level (F-test). This is probably a statistical aberration.

[2]Includes dilaudid, minor tranquilizers, and other drugs.

[3]For NTA includes holding a job, keeping a house, attending school or vocational training. For ASA includes only holding a job.

Categories of Success (Recovery)

Extent of Recovery	Engage in Illicit Drug Use[1]	Arrested	Prosocial Employment
Full	No	No	Yes
Partial-I	No	No	No
Partial-II	No	Yes	Yes
Partial-III	No	Yes	No
Partial-IV	Yes, but not daily	No	Yes
Marginal-I	Yes, but not daily	Yes	Yes
Marginal-II	Yes, but not daily	Yes	No
Marginal-III	Yes, but not daily	No	No
Failure	Yes, daily or incarcerated		

Table III-9 indicates the behavioral outcomes, expressed in terms of extent of recovery, achieved by clients in both the NTA and ASA programs. The category "Partial" includes all four Partial categories and "Marginal" includes all three Marginal categories.

TABLE III-9
EXTENT OF RECOVERY

Extent of Recovery	NTA	ASA
Fully	20	50
Partially	37	33
Marginally	23	10
Failure	20	7
Total	100	100
n=	189	374

[1] Except for marijuana.

The ASA program reported a substantially higher percentage of "fully recovered" clients and a great deal fewer "failures." The higher ASA success rate should be regarded with caution: (1) a substantially lower proportion of ASA clients were heroin users (80 compared to 98 percent); (2) the post-treatment employment data for ASA are probably inflated (as noted in Part II); (3) the types of programs were different in NTA and ASA; (4) the low ASA response rate, biases in the sampling process, and the large proportion of graduates, clients still in treatment, and clients who had been in treatment for unusually long periods of time all act to bias the results in the direction of higher success rates for ASA.

Analysis of Different Client Groupings

The definitions of the comparison group in both the Washington, D.C., and New York City studies were, necessarily, rather arbitrary. Both consisted of clients who had left treatment within five days of entry. However, 20 percent of the NTA comparison group members and 42 percent of the ASA comparison group members subsequently re-entered treatment. Thus, the comparison groups were not as pure as one would like.

In view of this "contamination" of the comparison groups, different groupings seemed to be of interest. Because of comparison group contamination, "purer" comparison groups were established consisting of clients who never received more than one day of treatment. However, in the case of ASA, insufficient numbers of persons appeared in the samples; therefore, that comparison group included persons with no more than five days of treatment.

Relationships between total time in treatment and outcomes were analyzed by partitioning clients into groups depending upon *total* length of time spent in treatment. Thus, if a client entered treatment once for ten days and a second time for 50 days, his total time in treatment would be 60 days.

The results of these analyses may be summarized briefly:

- NTA clients' behavioral changes were essentially the same whether they stayed in treatment one day or five years (or shorter periods of time).
- Changes in ASA clients' behavior were generally not associated with total time spent in treatment. However, clients in treatment more than 364 days were signifi-

---

1 Except those in treatment 6-14 days.

cantly more likely to become employed than those in treatment for shorter periods.[1] Changes in ASA clients' behavior were unrelated to the number of treatment episodes.[1]

---

[1] No analysis was conducted of the relationship between NTA clients' behavioral changes and the number of treatment episodes.

Chapter IV

A SEARCH FOR EXPLANATORY FACTORS

We look again at possible reasons why there are few significant differences in the behavior of former clients sampled among groups and we search for factors that might explain outcomes. First to be examined are the backgrounds and characteristics of the clients to determine whether there are significant differences among groups. Second, possible differences in the groups are examined in terms of subsequent treatment and types of participation in NTA and ASA. Third, possible interpretations are analyzed through multivariate analyses. Finally, an analysis is made of the services actually received by the clients.

Client Backgrounds and Characteristics

The following client background and characteristic variables are examined in this section:

- Sex
- Race
- Age
- Highest grade completed in school
- Marital status
- Living with someone
- Age first used heroin
- Treatment prior to entering NTA or ASA
- Treatment after leaving NTA or ASA
- Type of participation in NTA or ASA

In summary, no significant differences were found for NTA clients among the major groups.

In contrast, for ASA clients, statistically significant differences were found for the following variables:

- Age — methadone maintenance clients were significantly older than members of other groups.
- Marital status — the percentage of clients who are unmarried (i.e., single, divorced or widowed) differs among each of the groups, varying from 59 to 81 percent. The differences are statistically significant among the groups and between ambulatory unit clients and comparison and methadone maintenance clients as well as between methadone maintenance and therapeutic community clients.
- Age first used heroin — the earlier the age the individual first uses heroin, the more he is believed to have adopted heroin use as a long-term life style. A significant tendency is shown among methadone maintenance clients to begin heroin use at a later age than clients in other groups.
- Treament prior to entering ASA — significantly higher proportions of methadone maintenance and therapeutic community clients had treatment prior to entering ASA compared to ambulatory unit clients (39 and 34 percent compared to 21 percent respectively).
- Treatment after ASA — 42 percent of the control groups entered treatment subsequent to ASA compared to 21 to 46 percent of the treatment groups. These differences are statistically significant. These data raise serious questions regarding the adequacy of the comparison group.
- Type of participation — there are statistically significant differences in the percentage of clients who were forced by legal authorities to enter treatment among the groups (the range is 7 to 29 percent for the methadone maintenance and therapeutic community respectively).

Multivariate Analysis

Thus far, the clients' behavior has been analyzed in terms of a single variable at a time. A number of background and characteristic variables were examined for NTA and ASA to determine whether there were significant differences among the groups. The analysis for NTA indicated that the groups were homogeneous with respect to all background and demographic variables involved in the study. They therefore were collapsed into one group and examined to see whether combinations of characteristics can explain variances in the dependent variables (i.e., outcomes).

For ASA, the examination of characteristics showed that there were a number of significant differences among the groups. Because these groups were not homogeneous, each was examined separately to determine whether combinations of characteristics could explain differences in dependent variables. Table IV-1 depicts the dependent and independent variables included in stepwise multiple regressions

TABLE IV-1
VARIABLES INCLUDED IN STEPWISE MULTIPLE REGRESSIONS

Independent Variables	NTA	ASA
Sex	X	X
Race	X	X
Age	X	X
Highest grade completed	X	X
Married	X	X
Living with someone	X	X
Caretaker's work history	X	X
Heroin use 2 months before entering treatment	X	X
Prior drug treatment	X	X
Drug treatment after leaving	X	
Voluntary vs. involuntary participation	X	X
Major source of income 2 months before entering treatment (job, other)	[1]	X
Number of associates using drugs 2 months before entering treatment	X	X
Number of associates using drugs 2 months after leaving treatment	[1]	X
Number of associates using drugs past 2 months	[1]	X
Job 2 months before entering treatment (yes, no)	[1]	X
Job 2 months after leaving treatment (yes, no)	[1]	X
Lived at one place in the last 2 months	X	
Used heroin in the last 2 months[2]	X	
Total arrests in the last 2 months[2]	X	
More than one drug[2]	X	

[1] Included in factor analysis only; not used in stepwise regression due to multicolinearity.
[2] Also used alternatively as dependent variable.

TABLE IV-1 (continued)

	NTA	ASA
Employed in the last 2 months[2]	X	
Number of years gone to school since leaving treatment	X	
Longest period of time client lived in one place during 2 months prior to interview	X	
Number of places lived during last 3 years	X	
Days sick in bed during 2 months prior to being interviewed	X	
What adults the client lived with most of the time until age fifteen (parents, other)	X	
Years of school by client	X	
Drug use by persons in client's household when growing up	X	
Was the amount of time spent in the clinic at each visit enough?	X	
Was methadone maintenance or another activity most helpful?	X	
Number of arrests	X	
Was client incarcerated during the 6 months prior to first entering treatment?	X	
Longest time client held a job	X	
Number of days client worked during the 2 months before first entering treatment	X	
Source of funds 2 months before first entering treatment (illegal activities or other)	X	
Source of funds 2 months before entering treatment (Social Security, VA benefits or unemployment; other)	X	
Dependent Variables		
Used heroin last 2 months	X	X
More than one drug used last 2 months	X	
Cigarettes used last 2 months	X	
Alcohol used last 2 months	X	
Total arrests last 2 months	X	
Number of days worked last 2 months	X	
Illegal activities last 2 months	X	
Major source of income last 2 months (job, other)		X
Job held last 2 months		X

conducted for NTA and ASA respectively. Separate regressions were run for each of the dependent variables indicated. In the case of NTA, all treatment program clients were collapsed into one group for the reason previously indicated. For ASA clients, separate regressions were run for each of the three treatment groups: methadone maintenance, ambulatory, and residential therapeutic community.

The highest multiple correlation coefficient squared (R^2) for the NTA multiple regression runs was .23, indicating that none of the independent variables, when used in a linear relationship, showed a useful reduction in the dependent variable's variance. The correlation coefficients were also quite low, indicating no useful reduction in the independent variable. Therefore, none of these independent variables explained the behavioral outcomes.

A substantially similar pattern occurred with the ASA sample. As indicated previously, separate stepwise multiple regressions were run for each of the dependent variables for each of the three treatment groups. Only two of the squared multiple correlation coefficients exceeded 0.27; both of these were for the ambulatory group. An R^2 of 0.46 was shown for the dependent variable "major source of income (job, other)." However, 32 percent of the variance was explained by one independent variable: that the client held a job during the period two months after leaving treatment. All the other independent variables accounted for only 14 percent of the variance (including colinearity). Another regression run for the ambulatory group showed an R^2 of 0.43. However, 28 percent of the variance in the dependent variable "whether a job was held in the past two months" is explained by the same independent variable as in the previous regression run. The combined explanatory power of the other independent variables is only 15 percent (including colinearity). This relationship seems rather obvious: that an individual who was employed during the period two months after leaving treatment is more likely to be employed during the two months prior to the interview than one who is not so employed. However, it does not hold for clients outside of ambulatory programs. We conclude that one can draw very little in the way of conclusions from this relationship and that essentially none of these independent variables explains the behavioral outcomes.

Services Received by Clients

Nearly all the NTA treatment group clients received either methadone maintenance or methadone detoxification. However, few of the clients reported that they received supportive services. Only 43 percent of the maintenance clients and 55 percent of the abstinence clients stated that they had received individual counseling. This surprisingly low percentage could be partially attributable to clients' not necessarily perceiving the types of encounters received with NTA staff as being "individual counseling" per se. Only 17 percent of the NTA clients reported receiving group counseling, and even smaller percentages reported receiving job training, referral, placement counseling, rehabilitation counseling, or help in getting a job.

Analyses of services received by ASA clients is made very difficult by the extremely low response rates to questions concerning receipt of these services. Only the individual and group counseling categories represent 75 percent or more of the respondents; the other services range from 23 to 52 percent respondent representation. Since such low response rates may yield spurious data, only the individual and group counseling services will be discussed.

Eighty-seven to 93 percent of ASA clients in each of the treatment groups stated that they had received individual counseling. While nearly all ambulatory unit and therapeutic community respondents participated in group counseling (94 and 97 percent, respectively), roughly half (51 percent) of the methadone maintenance respondents did so. Such variation in service participation may be attributed to differing emphases and types of services offered in particular treatment modalities.

Reported receipt of services is unrelated to outcome for both the NTA and ASA samples.

Chapter V

DISCUSSION[1]

This comparative analysis of NTA and ASA programs raises many issues and tests numerous hypotheses. The results raise questions with respect to some of the common assumptions pertaining to treatment programs.

One is struck first by the very large behavioral change experienced by these clients. However, the data suggest that the effects of treatment cannot be separated from other factors. Moreover, clients' behavioral change was not only unrelated to presence and type of treatment, but was unrelated to clients' demographic or background characteristics as well. This absence of differences is surprising.

The "maturing out" hypothesis that has been advanced seems inadequate to explain these findings. In that formulation, the addict is seen as reaching a point at which the rigorous addict lifestyle is felt to be no longer feasible and/or desirable. The addict is forced to explore alternatives to heroin use and all that is involved in maintaining his use of heroin. Whether or not that phenomenon of maturing out exists in fact, it does not appear to fit the NTA data, if only because of the limited time frames involved. Addicts were interviewed as little as one year and no more than four years after leaving NTA. There were no significant differences in outcomes in terms of time elapsed since leaving NTA. All ASA clients were interviewed more than three years after leaving the program; because no measurements were taken (say) one or two years after leaving treatment, there is no way to test this hypothesis.

---

1 Much of the discussion in this chapter is drawn from an unpublished paper: Marvin R. Burt, Barry S. Brown, and Robert L. Dupont, "Evaluation of a Large Multi-Modality Drug Program" (processed) .

Three other efforts at explanation may have greater merit. Forces work to help bring about change in the behavior of drug abusers. The entirely outside the traditional treatment process may have been at community itself may have changed. Illicit drug use may have become increasingly unacceptable as the real dangers of certain drugs (e.g., heroin) became known. If what was once "cool" became foolish and weak, it may well have become necessary to reassess activity in regard to that behavior. Whether or not this describes intellectual and behavioral changes in the decade 1965-1975 in Washington, D.C., and New York City is uncertain, but two points are worth noting.

First, in a 1975 study conducted among juvenile users and non-users of heroin in the District of Columbia it was found that non-users were most likely to relate their nonuse of heroin to information that only became available in the early 1970's. The juvenile nonusers reported firsthand knowledge of persons who became involved with heroin and whose behavior deteriorated and lives were threatened as a consequence. Since the peak years of heroin use in the District were 1966-1968, this was information simply not available to their elders — the addicts in this study. It suggests, but by no means confirms, a dramatic change in awareness and thinking about heroin by the time the study was undertaken.[1] We are not aware of a similar study in New York City.

A second explanation for the lack of differences between treatment and control groups may lie in the data itself. In this regard, it was hypothesized that persons who once have made a commitment to seek change, i.e., who enter treatment, and then drop out of treatment immediately thereafter represent a very select group of persons and are improperly cast into a control group. In this formulation, that group would consist, at least largely, of persons who had not quit on their resolve to seek behavioral change, but merely quit on the means to accomplish that change as posed by the treatment program.

Another explanation lies in the role of the criminal justice system's efforts to reduce the supply of illicit drugs and make the abuser's lifestyle more difficult to maintain. The number of arrests made by the District of Columbia Metropolitan Police Department

---

[1] Starlett R. Craig and Barry S. Brown, "Comparison of Youthful Heroin Users and Non-users From One Urban Community," *International Journal of the Addictions*, 10 (1): 53-64, 1975.

did not vary markedly during the period in question, but purity of heroin decreased markedly and the price of heroin increased substantially, making it more difficult for a heroin addict to obtain the drug.

Similar data specific to New York City are lacking. Strict federal controls were instituted on the dispensing of methadone and (later) amphetamines.

It seems reasonable to expect these substantial changes in availability, purity, and price of illicit drugs to result in decreased illicit drug taking.

In any event, a review of the findings from this study cannot help but raise further questions. One is struck not only by the relatively high rate of prosocial behavioral change taking place within the NTA and ASA samples surveyed, but also by the fact that change takes place irrespective of the type of treatment initiated and, to a considerable extent, irrespective of whether or not treatment is instituted. In NTA, clients receiving no treatment realized behavioral changes as great as clients receiving treatment. In ASA, a similar, though not as uniform, pattern was seen.

The results of this study cause us to re-examine some commonly held assumptions regarding the treatment process. First is the common assumption that it is desirable to keep clients in treatment for extended periods of time. NTA clients did equally well whether they stayed in treatment one day or five years (or shorter periods of time). Changes in ASA clients' behavior were generally not associated with total time spent in treatment.[1]

The study raises questions with respect to the comparative virtues of methadone maintenance vs. detoxification. Neither modality was found to be superior to the other in NTA. Again, perhaps treatment programs should be flexible, as was NTA, with respect to the modality in which the clients are placed.

The study also raises questions with respect to the comparative virtues of ASA's methadone maintenance, ambulatory, and residential therapeutic community programs. No modality was found to be clearly superior to the others, although the residential therapeutic community had a slightly higher proportion of clients achieving full

---

[1] Except those in treatment 6-14 days. (However, clients in treatment more than 364 days were significantly more likely to become employed than those in treatment for shorter periods. Pehaps the client himself is the best judge of how long a period of treatment is sufficient.)

recovery. The difference was due to their higher post-treatment employment level.

There has been a great deal of interest in demographic and background correlates of success in drug treatment. Some studies have produced limited evidence showing that clients with certain characteristics do better in treatment than others. In this study, demographic and background factors failed to explain success in treatment or lack thereof.

Chapter VI

IMPLICATIONS FOR TREATMENT AND RESEARCH

Implications for Treatment

The findings of these studies should be extrapolated beyond the New York City and Washington, D.C., scenes with considerable caution. However, the substantial similarity in the findings and their implications for treatment provide compelling reasons for other treatment programs seriously to consider them.

Demographic and Background Factors Do Not Explain or Predict Outcomes

There has been a great deal of attention in the drug abuse field to developing typologies of clients who are more successful in particular types of treatment and even developing instruments for use in assigning clients to particular modalities. Findings of this study suggest that such attempts are of little practical use insofar as the variables considered in these studies are concerned. Demographic and background factors did not explain behavioral outcomes and thus are of little predictive value. Among the factors considered important by some experts, for example, is whether a client entered the program voluntarily or under pressure from the criminal justice system. The results of these studies indicate that this factor is unimportant and has no predictive value.

Outcomes Are Not Related to Type of Treatment

NTA assigned clients to modality by using professional judgment combined with the clients' preference. The principal choices were methadone maintenance and methadone detoxification, with a very limited number of clients being referred to residential therapeutic communities. ASA had a wider range of programs available, but did not necessarily process all clients through central intake as did NTA.

Whatever the rationale for assigning clients to a modality, the clients did equally well virtually irrespective of type of modality to which assigned. This, of course, is different from saying that random assignment to modality is as good as assignment based upon professional judgment. However, the similarity in outcomes among modalities is striking. Perhaps the debate regarding the relative virtues of different types of modalities should be couched in different terms. The results of this study tend to support the existence of various types of modalities and do not indicate the clear superiority of any one type over others.

The Amount of Time a Client Spends in Treatment Has Little Significance

It has been widely assumed that clients should be retained in treatment for extended periods of time. This assumption has been based on the belief that more treatment is better than less and that there is a positive association between the length of time spent in a particular treatment episode and desirable behavioral outcomes. The data from this study refute this belief. In both the NTA and ASA samples, outcomes were unrelated to the amount of time spent in treamtent for a particular episode. For the Washington, D.C., sample, outcomes were also unrelated to *total* time spent in treatment (including all episodes). For the New York City sample, outcomes were unrelated to *total* time spent in treatment with the exception of employment; clients in treatment for more than one year experienced a somewhat higher employment rate than other clients.

This finding has implications for evaluation methodology as well. Since retention in treatment for a particular episode has no relationship to later changes in client behavior, why should this be an evaluation criterion? Further, from a standpoint strictly of cost effectiveness, shorter treatment might be more cost-effective because similar outcomes could be achieved for a lower cost per patient. This conclusion requires further investigation to include specific cost-effectiveness analyses of a variety of different types of treatment episodes for different types of modalities in different settings.

Research Issues Raised by This Study

Contribution of Each Major Type of Service

This study addressed the issue of the comparative effectiveness of major modalities of treatment (as defined) in Washington, D.C., and New York City. The analysis was not service specific. Effectiveness was not assessed in terms of the specific services received within each modality but in terms of the modality in which clients were treated. It is possible that the outcomes would have been quite different had different mixes of services been employed. For example, few of the NTA clients received group or employment counseling. It is of interest to know whether the outcomes would have been substantally different if these services had been received. Further, there are substantial differences in the mixture of services offered by each of the modalities examined — methadone maintenance, methadone detoxification, residential therapeutic community, and ambulatory programs. Answering this question would require either better record keeping on the part of the programs in question, to include the specific services received by clients, and/or a more detailed questionnaire to obtain this information from each of the clients.

Since no demographic or background characteristics were found to be related to treatment outcome, this might help in a search for factors which do relate to outcome.

The Effect of the Community

It is believed that the attitudes of the community (its people, systems, institutions, norms, etc.) may have an influence on both drug-taking behavior and drug treatment. This could have a substantial impact on the apparent effectiveness of drug treatment. Studies should be made of the relationships between community attitudes and the effectiveness of drug treatment. If, as we suspect, there is a strong positive association, the implications are potentially enormous. Such studies could help to xeplain the high recovery rate among drug abusers who seek but do not receive treatment.

Relationships Between Law Enforcement; Supply, Price, and Purity of Illegal Drugs; and Treatment Entry and Outcomes

It is believed that there are relationships between these factors and that they are important in understanding and explaining treatment outcomes.

There are probably strong interactions between these phenomena which are not well understood and which may act to confound follow-up study results.

A study could be conducted in a number of cities relating drug-related arrest and incarceration data, and Drug Enforcement Administration and local police drug seizure data (price, purity, quantity) to treatment program entry rates and outcomes.

Follow-up studies should include consideration of these factors in interpreting treatment outcomes.

The Motivation of Addicts Upon Entering Treatment

Since merely going through intake seems to be related to recovery, studies should be made of what motivates an addict to seek treatment in the first place; specifically, what interaction of addict motivational and program factors contribute to recovery. A related issue is what motivational factors distinguish persons who only go through intake from those who continue in a therapeutic process.

Investigation of "Comparison Groups"

Since the comparison groups had such high recovery rates, it is of interest to know what these individuals did while the experimental groups were in treatment. Of course, it would be difficult to determine this for the NTA or ASA groups, but this aspect could be included in any new treatment evaluation studies.

The Intake Process

It is of interest to know precisely how persons are assigned to modalities.

The Need for Better Control/Comparison Groups

Both the NTA and ASA studies experienced substantial difficulties because of the contamination of comparison groups. This problem was, of course, more severe with the ASA groups (of which about 30% later re-entered treatment) than with the NTA ones (of which about 16% later re-entered treatment). While it was possible to "purify" these groups, this resulted in such a small group that only limited analyses could be performed. This problem might be handled in one of several ways:

- Control/comparison groups may be formed from clients who have applied for treatment but have *never* received any. Our experience is that there will be very few people in this category, but if there is a sufficiently large universe from which to draw the sample, it can be done.

- Control groups can consist of persons who *never* applied for treatment. This type of individual would probably be a very hardcore addict who is unmotivated toward recovery. Therefore, it could be argued that this individual is so completely different from a person who is motivated to seek treatment that he would be improperly cast as a member of a control group. Based on our experience in the NTA study, we have no doubt that such individuals can be tracked and interviewed by using ex-addict interviewers.

- In a prospective study, persons can be assigned randomly to treatment and control groups. This is probably legally and ethically possible to carry out in communities where there are insufficient treatment resources to meet the demands for treatment. However, it is probably difficult to find such conditions due to the high priority placed upon treating drug addicts. This is the option which conceptually comes closest to meeting the requirements of a classical control group.

Need for a Systematic, Comprehensive Evaluation Program

There is definitely a need for more follow-up studies. These should be designed to test specific hypotheses concerning the efficacy of various types of treatments and various types of settings. One general approach is to select certain existing programs in which variations in programs and settings are allowed to occur naturally. Thus, programs can be selected which offer different modalities, different mixes of services within the modalities, have different types of clientele, and are offered in different settings. Client samples can be drawn from each of these programs, as well as comparison/control groups. Follow-ups can then be conducted to determine the behavior of the sample clients, how behavior has changed since the period immediately before entering treatment, and how the behavior varies from that of members of comparison/control groups.

An alternative approach, which would require substantially more lead time, would be to fund a series of planned variation demonstration programs. These demonstrations would be carefully designed so that each consists of a specified mix of services, serves specified types of clients, and operates in specified settings. These may be operated as field experiments in which certain variables (e.g., mixes of services) are systematically manipulated and changes in the impacts of these manipulations are measured. Through this process, the researchers may gain considerable insight into the efficacy of different types of treatment as compared to the first type of demonstration.

One issue that should be addressed within the context of the evaluation program is the relationship of varying times in treatment to outcomes (to include all episodes).

Cost-Effectiveness of Treatment

An issue that will continue to arise as results of follow-up studies are published is the cost-effecitveness of alternaitve types of treat‑ ment. The results of this study raise questions as to the common assumption that more treatment is better than less, an assumption which is at least implicit in many current treatment programs. If these findings are replicated by other studies, it may prove difficult to justify lengthy periods of treatment for high proportions of clients. Future evaluations should include serious consideration of the cost of providing treatment and the relative cost-effectiveness of different types of treatments.

APPENDIX A
SIGNIFICANT STATISTICAL TESTS

HEROIN

N T A

SIGNIFICANT TESTS

Variable Description	Group	T-Test	DF	Significance
2 Before vs 2 After	Maintenance	13.2	92	<.001
	Abstinence	14.0	95	<.001
	Comparison	11.2	99	<.001
2 Before vs Last 2	Maintenance	16.1	92	<.001
	Abstinence	18.1	95	<.001
	Comparison	15.0	99	<.001

A S A

SIGNIFICANT TESTS

Variable Description	Group	F-Test	T-Test	DF	Significance
2 Before vs 2 After	Comparison	--	6.2	81	<.001
	Ambulatory Unit	--	10.6	107	<.001
	Methadone Maintenance	--	12.7	106	<.001
	Therapeutic Community	--	15.3	153	<.001
	Comp. vs Methadone Maintenance	--	-2.8	187	.031
	Comp. vs Therapeutic Community	--	-3.1	234	.014
	Among Groups	4.4	--	3	.005
2 Before vs Past 2	Comp.	--	13.6	81	<.001
	Ambulatory Unit	--	13.3	105	<.001
	Methadone Maintenance	--	18.9	109	<.001
	Therapeutic Community	--	20.9	152	<.001
	Among Groups	2.8	--	3	.041

COCAINE

N T A
SIGNIFICANT TESTS

Variable Description	Group	T-Test	DF	Significance
2 Before vs 2 After	Maintenance	5.9	92	<.001
	Abstinence	5.1	95	<.001
	Comparison	5.8	99	<.001
2 Before vs Last 2	Maintenance	6.7	92	<.001
	Abstinence	5.6	95	<.001
	Comparison	7.7	99	<.001

A S A
SIGNIFICANT TESTS

Variable Description	Group	F-Test	T-Test	DF	Significance
2 Before vs 2 After	Ambulatory Unit	--	3.2	81	.003
	Methadone Maintenance	--	3.2	107	.002
	Therapeutic Community	--	6.2	106	<.001
		--	7.2	153	<.001
	Among Groups	3.3	--	3	.021
2 Before vs Last 2	Ambulatory Unit	--	4.9	81	<.001
	Methadone Maintenance	--	3.7	105	<.001
	Therapeutic Community	--	7.7	110	<.001
	Ambulatory vs Methadone Maint.	--	6.0	152	<.001
		--	-3.3	215	.007
	Among Groups	3.1	--	3	.026

AMPHETAMINES

N T A

SIGNIFICANT TESTS

Variable Description	Group	T-Test	DF	Significance
2 Before vs 2 After	Comparison	2.9	99	.006
2 Before vs Last 2	Maintenance	2.7	92	.008
	Abstinence	4.2	95	<.001
	Comparison	4.3	99	<.001

A S A

SIGNIFICANT TESTS

Variable Description	Group	T-Test	DF	Significance
2 Before vs 2 After	Ambulatory Unit	2.3	107	.027
	Therapeutic Community	3.7	153	<.001
2 Before vs Last 2	Methadone Maintenance	3.1	108	.003
	Therapeutic Community	2.9	151	.004

BARBITURATES

N T A

SIGNIFICANT TESTS

Variable Description	Group	T-Test	DF	Significance
2 Before vs 2 After	Maintenance	3.2	92	.002
	Comparison	2.5	99	.01
2 Before vs Last 2	Maintenance	3.5	92	<.001
	Comparison	2.9	99	.004

A S A

SIGNIFICANT TESTS

Variable Description	Group	T-Test	DF	Significance
2 Before vs 2 After	Ambulatory Unit	4.5	107	<.001
	Methadone Maintenance	3.4	106	<.001
	Therapeutic Community	5.1	153	<.001
2 Before vs Last 2	Ambulatory Unit	2.7	81	.008
	Methadone Maintenance	4.3	106	<.001
	Methadone Maintenance	4.6	108	<.001
	Therapeutic Community	5.1	151	<.001

ILLEGAL METHADONE

N T A
SIGNIFICANT TESTS

Variable Description	Group	T-Test	DF	Significance
2 Before vs 2 After	Maintenance	3.5	92	<.001
	Abstinence	3.3	95	.002
	Comparison	3.5	99	<.001
2 Before vs Last 2	Maintenance	4.9	92	<.001
	Abstinence	5.4	95	<.001
	Comparison	5.3	99	<.001

A S A
SIGNIFICANT TESTS

Variable Description	Group	T-Test	DF	Significance
2 Before vs 2 After	Methadone Maintenance	2.6	106	.012
	Therapeutic Community	3.4	153	<.001
2 Before vs Last 2	Comparison	2.2	80	.032
	Ambulatory Unit	2.2	105	.028
	Methadone Maintenance	3.2	109	.002

LEGAL METHADONE

N T A

SIGNIFICANT TESTS

Variable Description	Group	T-Test	DF	Significance
2 Before vs 2 After	Abstinence	3.1	95	.003

DILAUDID

N T A

SIGNIFICANT TESTS

Variable Description	Group	T-Test	DF	Significance
2 Before vs Last 2	Maintenance	2.2	92	.03
	Abstinence	2.8	95	.006

MINOR TRANQUILIZERS

N T A

SIGNIFICANT TESTS

Variable Description	Group	T-Test	DF	Significance
2 Before vs 2 After	Comparison	2.2	99	.03

HALLUCINOGENS
A S A

SIGNIFICANT TESTS

Variable Description	Group	T-Test	DF	Significance
2 Before vs 2 After	Ambulatory Unit	2.7	107	.009
	Therapeutic Community	3.6	153	<.001
2 Before vs Last 2	Ambulatory Unit	2.3	105	.024
	Therapeutic Community	2.7	151	.008

ALCOHOL USE
A S A

SIGNIFICANT TESTS

Variable Description	Group	T-Test	DF	Significance
2 Before vs Last 2	Ambulatory Unit	-2.6	85	.012

CIGARETTE USE
A S A

SIGNIFICANT TESTS

Variable Description	Group	T-Test	DF	Significance
2 Before vs 2 After	Ambulatory	2.1	99	.035
	Therapeutic Community	4.1	147	<.001
2 Before vs Last 2	Ambulatory	18.3	101	<.001
	Methadone Maintenance	18.4	107	<.001
	Therapeutic Community	22.3	148	<.001
	Comparison	13.8	77	<.001

MARIJUANA

N T A

SIGNIFICANT TESTS

Variable Description	Group	T-Test	DF	Significance
2 Before vs 2 After	Maintenance	2.0	92	.05
	Comparison	3.4	99	.002
2 Before vs Last 2	Maintenance	2.3	92	.02
	Comparison	2.0	99	.05

A S A

SIGNIFICANT TESTS

Variable Description	Group	F-Test	T-Test	DF	Significance
2 Before vs 2 After	Comparison	--	2.8	81	.007
	Ambulatory Unit	--	4.3	107	<.001
	Methadone Maintenance	--	4.0	106	<.001
	Therapeutic Community	--	8.0	153	<.001
	Comp. vs. Therapeutic Commun.	--	3.0	234	.017
	Therapeutic Commun. vs Meth.Maint.	--	3.3	259	.008
	Among Groups	5.1	--	3	.002
2 Before vs Last 2	Comparison	--	2.4	82	.019
	Ambulatory Unit	--	3.4	105	.002
	Methadone Maintenance	--	2.0	109	.049
	Therapeutic Community	--	5.0	153	<.001

OTHER DRUGS

N T A

SIGNIFICANT TESTS

Variable Description	Group	T-Test	DF	Significance
2 Before vs 2 After	Maintenance	2.3	92	.03
	Comparison	2.6	99	.01
2 Before vs Last 2	Maintenance	2.1	92	.04
	Abstinence	2.0	95	.05
	Comparison	2.9	99	.005

A S A

SIGNIFICANT TESTS

Variable Description	Group	T-Test	DF	Significance
2 Before vs Last 2	Therapeutic Community vs Meth. Maint.	3.1	211	.014

ARRESTS

N T A

SIGNIFICANT TESTS

Variable Description	Group	X^2 Test	DF	Significance
2 Before vs Last 2	Maintenance	10.5	1	<.005
	Abstinence	14.5	1	<.005
	Comparison	14.0	1	<.005

A S A

SIGNIFICANT TESTS

Variable Description	Group	X^2 Test	DF	Significance
2 Before vs 2 After	Methadone Maintenance	10.1	1	.002
	Ambulatory	5.6	1	.012
	Therapeutic Community	28.6	1	<.001
2 Before vs 2 After	Comparison	11.7	1	<.001
	Methadone Maintenance	20.0	1	<.001
	Ambulatory	23.1	1	<.001
	Therapeutic Community	37.6	1	<.001

INCARCERATIONS

N T A

SIGNIFICANT TESTS

Variable Description	Group	x^2 Test	DF	Significance
2 Before vs Last 2	Comparison	4.5	1	.05

A S A

SIGNIFICANT TESTS

Variable Description	Group	x^2 Test	DF	Significance
2 Before vs 2 After	Therapeutic Community	36.7	1	<.001
	Comparison	6.1	1	.011
2 Before vs Last 2	Methadone Maintenance	5.4	1	.02
	Ambulatory	4.5	1	.04
	Therapeutic Community	35.6	1	<.001
	Comparison	8.6	1	.003

EMPLOYMENT STATUS

N T A

SIGNIFICANT TESTS

Variable Description	Group	T Test	F Test	X^2 Test	DF	Significance
2 Before vs 2 After	Abstinence	-2.2	--		95	.028
2 Before vs Last 2	Abstinence Maint. vs	-4.7 3.5	-- --		95 185	<.001 .003
	Abstinence vs Comparison	-2.9	--		194	.014
	Among Groups	--	7.0		2	.002
Last 2	Maint. vs Abstinence			4.8	1	.05
	Abstinence vs Comparison			4.2	1	.05

A S A

SIGNIFICANT TESTS

Variable Description	Group	T Test	F Test	DF	Significance
2 Before vs 2 After	Ambulatory	3.8	--	105	<.001
	Methadone Maintenance	2.2	--	92	.028
	Therapeutic Community	5.4	--	151	<.001
	Comparison vs Therapeutic Community	-3.3	--	229	.008
	Among Groups	--	4.8	3	.003
2 Before vs Last 2	Comparison	2.7	--	82	.009
	Ambulatory	5.9	--	106	<.001
	Methadone Maintenance	4.1	--	108	<.001
	Therapeutic Community	9.0	--	152	<.001
	Comparison vs Therapeutic Commun.	-3.5	--	234	.004
	Therapeutic Commun. vs Meth. Maint.	-3.4	--	260	.006
	Among Groups	--	6.5	3	<.001

AGE OF CLIENT AND MARITAL STATUS

A S A

SIGNIFICANT TESTS

Variable Description	Group	T Test	F Test	X^2 Test	DF	Significance
Age of Client	Among Groups	--	--	93.143	15	<.001
	Among Groups	--	30.096	--	3	<.001
	Comparison vs Methadone Maint.	-4.436	--	--	193	<.001
	Comparison vs Methadone Maint.	3.678	--	--	235	.002
	Ambulatory vs Methadone Maint.	-6.569	--	--	218	<.001
	Methadone Maint. vs Therapeutic Commun.	9.581	--	--	264	<.001

SIGNIFICANT TESTS

Variable Description	Group	T Test	F Test	X^2 Test	DF	Significance
Marital Status	Among Groups	--	6.827	--	3	<.001
	Comparison vs Ambulatory	3.479	--	--	189	.004
	Ambulatory vs Methadone Maint.	-3.678	--	--	217	.002
	Methadone Maint. vs Therapeutic Commun.	2.847	--	--	263	.029

SUBSEQUENT DRUG TREATMENT

A S A

SIGNIFICANT TESTS

Variable Description	Group	T Test	F Test	X^2 Test	DF	Significance
Subsequent Drug Treatment	Post-ASA Treat. vs No Post-ASA Treatment	--	--	25.5	3	<.001
	Methadone Maint. vs Ambulatory	--	--	12.5	1	<.001
	Methadone Maint. vs Therapeutic Community	--	--	15.1	1	<.001
	Therapeutic Commun. vs Comparison	--	--	9.9	1	<.01
	Ambulatory vs Comparison	--	--	8.3	1	<.01

TYPE OF PARTICIPATION

A S A

SIGNIFICANT TESTS

Variable Description	Group	T Test	F Test	X^2 Test	DF	Significance
Type of Participation in ASA	Among Groups	--	--	21.1	3	<.001
	Methadone Maint. vs Therapeutic Community	--	--	17.18	1	<.001
	Methadone Maint. vs Comparison	--	--	10.05	1	<.01
	Ambulatory vs Therapeutic Community	--	--	4.64	1	<.05

AGE FIRST USED HEROIN

A S A

SIGNIFICANT TESTS

Variable Description	Group	T Test	F Test	X^2 Test	DF	Significance
Age First Used Heroin	Among Ages	5.847	--	41.8	12	<.001
	Methadone Maint. vs Therapeutic Community	--	--	--	258	<.001
	Among Groups	--	9.5	--	3	<.001

PRIOR DRUG TREATMENT

A S A

SIGNIFICANT TESTS

Variable Description	Group	T Test	F Test	X^2 Test	DF	Significance
Drug Treatment Before ASA	Pre-ASA Treat. vs no Pre-ASA Treatment	--	--	8.739	3	.03
	Ambulatory vs Methadone Maint.	--	--	7.61	1	<.01
	Ambulatory vs Therapeutic Community	--	--	4.219	1	<.025

APPENDIX B
FACTOR ANALYSIS RESULTS

FACTOR 1:   SOURCE OF INCOME

Variable	Factor Loading
Source of Income 2 Months Before	
Job	.37
Social Security, VA, Unemployment	.90
Welfare	.73
Spouse	.83
Relatives or Friends	.57
Source of Income 2 Months After	
Social Security, VA, Unemployment	.89
Welfare	.70
Spouse	.84
Relatives or Friends	.58
Source of Income Last 2 Months	
Illegal Activities	.36
Social Security, VA, Unemployment	.81
Welfare	.71
Spouse	.83
Relatives or Friends	.51

FACTOR 2:   ASSOCIATES' DRUG USE

Variable	Factor Loading
Number of Associates Entering NTA	
2 Months Before	.70
2 Months After	.84
Past 2 Months	.56
Number of Associates Using Drugs	
2 Months Before	.89
2 Months After	.77
Past 2 Months	.69

FACTOR 3: INCARCERATIONS

Variable	Factor Loading
Number of Times Incarcerated	.36
Number of Days Incarcerated	.49
Did Time Last 2 Months (Yes = 1)	.92
Number of Days Incarcerated 2 Months After	.42
Incarcerated 6 Months After (Yes = 1)	.91
Number of Days Incarcerated 2 Months Before	.38
Incarcerated 6 Months Before	.78

FACTOR 4: EMPLOYMENT

Variable	Factor Loading
Number of Days Employed	
2 Months Before	.79
2 Months After	.64
Source of Income 2 Months Before	
Job	.77
Relatives or Friends	-.43
Source of Income 2 Months After	
Job	.63
Relatives or Friends	-.38

FACTOR 5: ILLEGAL ACTIVITIES

Variable	Factor Loading
Heroin Use Past 2 Months	.41
Illegal Activities	
2 Months Before as Source of Income	.64
2 Months After as Source of Income	.68
Past 2 Months as Source of Income	.61

FACTOR 6: FURTHER CONTACT WITH NTA AFTER LEAVING

Variable	Factor Loading
Further Contact with NTA	.86
Frequency of Contact	.88
Treatment After NTA	.48

FACTOR 7:   ACTIVITIES AT NTA

Variable	Factor Loading
Adequacy of Time at NTA (0 = no, 1 = yes)	.61
Individual Counseling Participation (0 = no, 1 = yes)	.43
Methadone Detoxification Participation (0 = no, 1 = yes)	.47
Most Helpful Activity (0 = MM, 1 = other)	.73

FACTOR 8:   EMPLOYMENT PAST 2 MONTHS

Variable	Factor Loading
Number of Days Employed Past 2 Months	.88
Job Source of Income Past 2 Months	.79

FACTOR 9:   ACTIVITIES AT NTA

Variable	Factor Loading
Participation in:	
Group Counseling (0 = no)	.46
Tranquilizers/Muscle Relaxers (0 = no)	.62
Other (0 = no)	.57
Most Helpful Activity (0 = methadone maintenance, 1 = other)	.56

FACTOR 10:   SEX AND SOURCE OF INCOME

Variable	Factor Loading
Sex (0 = male, 1 = female)	.46
Source of Income--Welfare	
2 Months Before	.58
2 Months After	.65
Past 2 Months	.58

FACTOR 11:   MOST HELPFUL ACTIVITY

Variable	Factor Loading
Participated in Methadone Detoxification (0 = no, 1 = yes)	.36
Activity Most Helpful (0 = meth. maint., 1 = Other)	.73
Participated in Methadone Maintenance (0 = no, 1 = yes)	.78

FACTOR 12:   ARRESTS AND INCARCERATIONS

Variable	Factor Loading
Number of Times Busted	.69
Number of Times Incarcerated	.66

FACTOR 13:   ARRESTS AND INVOLUNTARY PARTICIPATION

Variable	Factor Loading
Participation in NTA (0 = voluntary, 1 = involuntary)	.53
Busted 6 Months Before	.67
Number of Days Incarcerated 2 Months Before	.38

FACTOR 14:   EMPLOYMENT

Variable	Factor Loading
Number of Days Employed 2 Months After	.40
NTA Helped Get Job 2 Months After	.66
NTA Helped Get Job Past 2 Months	.37
Source of Income--Job 2 Months After	.46